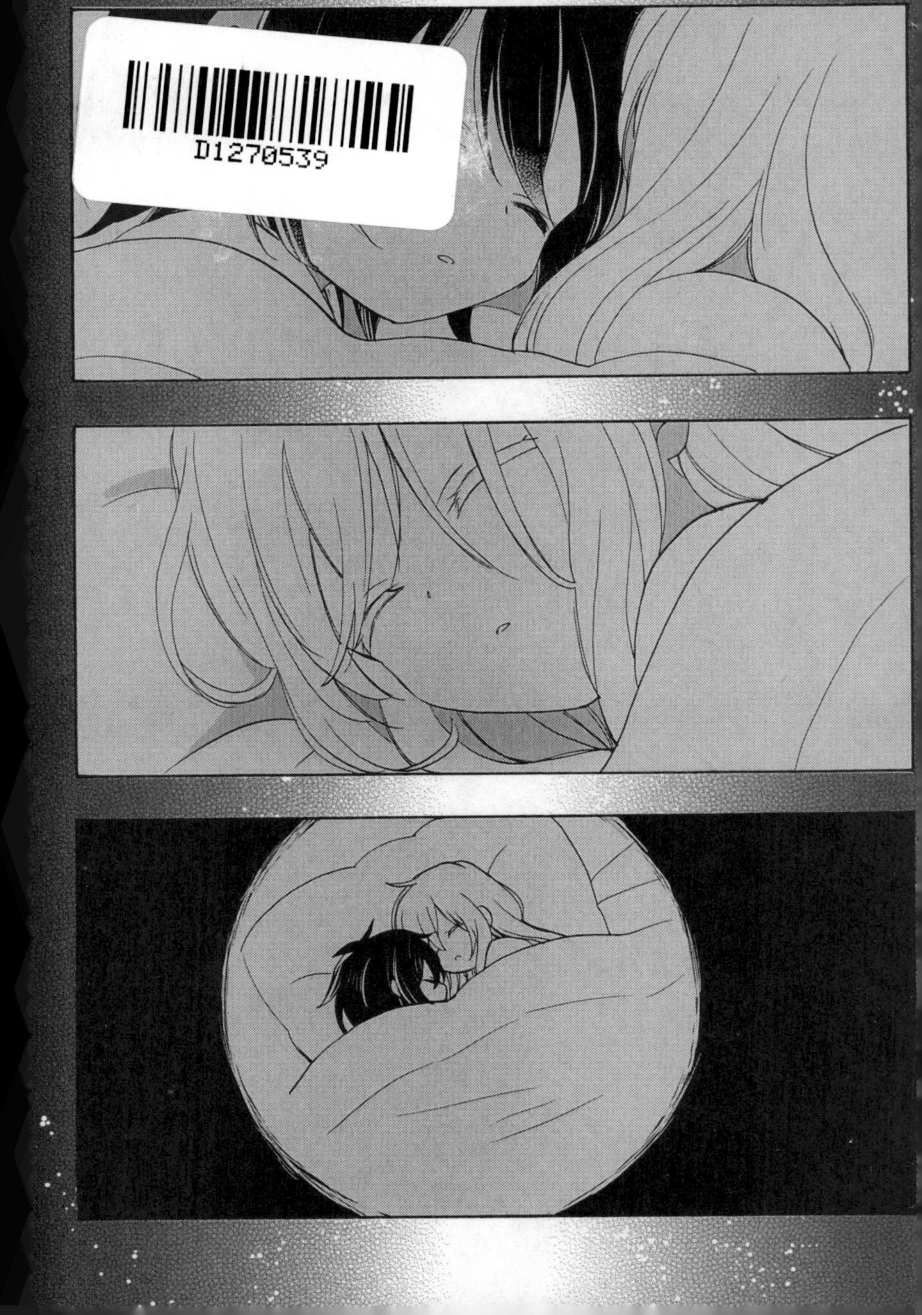

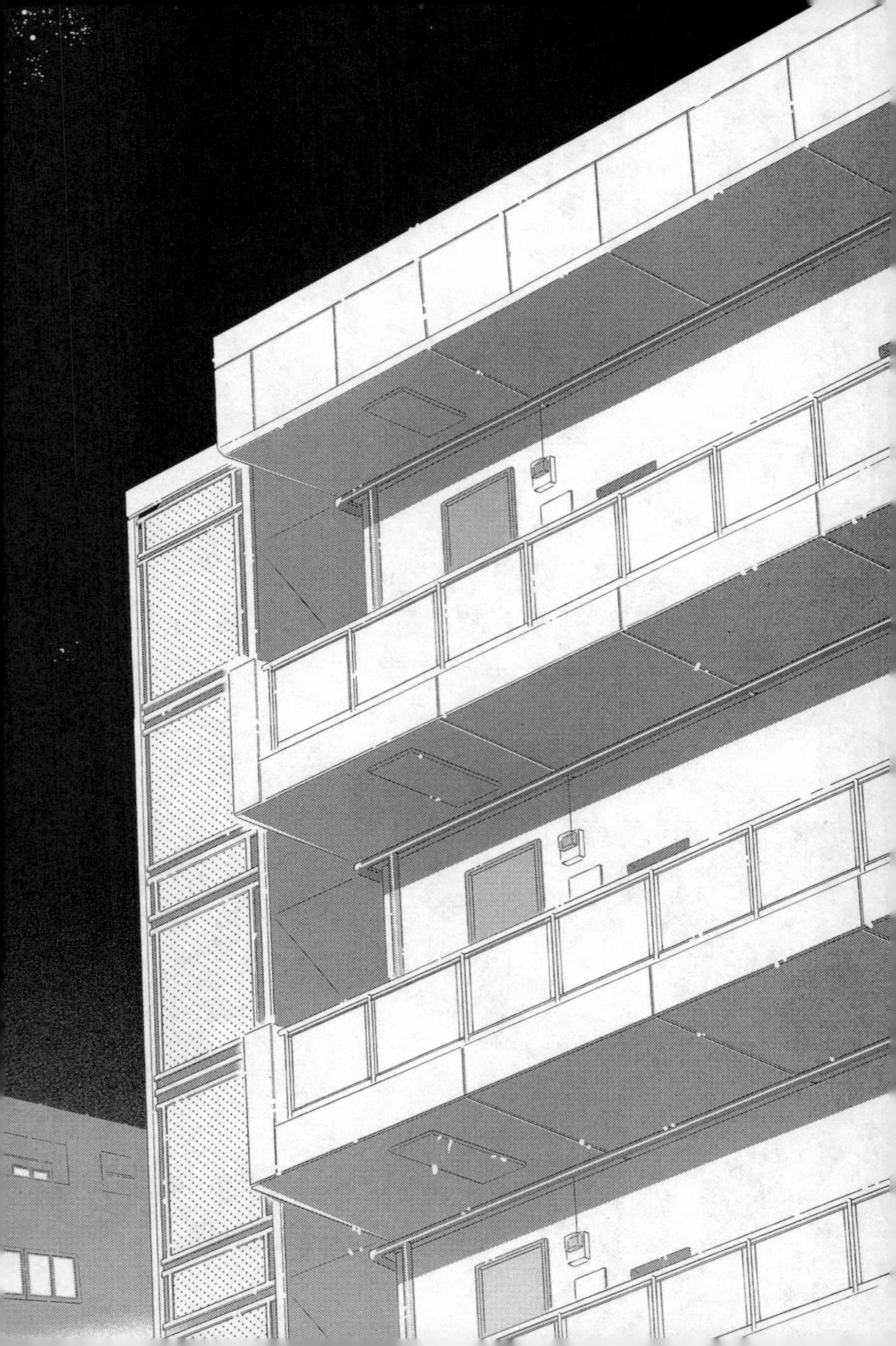

Happy sugar Life

Happy
Sugar
Life

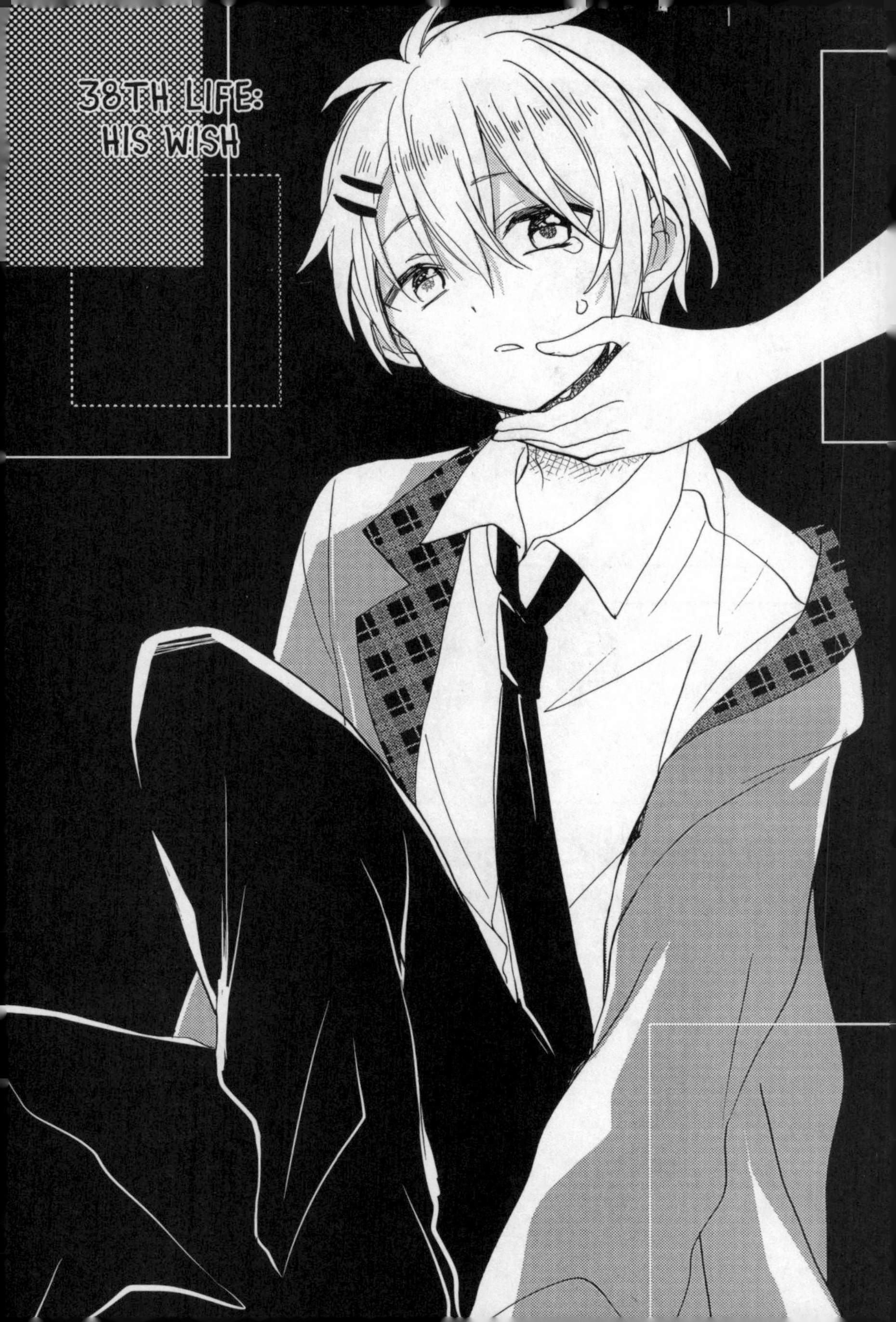
38TH LIFE:
HIS WISH

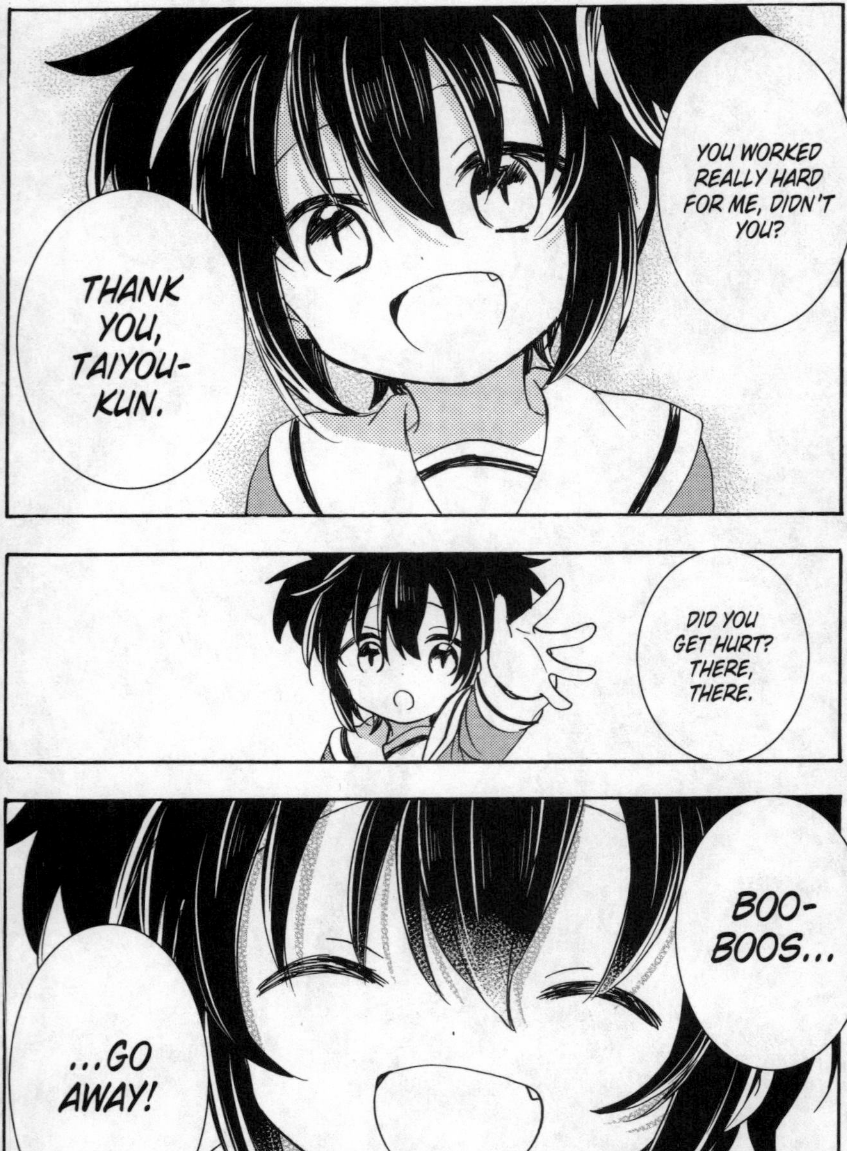
YOU WORKED REALLY HARD FOR ME, DIDN'T YOU?
THANK YOU, TAIYOU-KUN.
DID YOU GET HURT? THERE, THERE.
BOO-BOOS...
...GO AWAY!

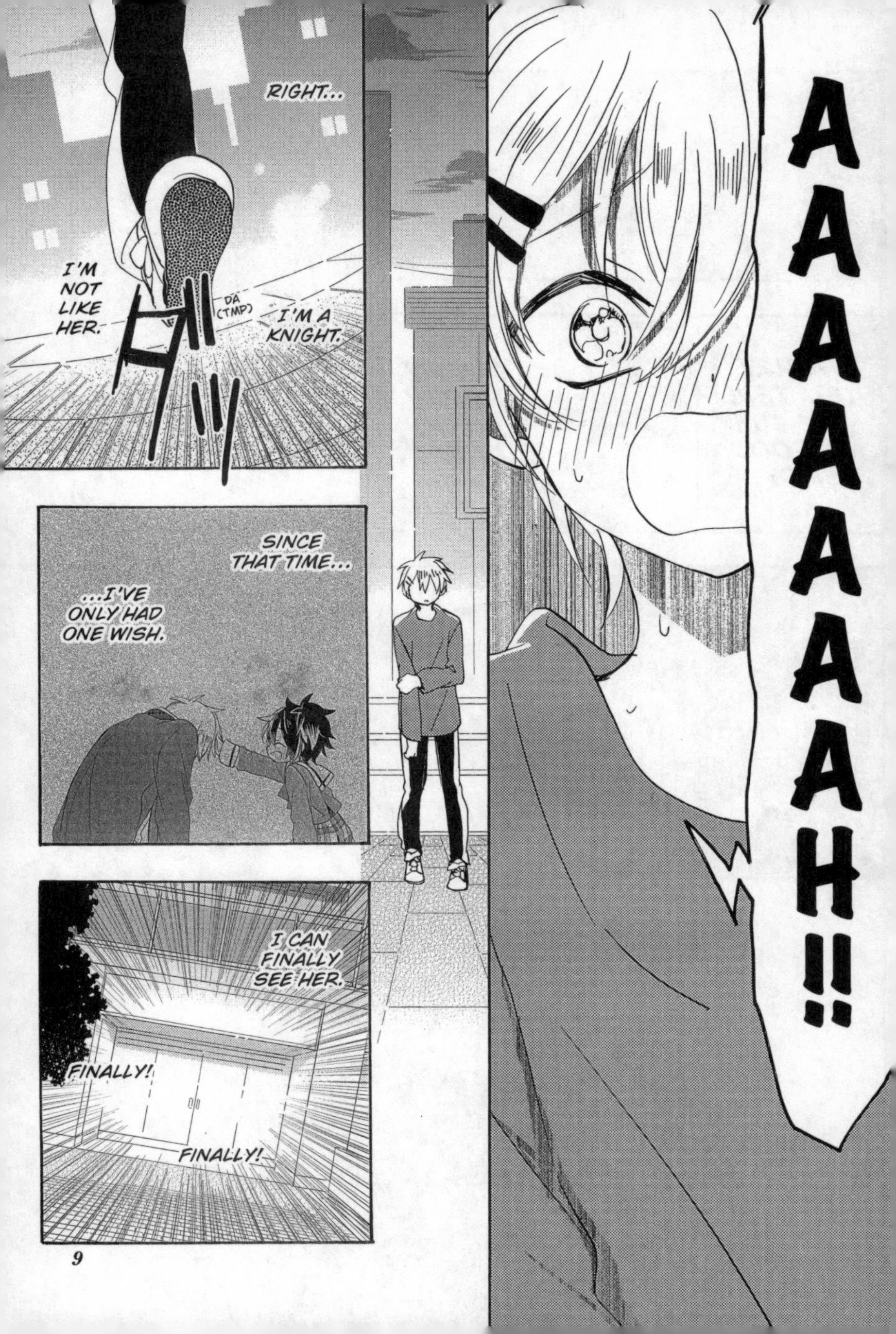
AAAAAAH!!
RIGHT...
I'M A KNIGHT.
DA (TMP)
I'M NOT LIKE HER.
SINCE THAT TIME...
...I'VE ONLY HAD ONE WISH.
I CAN FINALLY SEE HER.
FINALLY!
FINALLY!

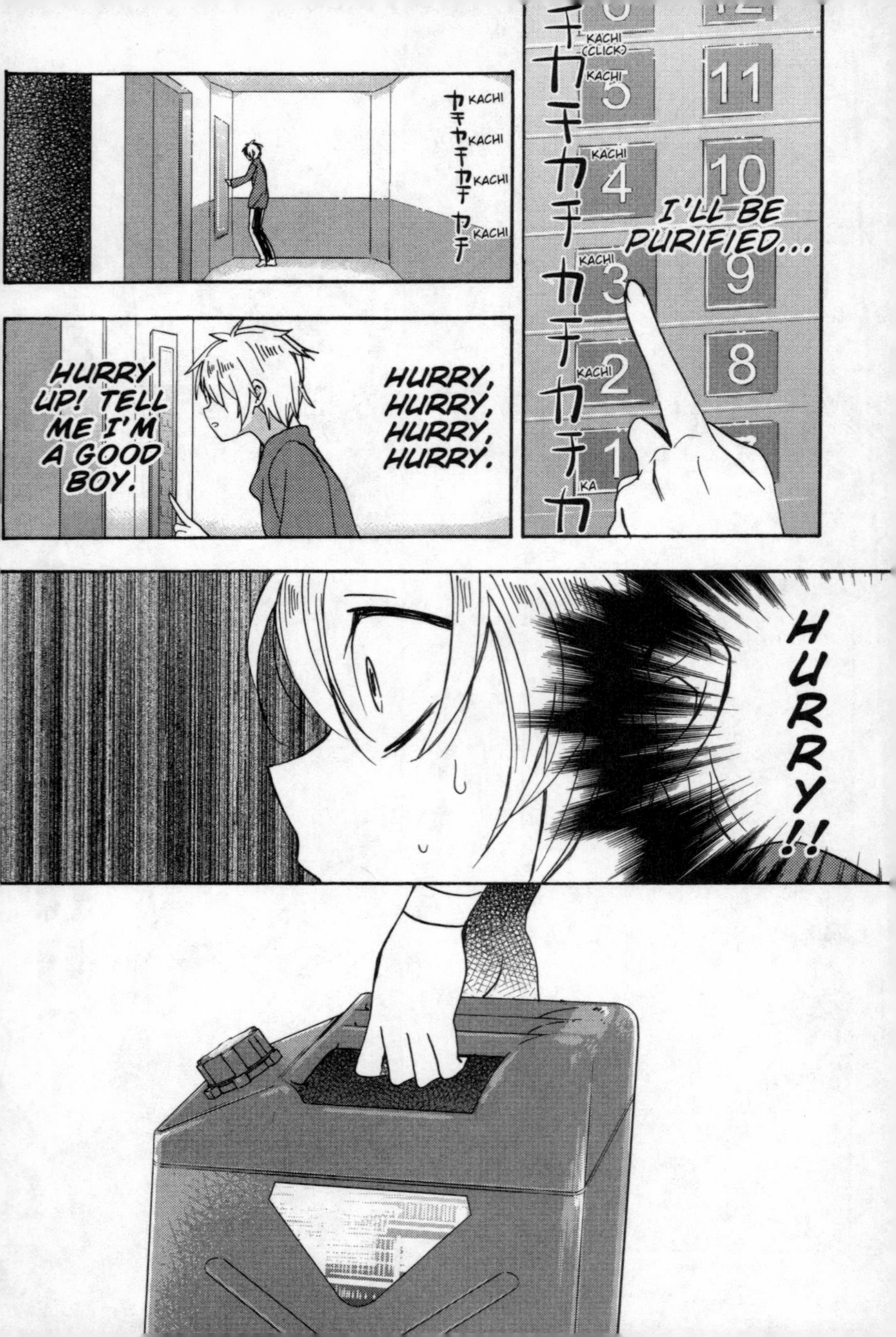
KACHI (CLICK)
KACHI
KACHI
KACHI
KACHI
KA
I'LL BE PURIFIED...
KACHI
KACHI
KACHI
KACHI
HURRY, HURRY, HURRY, HURRY.
HURRY UP! TELL ME I'M A GOOD BOY.
HURRY!!

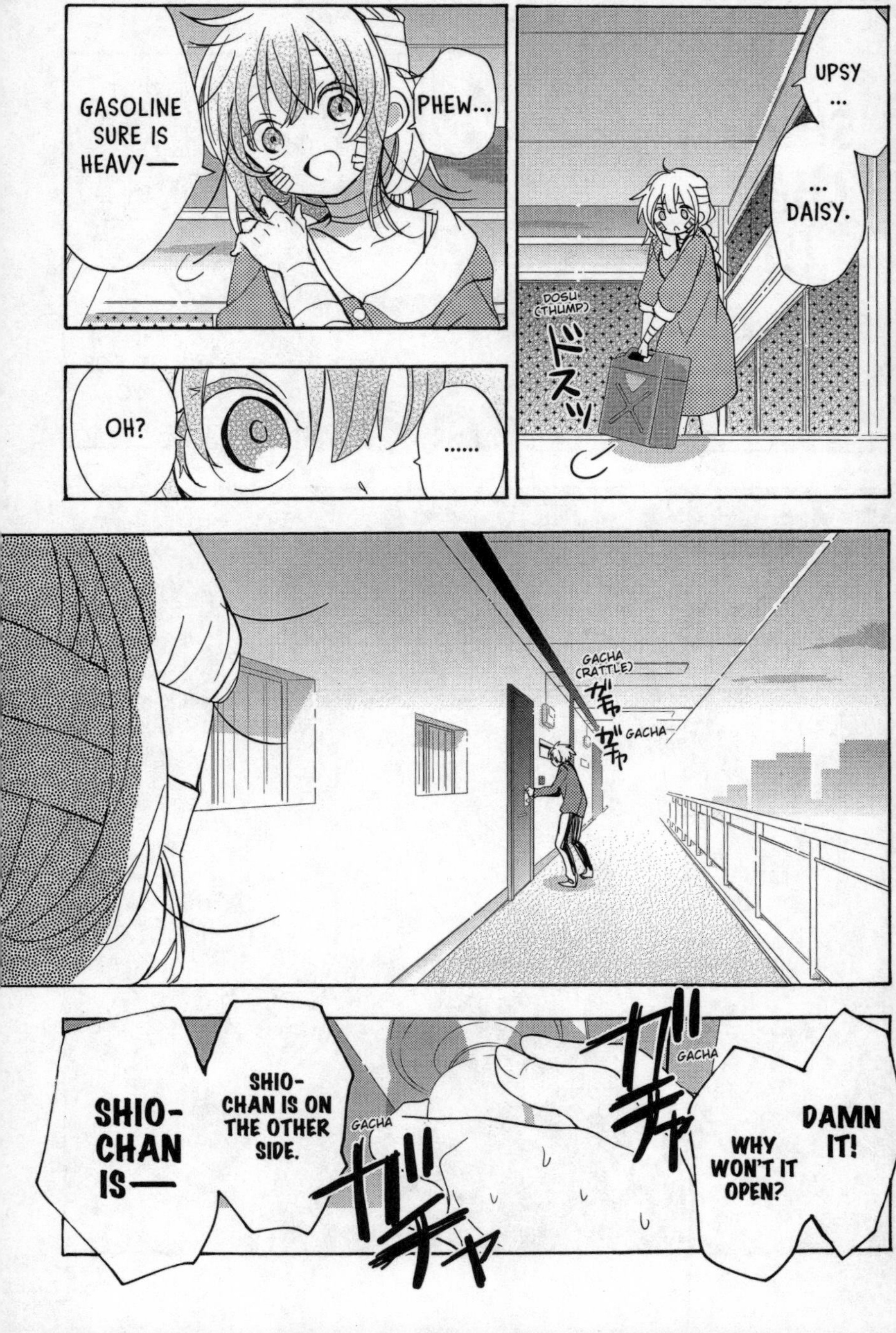
UPSY ...
... DAISY.
DOSU (THUMP)
ドスッ
PHEW...
GASOLINE SURE IS HEAVY—
......
OH?
GACHA (RATTLE)
ガチャ
GACHA
ガチャ
DAMN IT!
WHY WON'T IT OPEN?
GACHA
ガチャ
GACHA
ガチャ
SHIO-CHAN IS ON THE OTHER SIDE.
SHIO-CHAN IS—

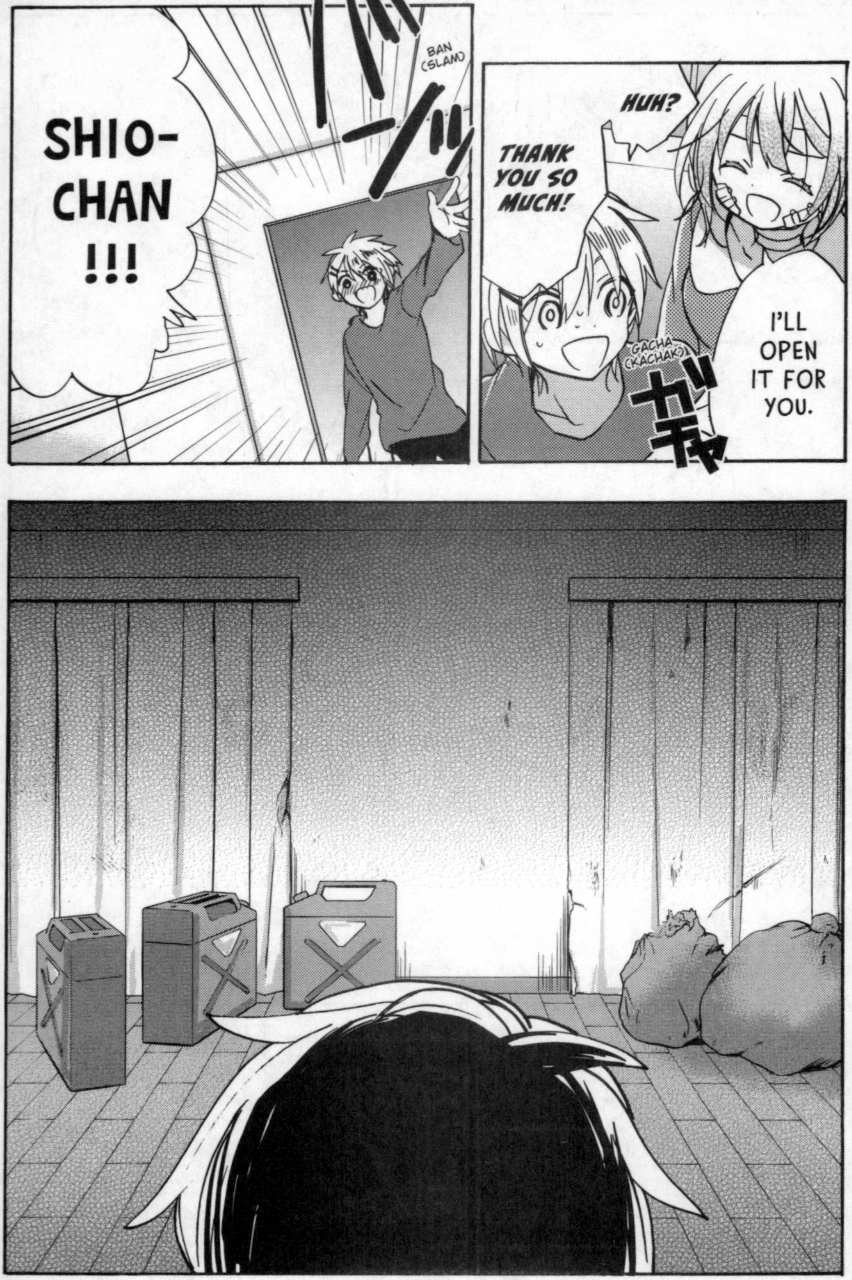
HUH?
THANK YOU SO MUCH!
I'LL OPEN IT FOR YOU.
GACHA (KACHAK)
ガチャ
BAN (SLAM)
SHIO-CHAN!!!

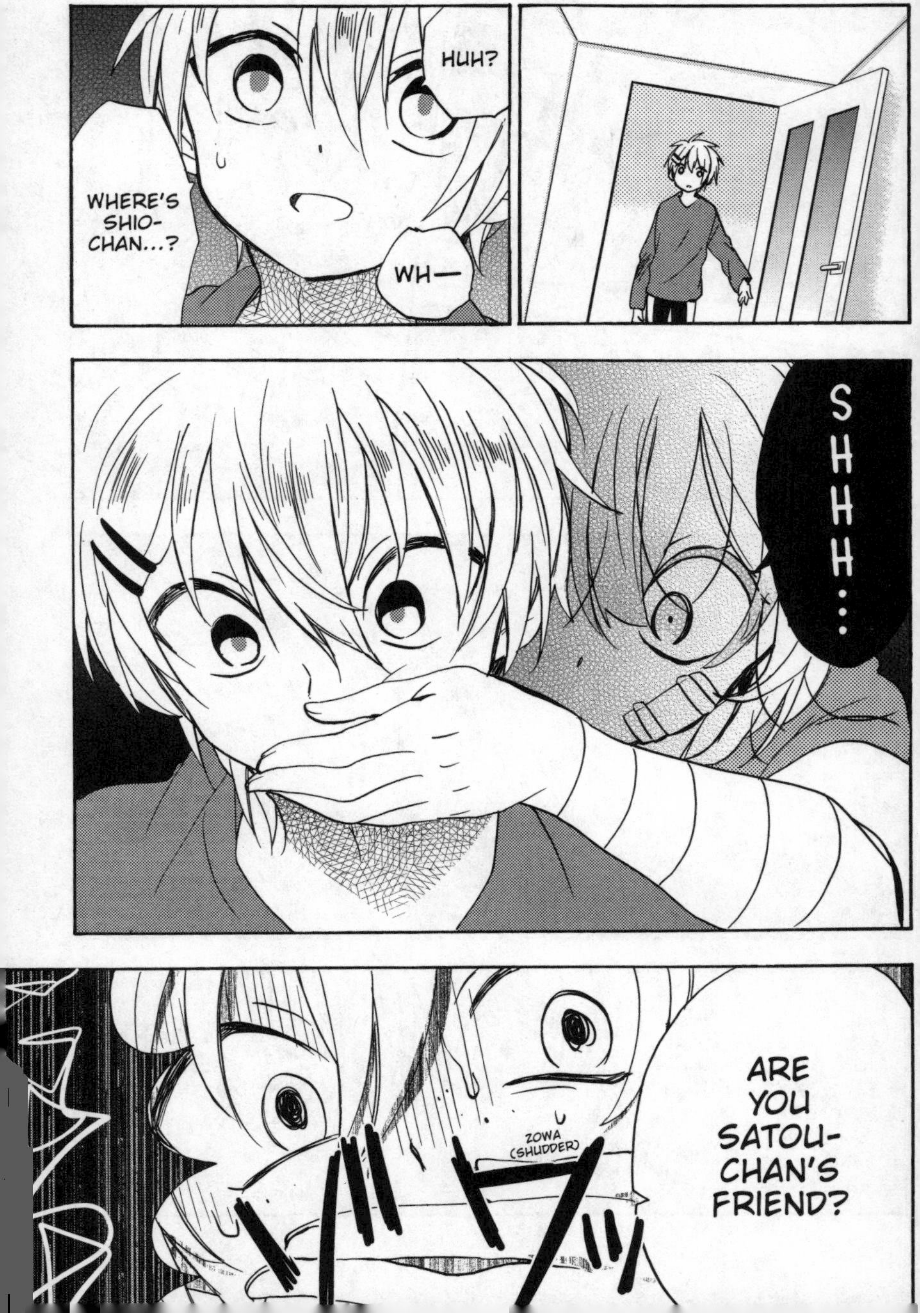
HUH?
WHERE'S SHIO-CHAN...?
WH—
SHHHH...
ARE YOU SATOU-CHAN'S FRIEND?
ZOWA (SHUDDER)

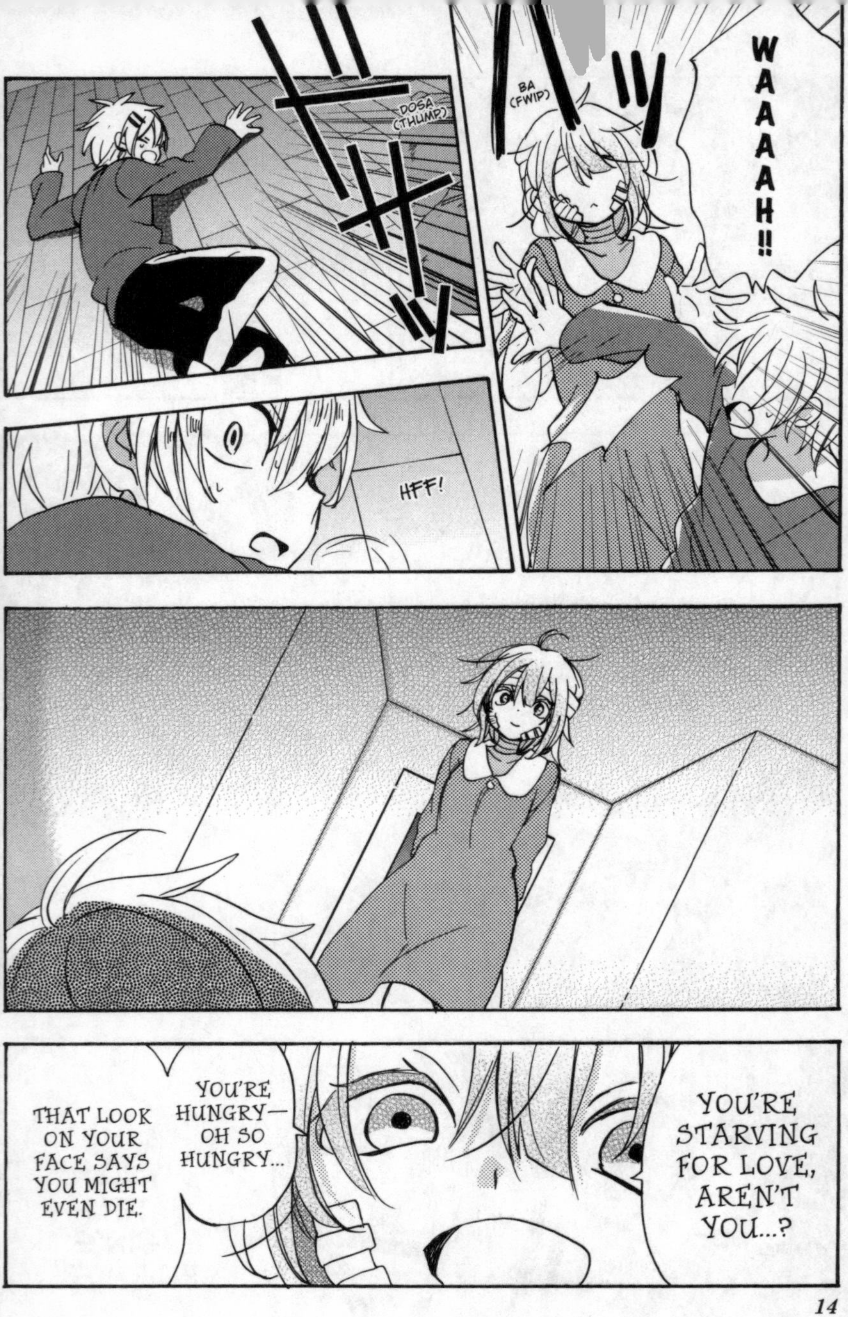
WAAAAAH!!
BA (FWIP)
DOSA (THUMP)
HFF!
YOU'RE STARVING FOR LOVE, AREN'T YOU...?
YOU'RE HUNGRY— OH SO HUNGRY...
THAT LOOK ON YOUR FACE SAYS YOU MIGHT EVEN DIE.

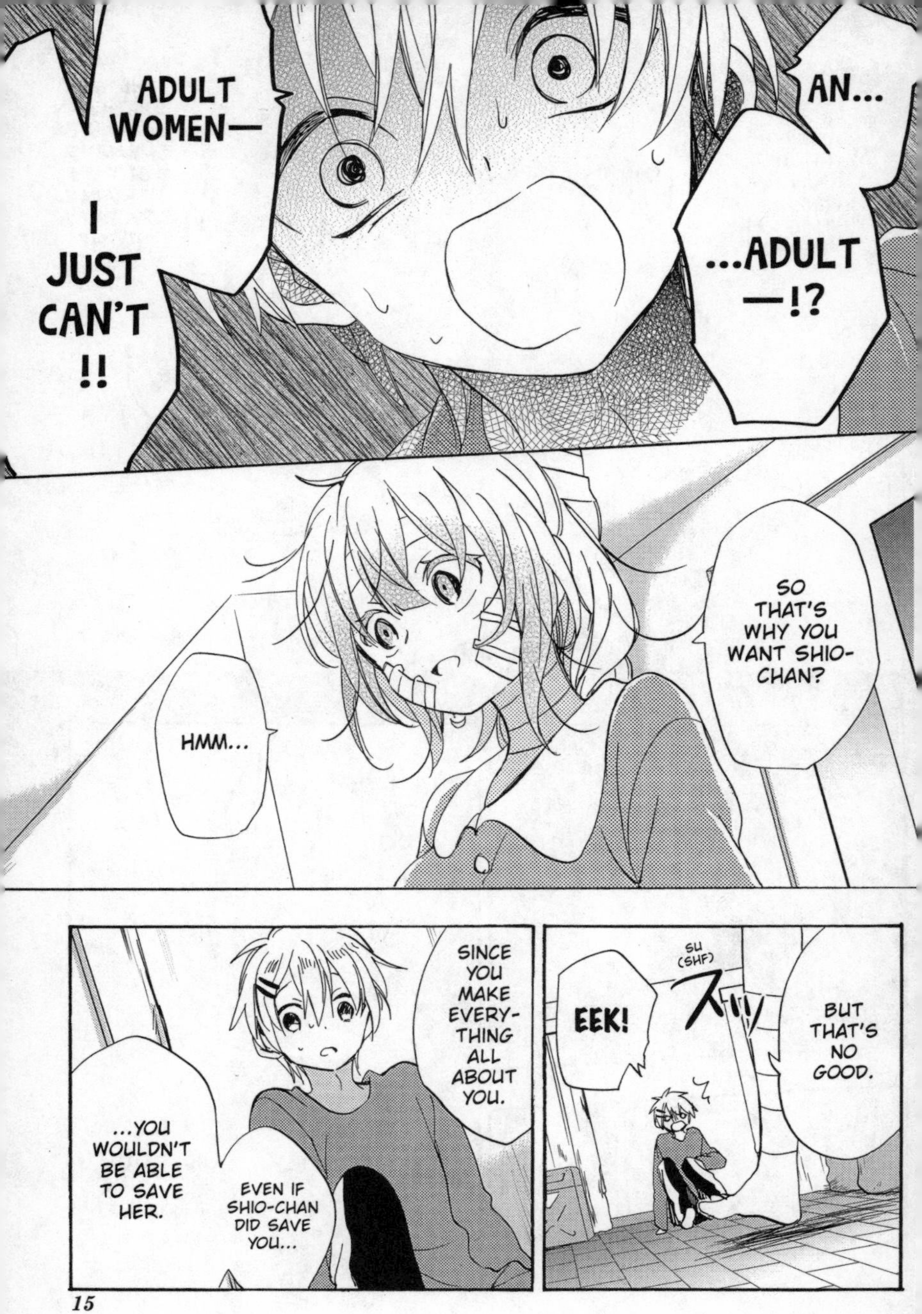
AN...
...ADULT—!?
ADULT WOMEN—
I JUST CAN'T!!
SO THAT'S WHY YOU WANT SHIO-CHAN?
HMM...
BUT THAT'S NO GOOD.
SU (SHF)
EEK!
SINCE YOU MAKE EVERY-THING ALL ABOUT YOU.
EVEN IF SHIO-CHAN DID SAVE YOU...
...YOU WOULDN'T BE ABLE TO SAVE HER.

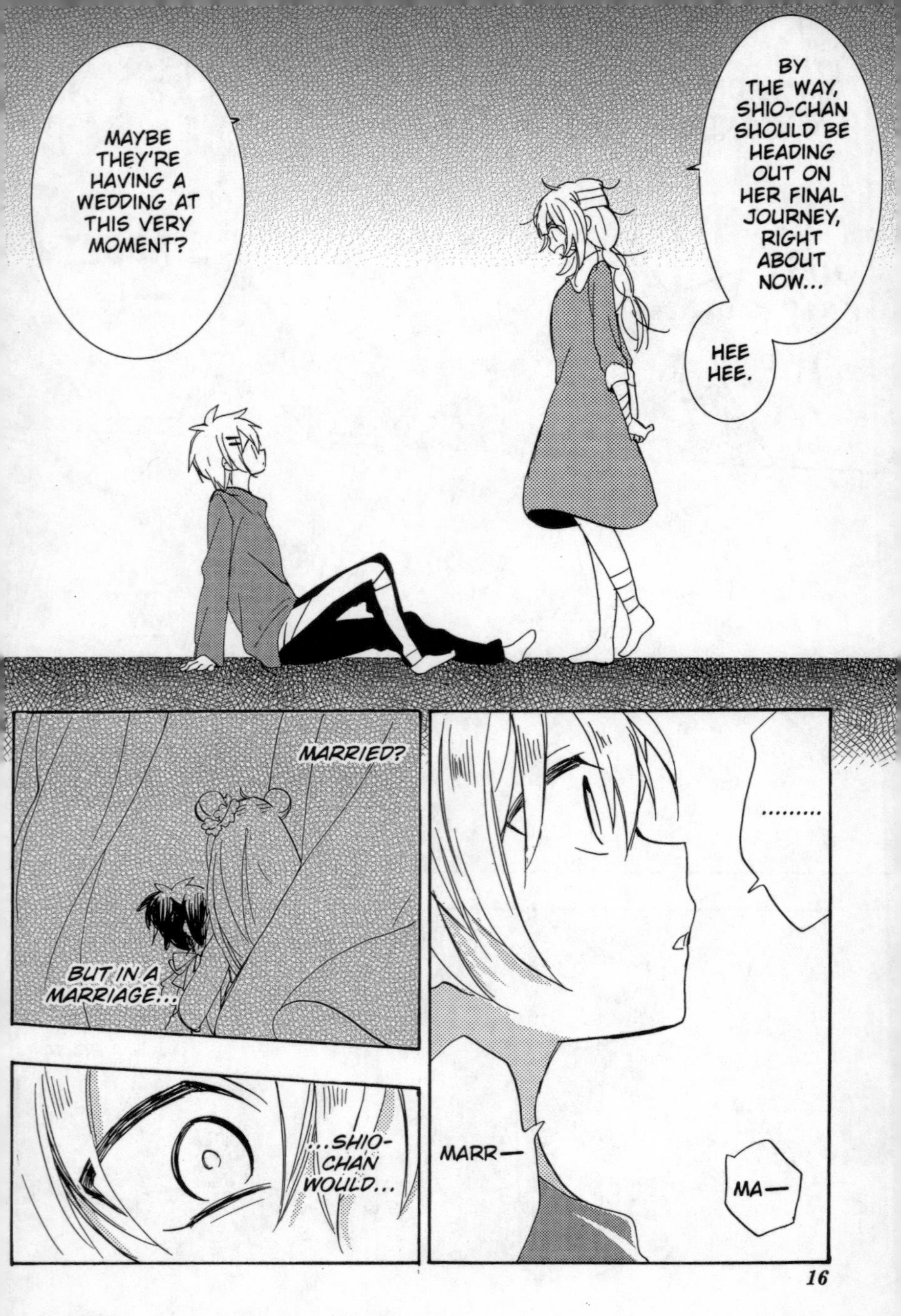
BY THE WAY, SHIO-CHAN SHOULD BE HEADING OUT ON HER FINAL JOURNEY, RIGHT ABOUT NOW...
HEE HEE.
MAYBE THEY'RE HAVING A WEDDING AT THIS VERY MOMENT?
....
MARR—
MA—
MARRIED?
BUT IN A MARRIAGE...
...SHIO-CHAN WOULD...

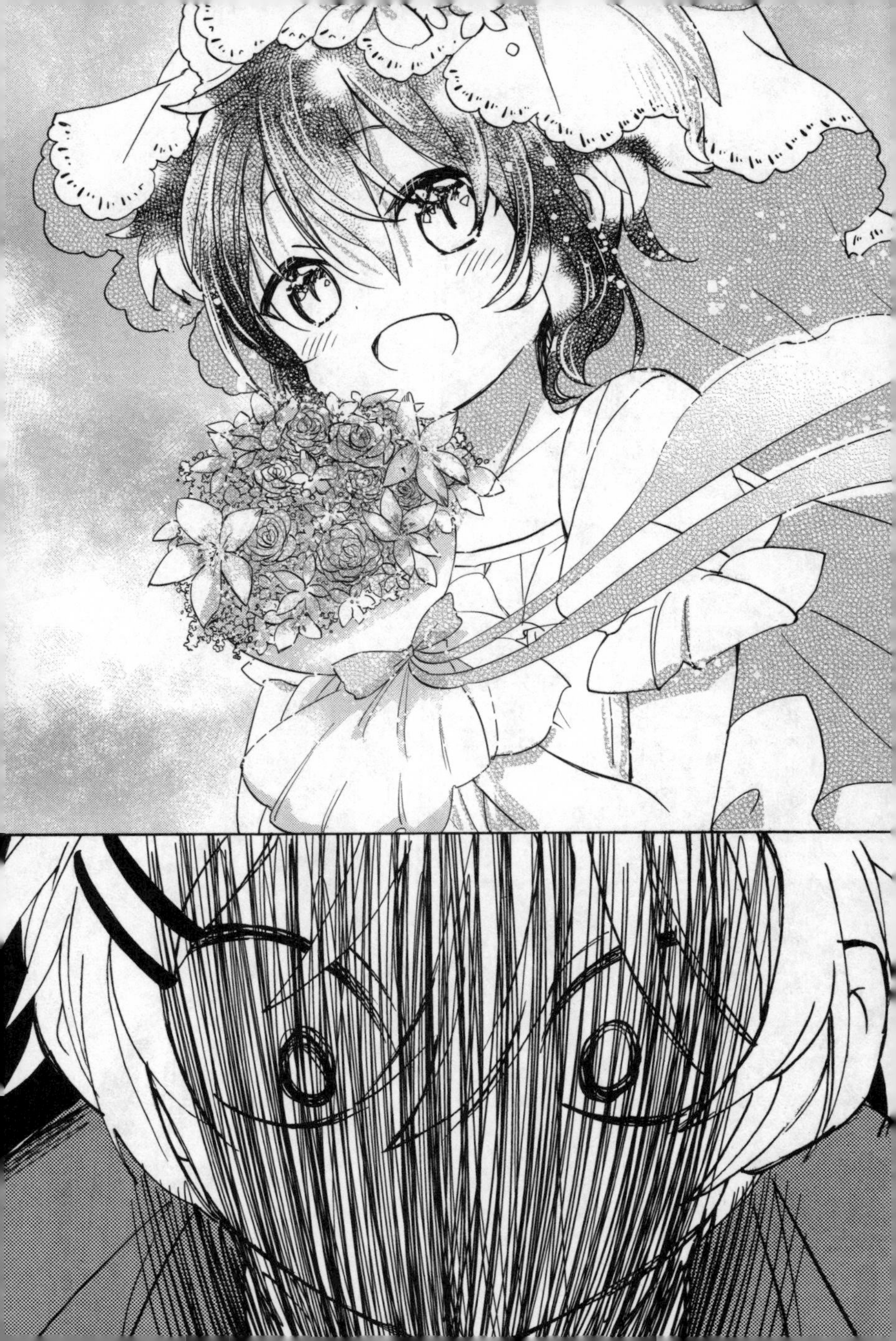

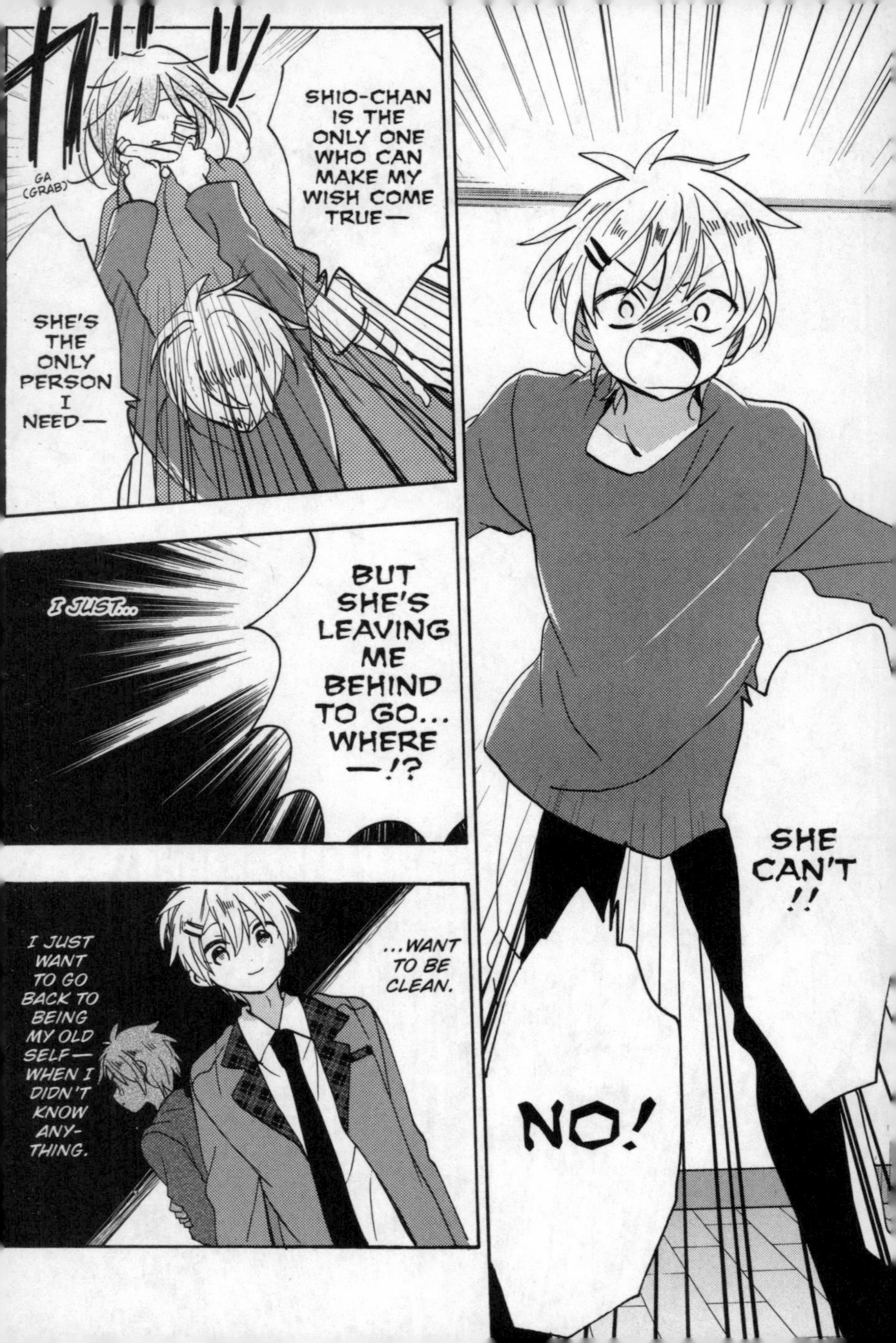
SHE CAN'T !!
NO!
SHIO-CHAN IS THE ONLY ONE WHO CAN MAKE MY WISH COME TRUE—
GA (GRAB)
SHE'S THE ONLY PERSON I NEED—
BUT SHE'S LEAVING ME BEHIND TO GO... WHERE—!?
I JUST...
...WANT TO BE CLEAN.
I JUST WANT TO GO BACK TO BEING MY OLD SELF—WHEN I DIDN'T KNOW ANYTHING.

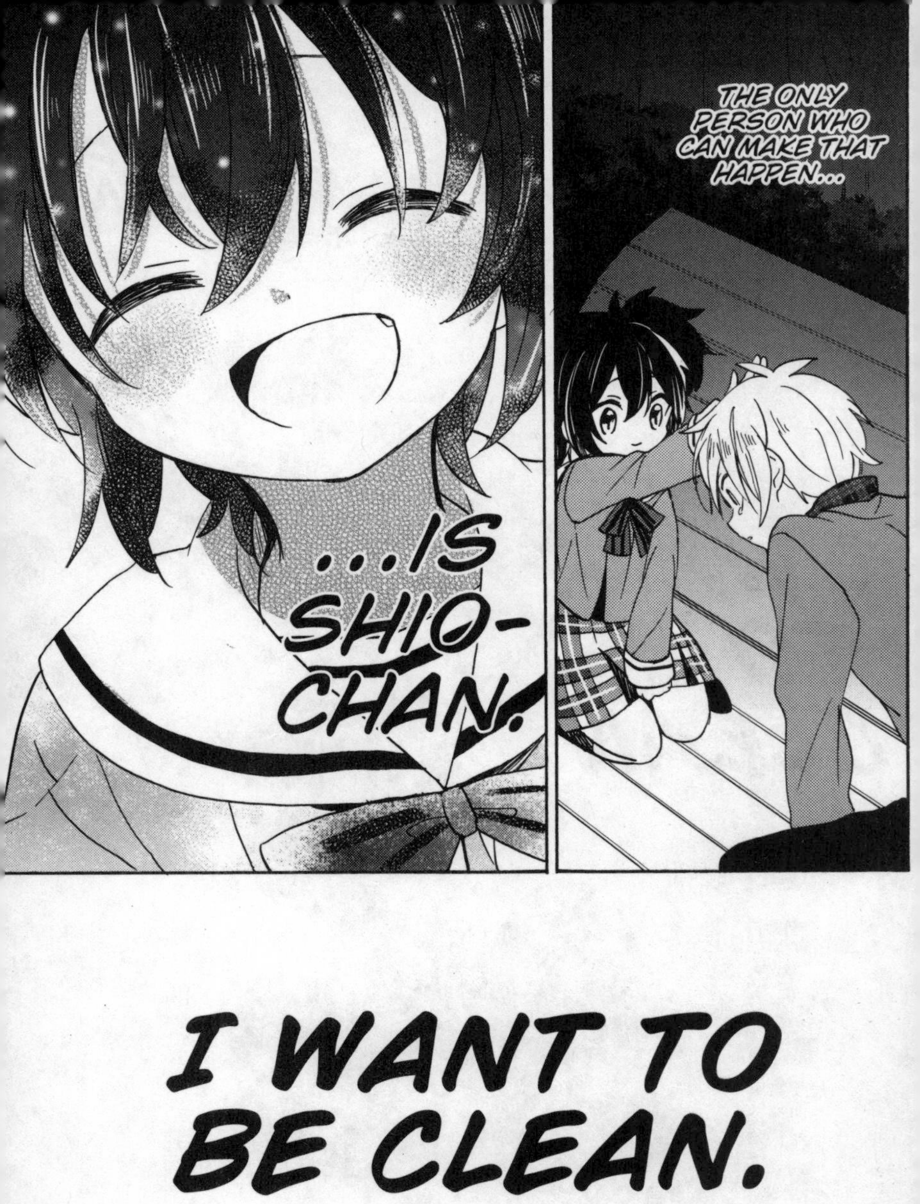
THE ONLY PERSON WHO CAN MAKE THAT HAPPEN...
...IS SHIO-CHAN.

I WANT TO BE CLEAN.

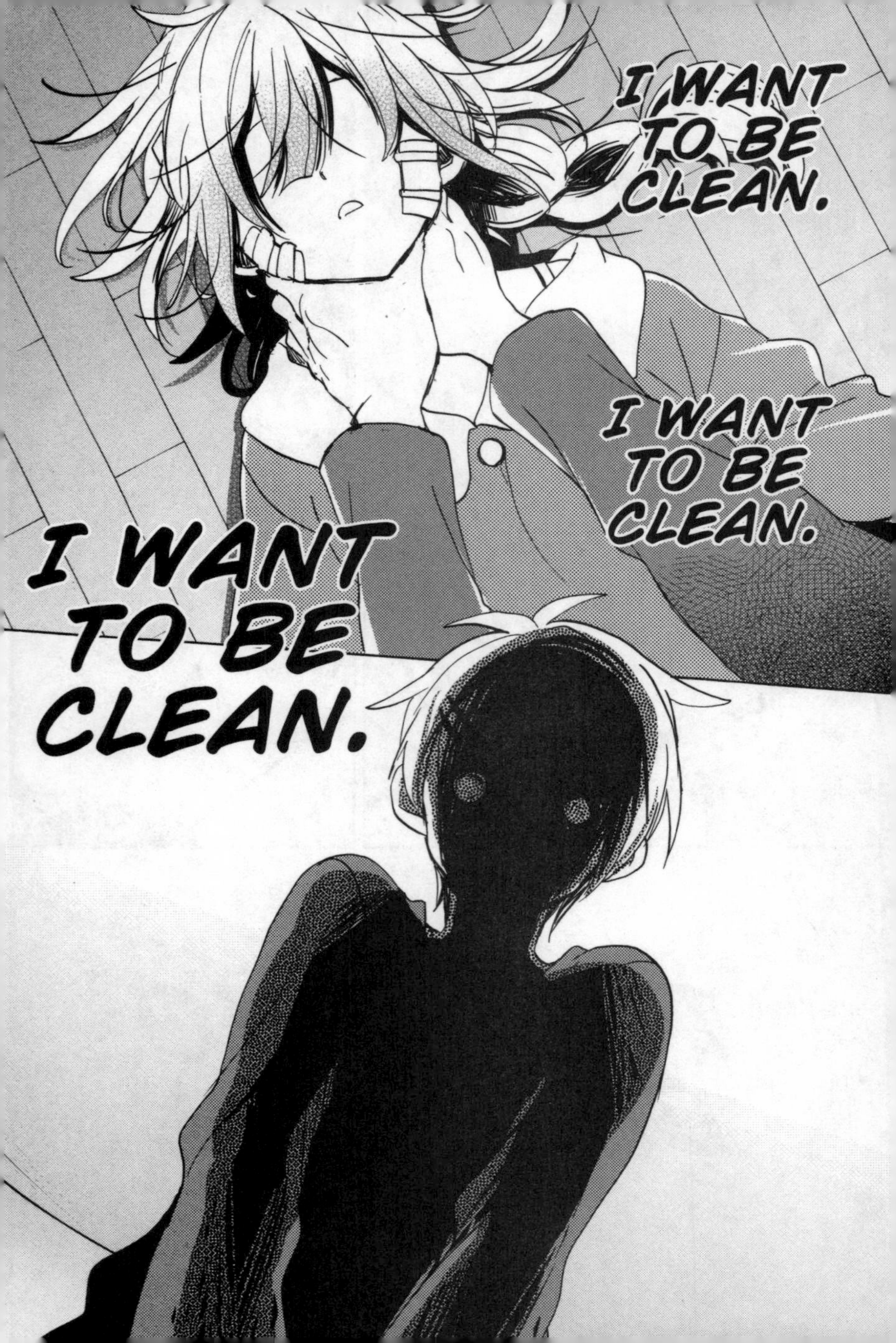
I WANT TO BE CLEAN.
I WANT TO BE CLEAN.
I WANT TO BE CLEAN.

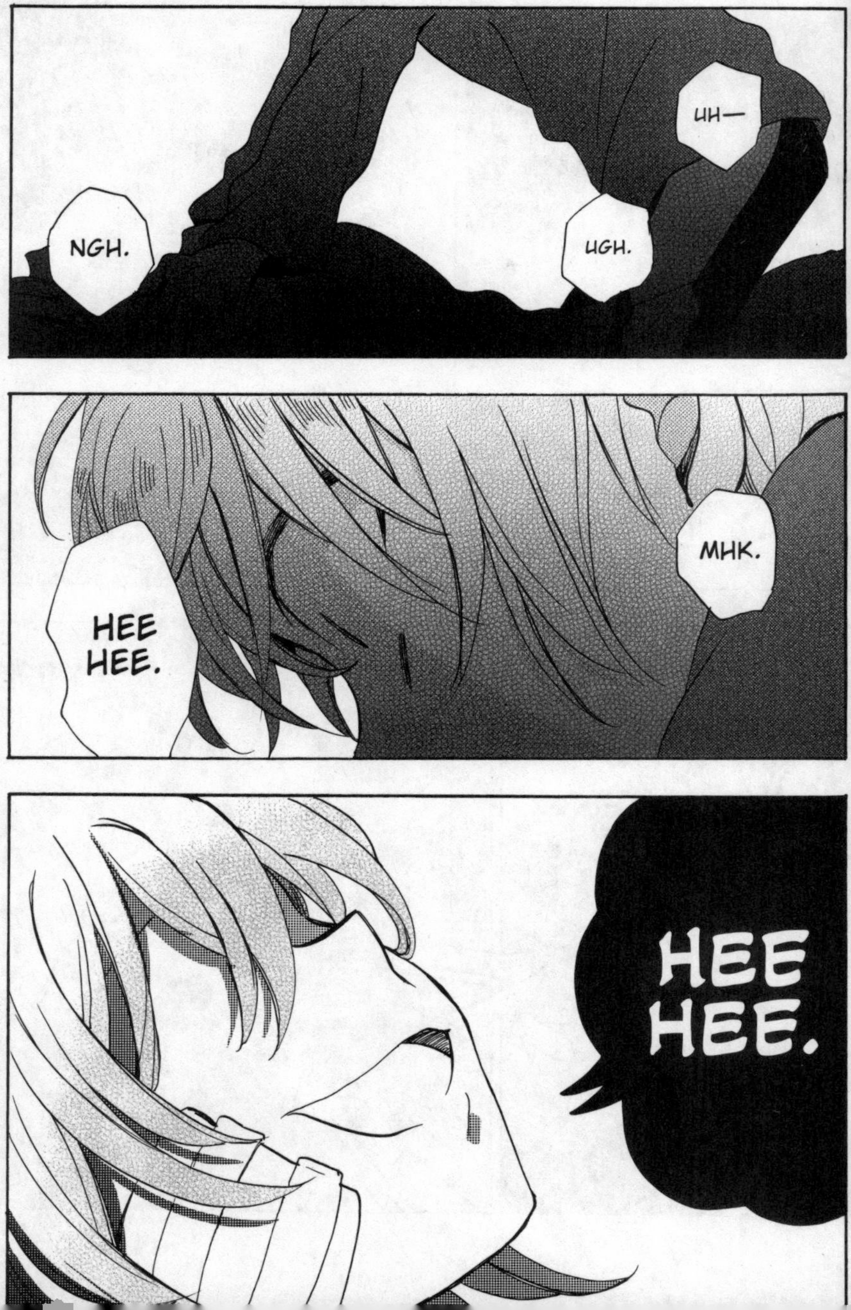
UH—
UGH.
NGH.
MHK.
HEE HEE.
HEE HEE.

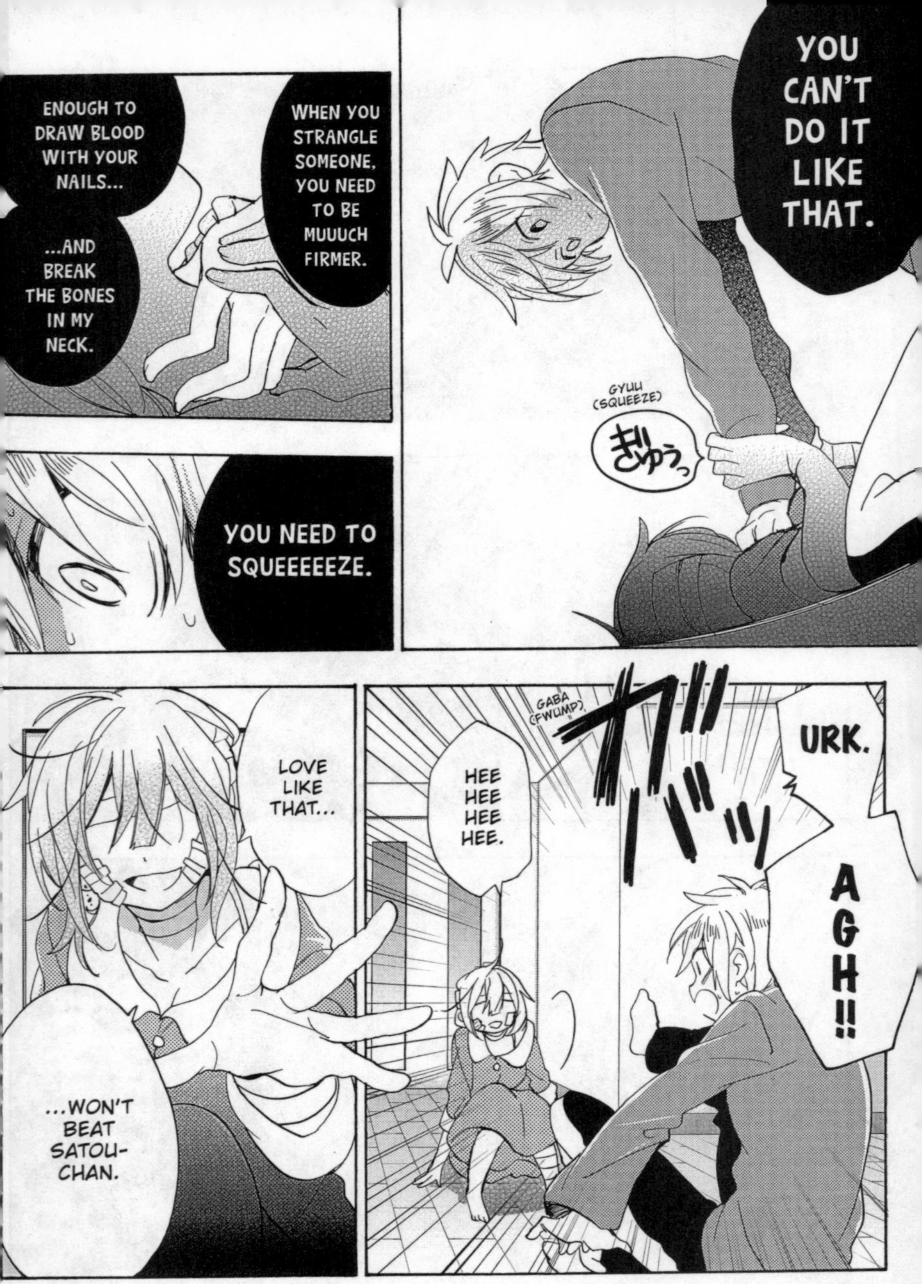
YOU CAN'T DO IT LIKE THAT.
GYUU (SQUEEZE)
ぎゅうっ
WHEN YOU STRANGLE SOMEONE, YOU NEED TO BE MUUUCH FIRMER.
ENOUGH TO DRAW BLOOD WITH YOUR NAILS...
...AND BREAK THE BONES IN MY NECK.
YOU NEED TO SQUEEEEEZE.
URK.
GABA (FWUMP)
ガバッ
HEE HEE HEE HEE.
AGH!!
LOVE LIKE THAT...
...WON'T BEAT SATOU-CHAN.

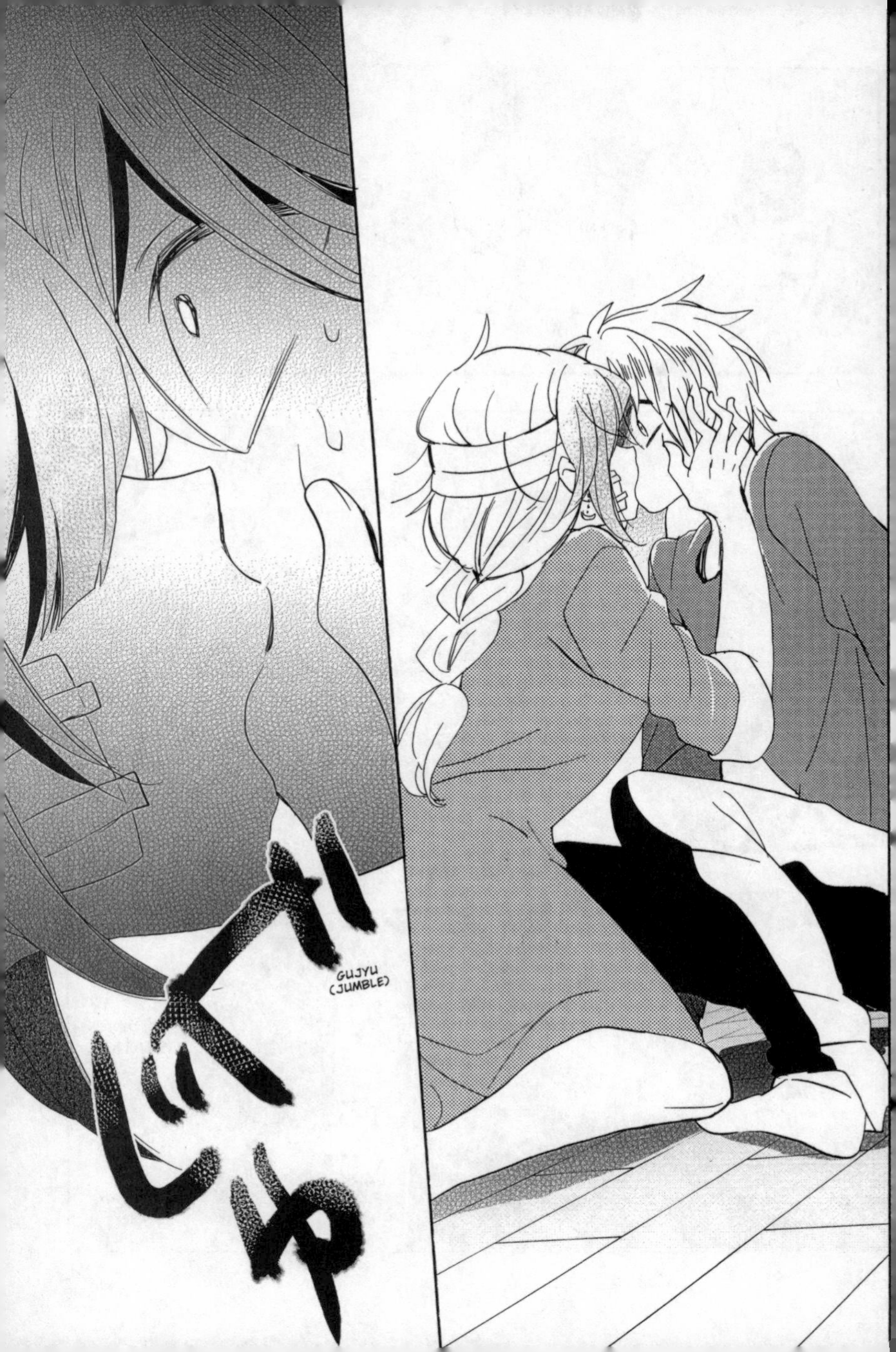
ぐじゅ
GUJYU
(JUMBLE)

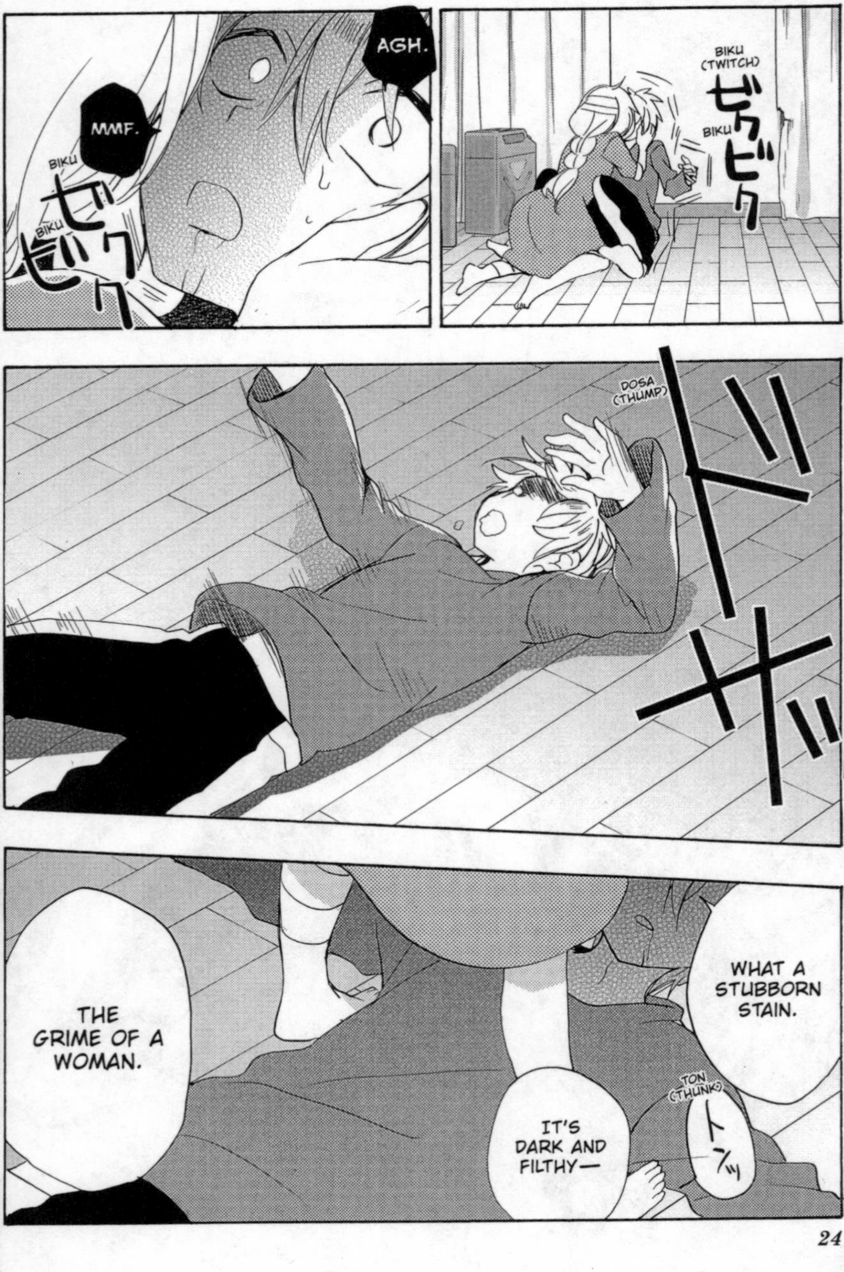
BIKU (TWITCH)
ビクビク
BIKU
AGH.
MMF.
BIKU
ビクビク
BIKU
DOSA (THUMP)
ドサッ
WHAT A STUBBORN STAIN.
TON (THUNK)
トンッ
IT'S DARK AND FILTHY—
THE GRIME OF A WOMAN.

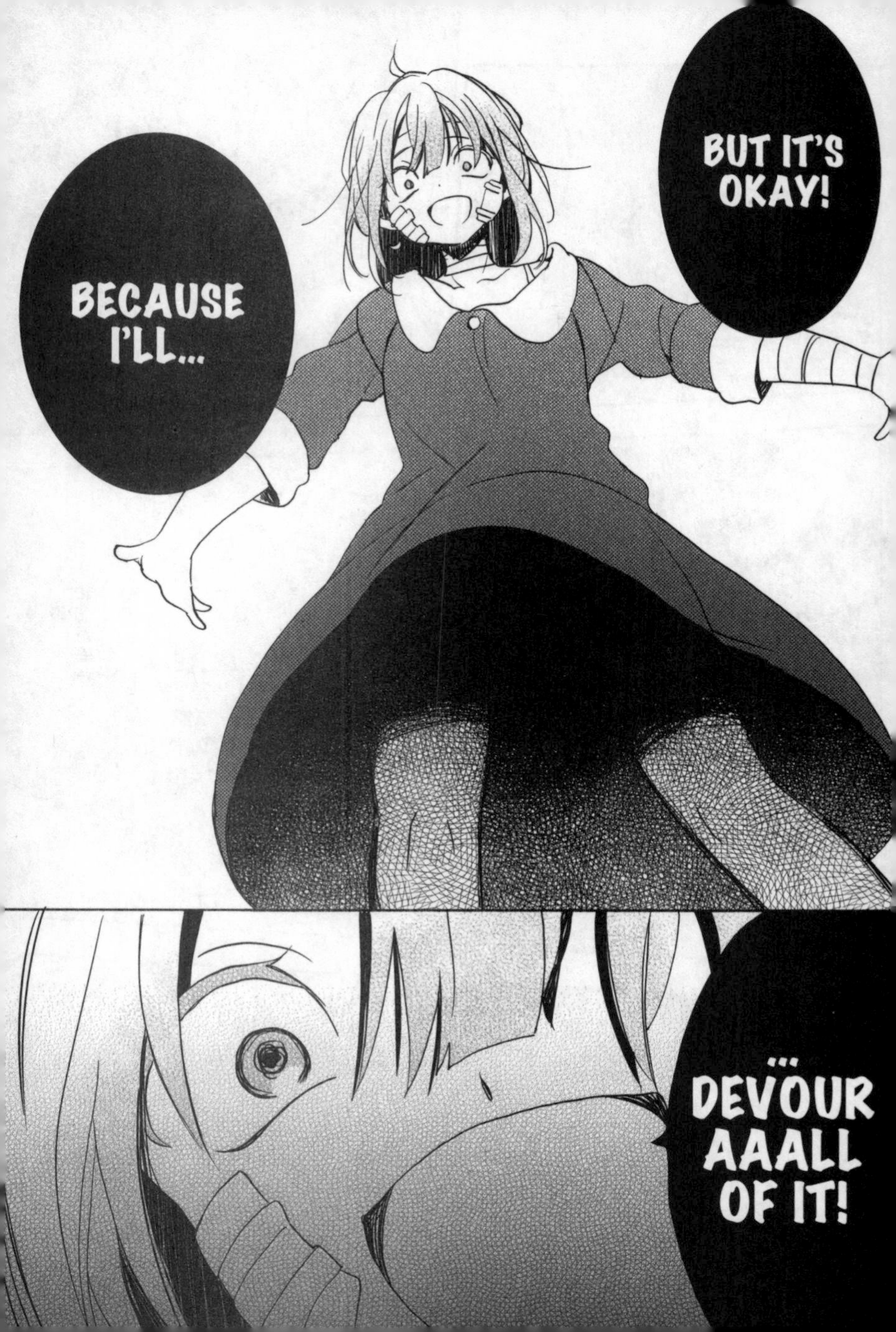
BUT IT'S OKAY!
BECAUSE I'LL...
...DEVOUR AAALL OF IT!

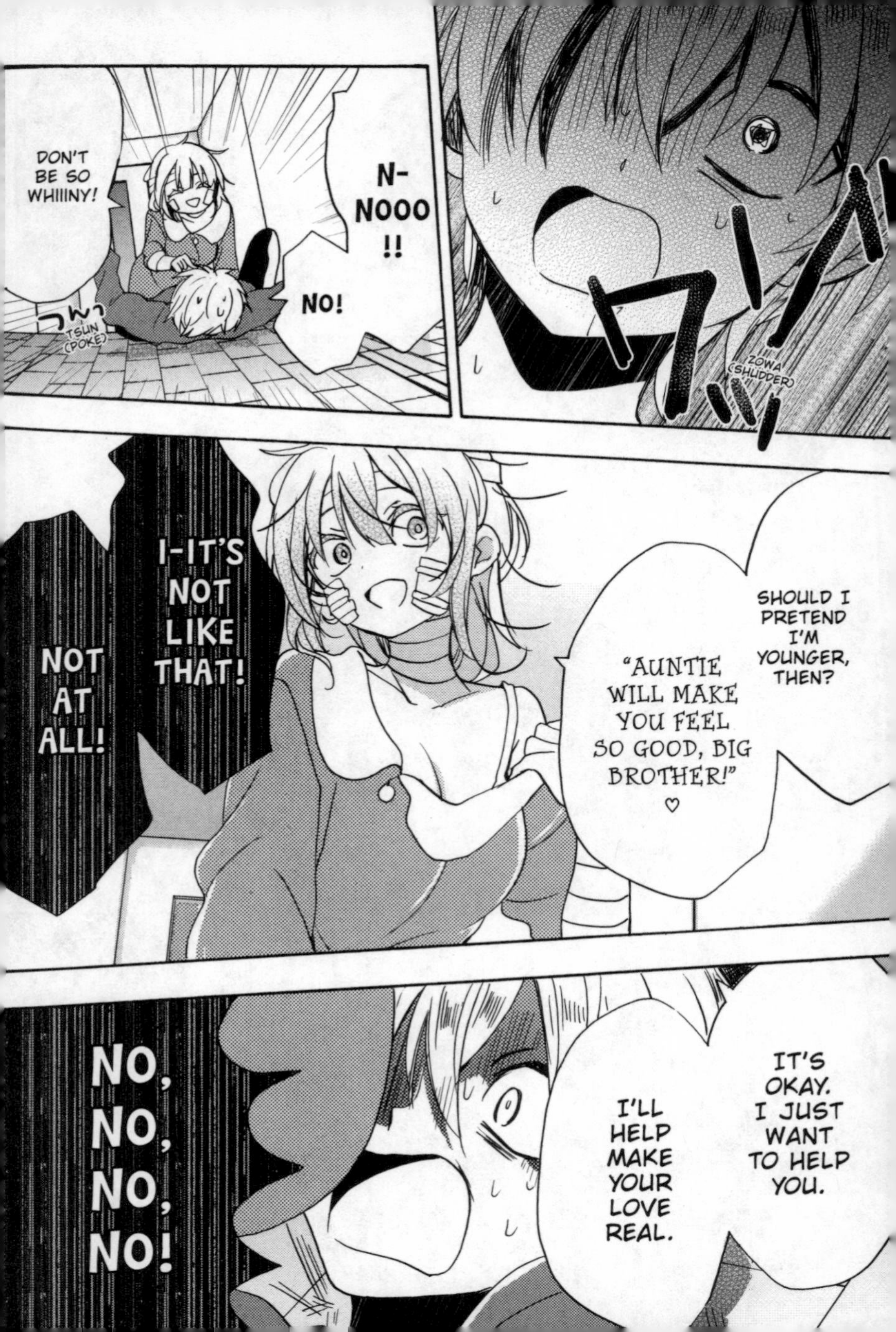
ZOWA (SHUDDER)
N-NOOO!!
NO!
DON'T BE SO WHIIINY!
TSUN (POKE)
SHOULD I PRETEND I'M YOUNGER, THEN?
"AUNTIE WILL MAKE YOU FEEL SO GOOD, BIG BROTHER!" ♡
I-IT'S NOT LIKE THAT!
NOT AT ALL!
IT'S OKAY. I JUST WANT TO HELP YOU.
I'LL HELP MAKE YOUR LOVE REAL.
NO, NO, NO, NO!

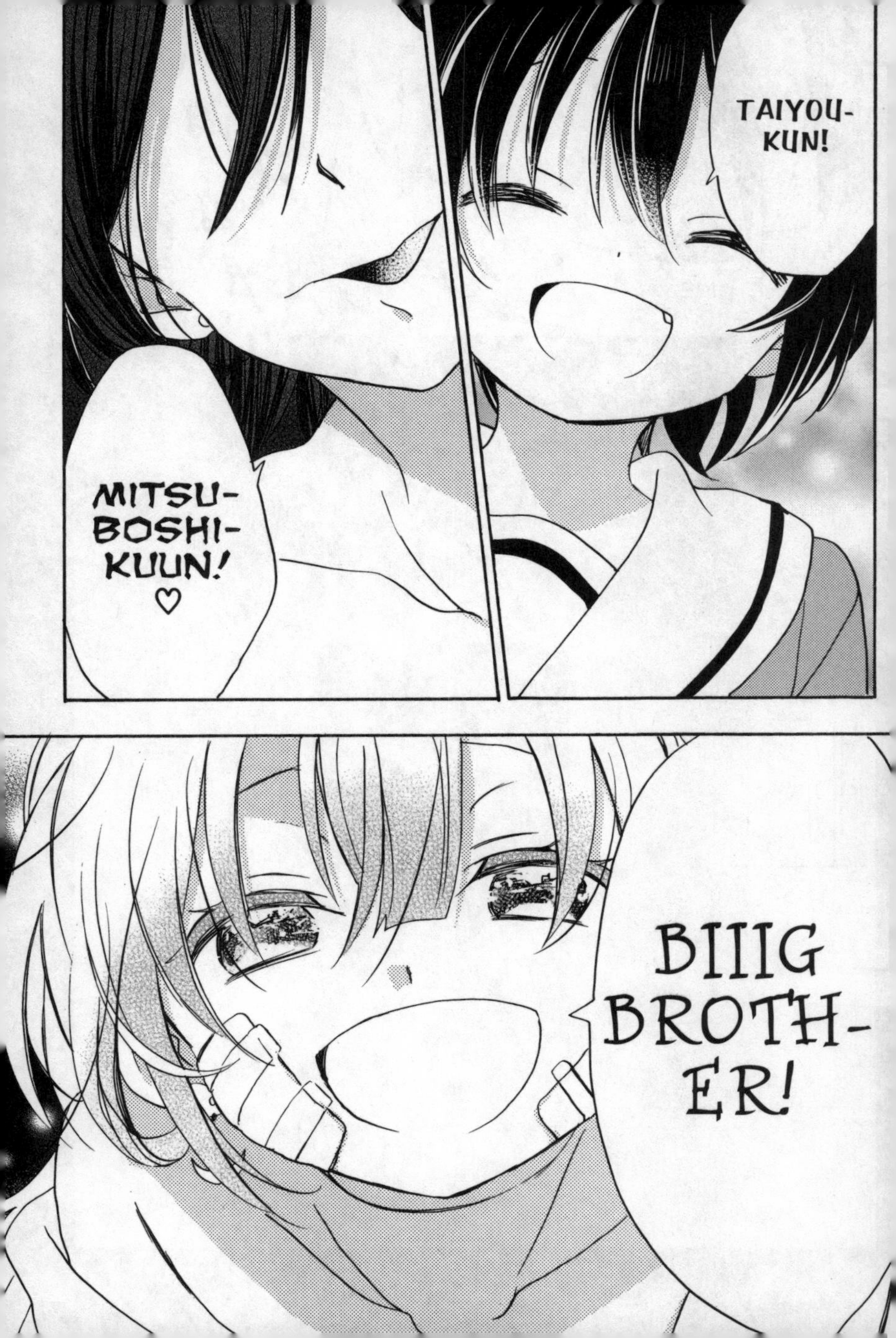
TAIYOU-KUN!
MITSU-BOSHI-KUUN! ♡
BIIIG BROTH-ER!

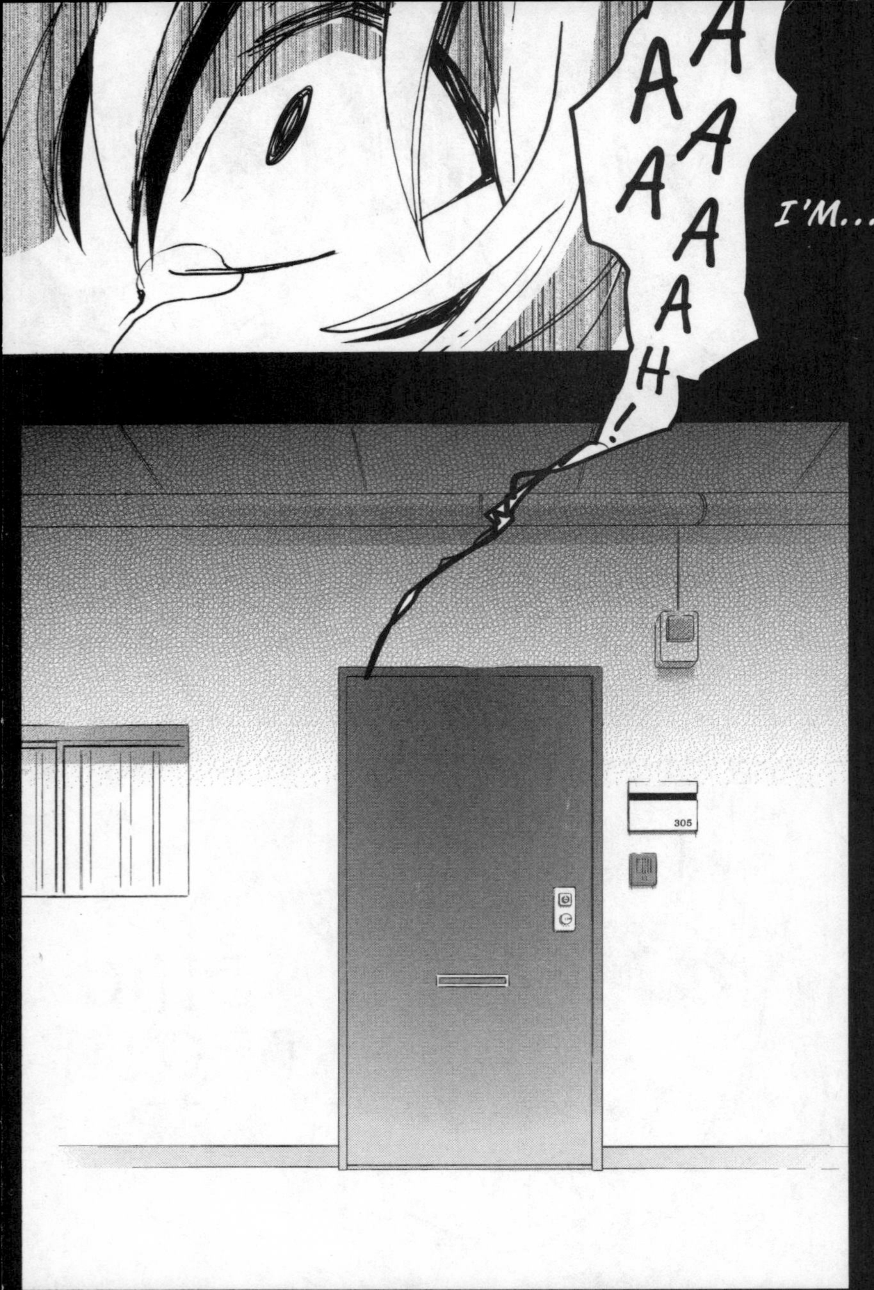
I'M...
AAAAAAH!
305

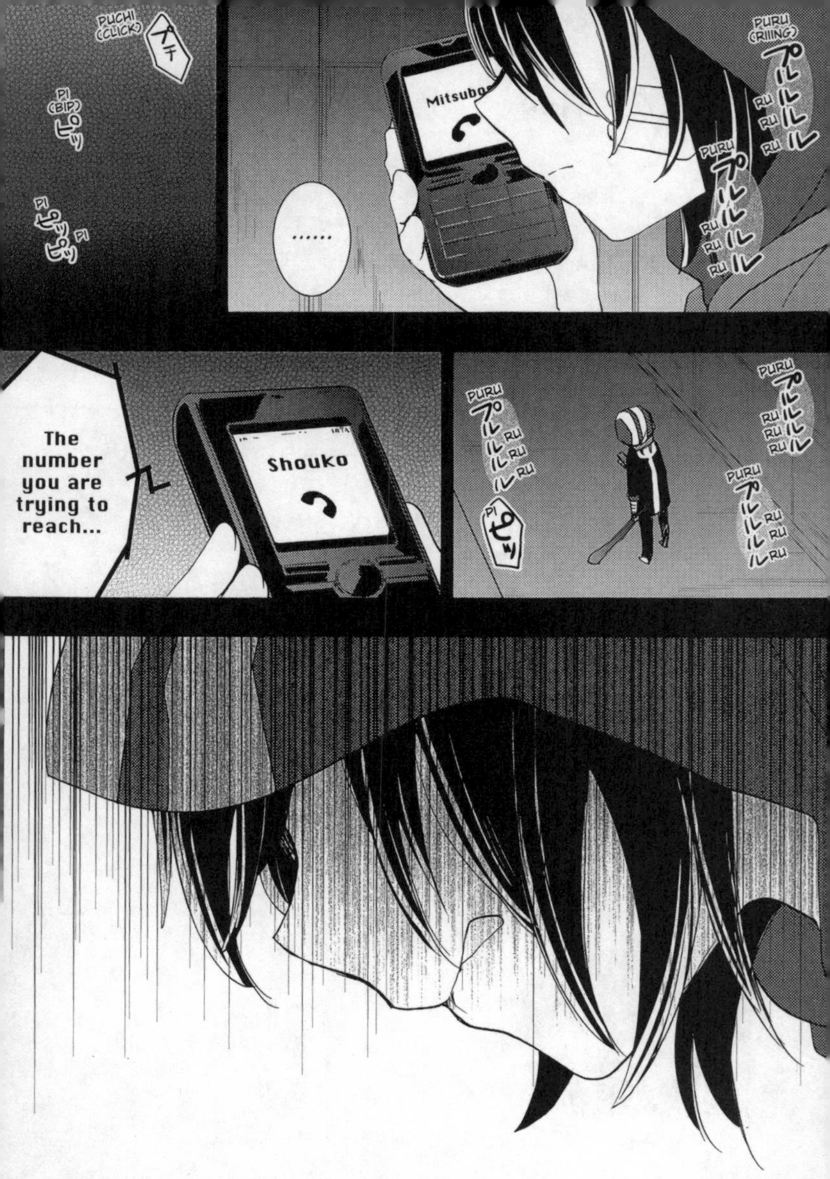
PURU (RIIING) プルルル
RU RU RU
PURU プルルル
RU RU RU
Mitsubos
......
PUCHI (CLICK) プチ
PI (BIP) ピッ
PI ピッ PI ピッ
PURU プルルル
RU RU RU
PURU プルルル
RU RU RU
PURU プルルル
RU RU RU
PI ピッ
Shouko
The number you are trying to reach...

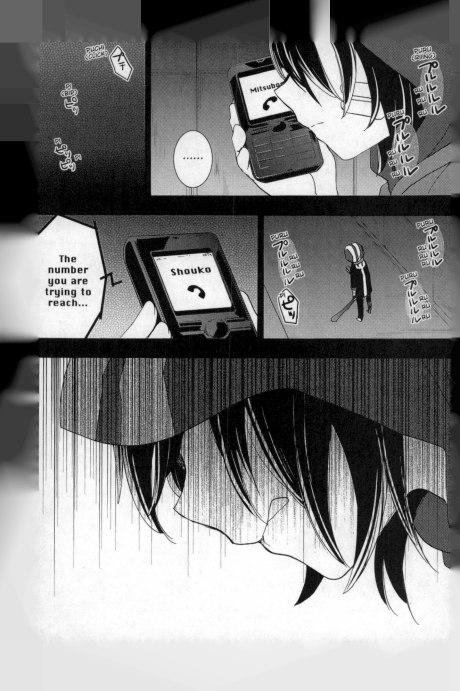

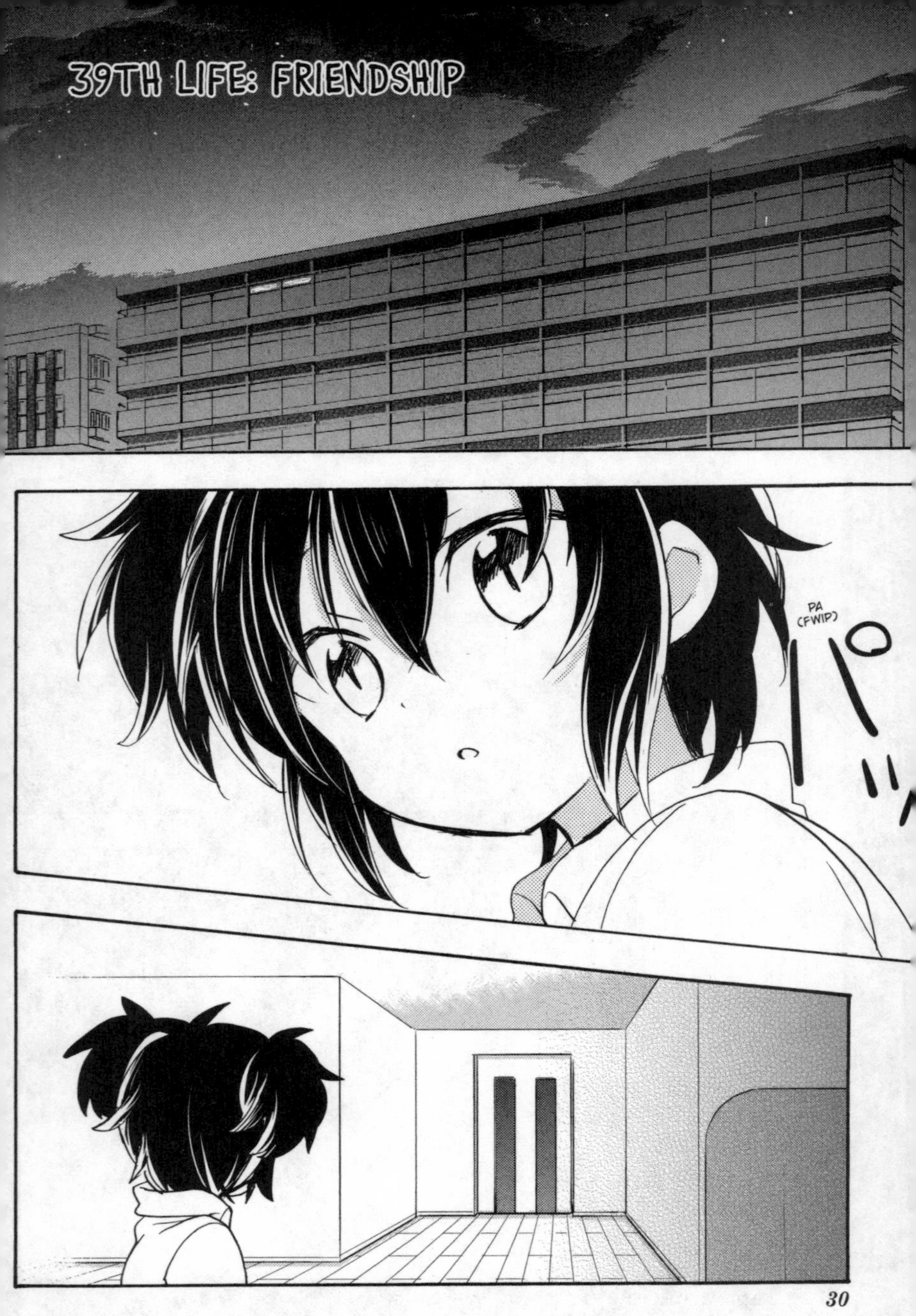
39TH LIFE: FRIENDSHIP
パッ
PA (FWIP)

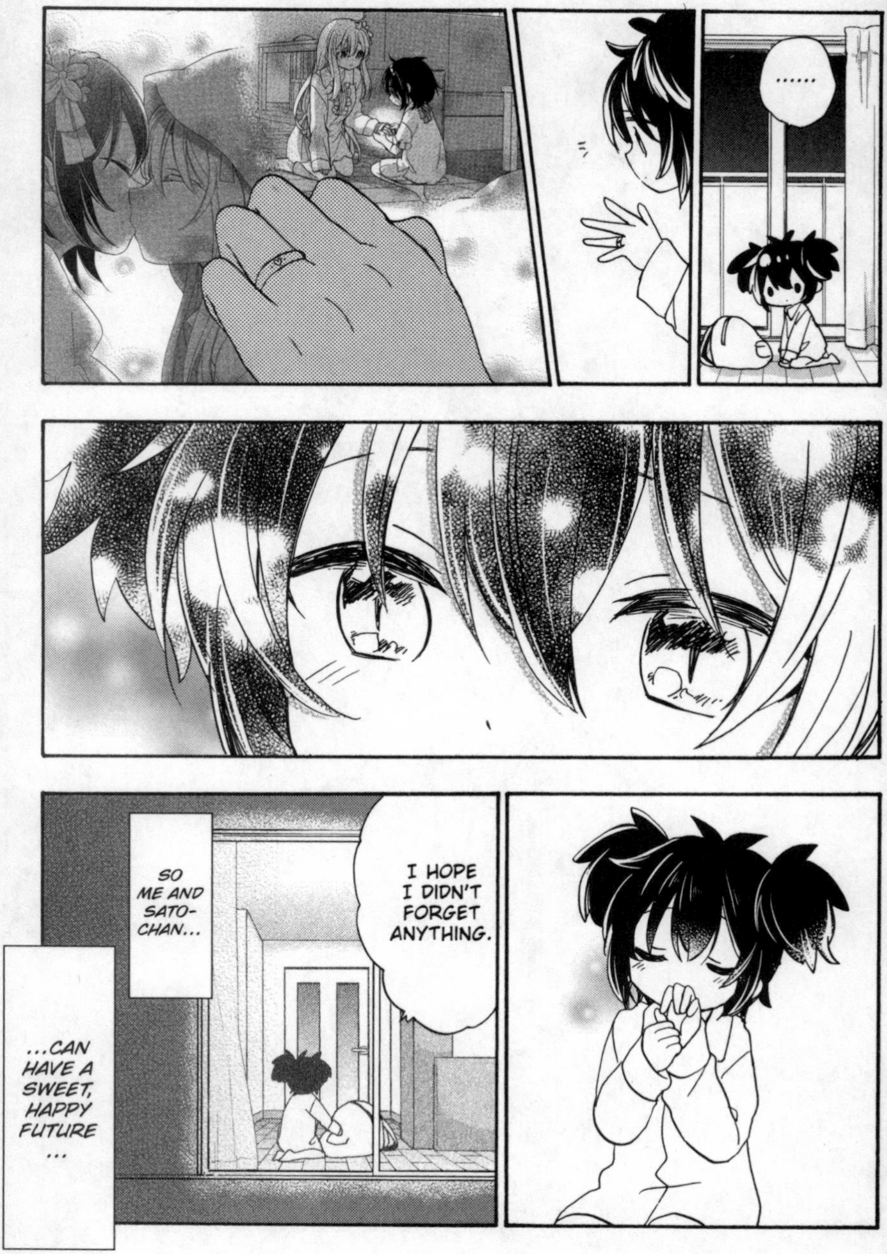
......
I HOPE I DIDN'T FORGET ANYTHING.
SO ME AND SATO-CHAN...
...CAN HAVE A SWEET, HAPPY FUTURE...

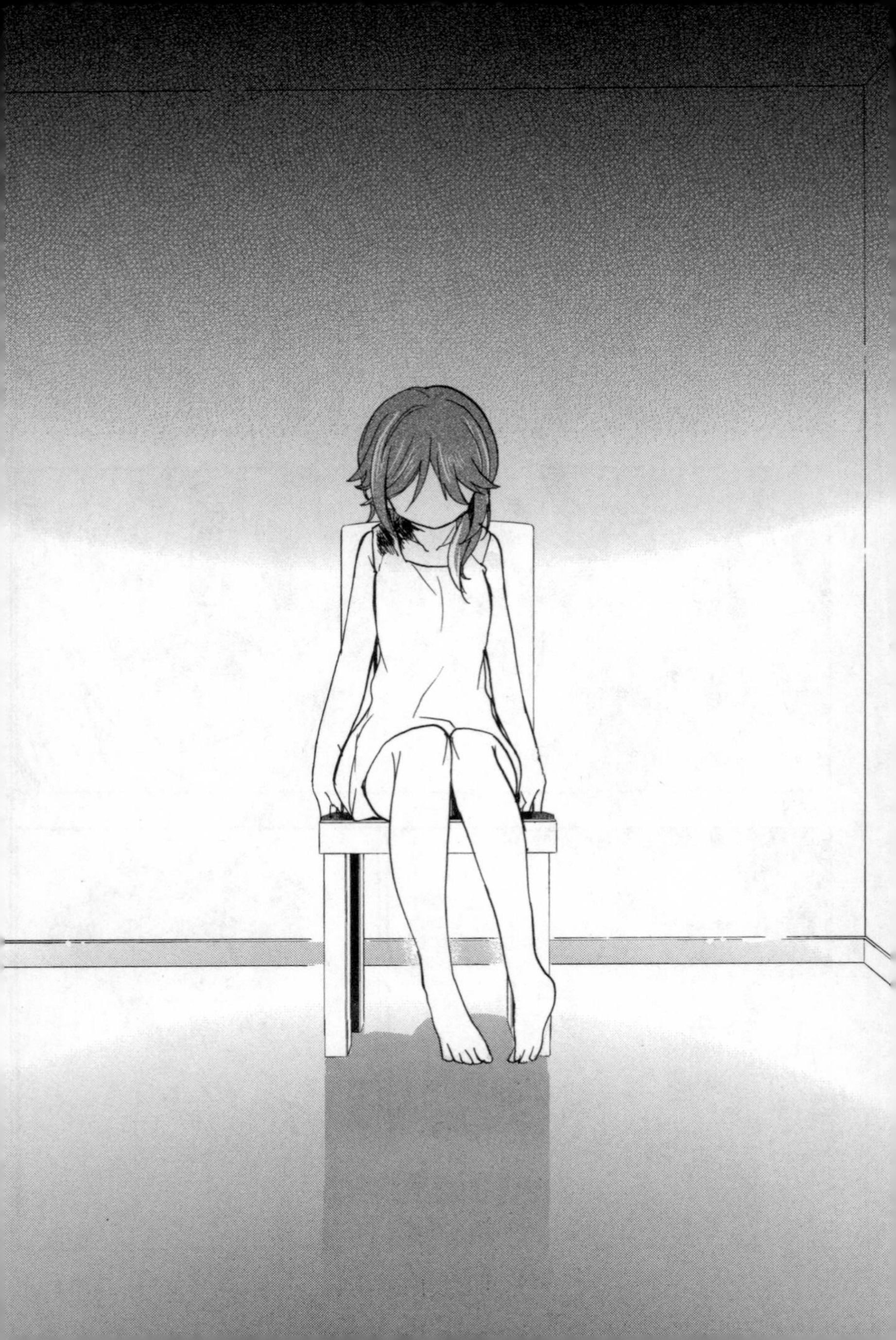

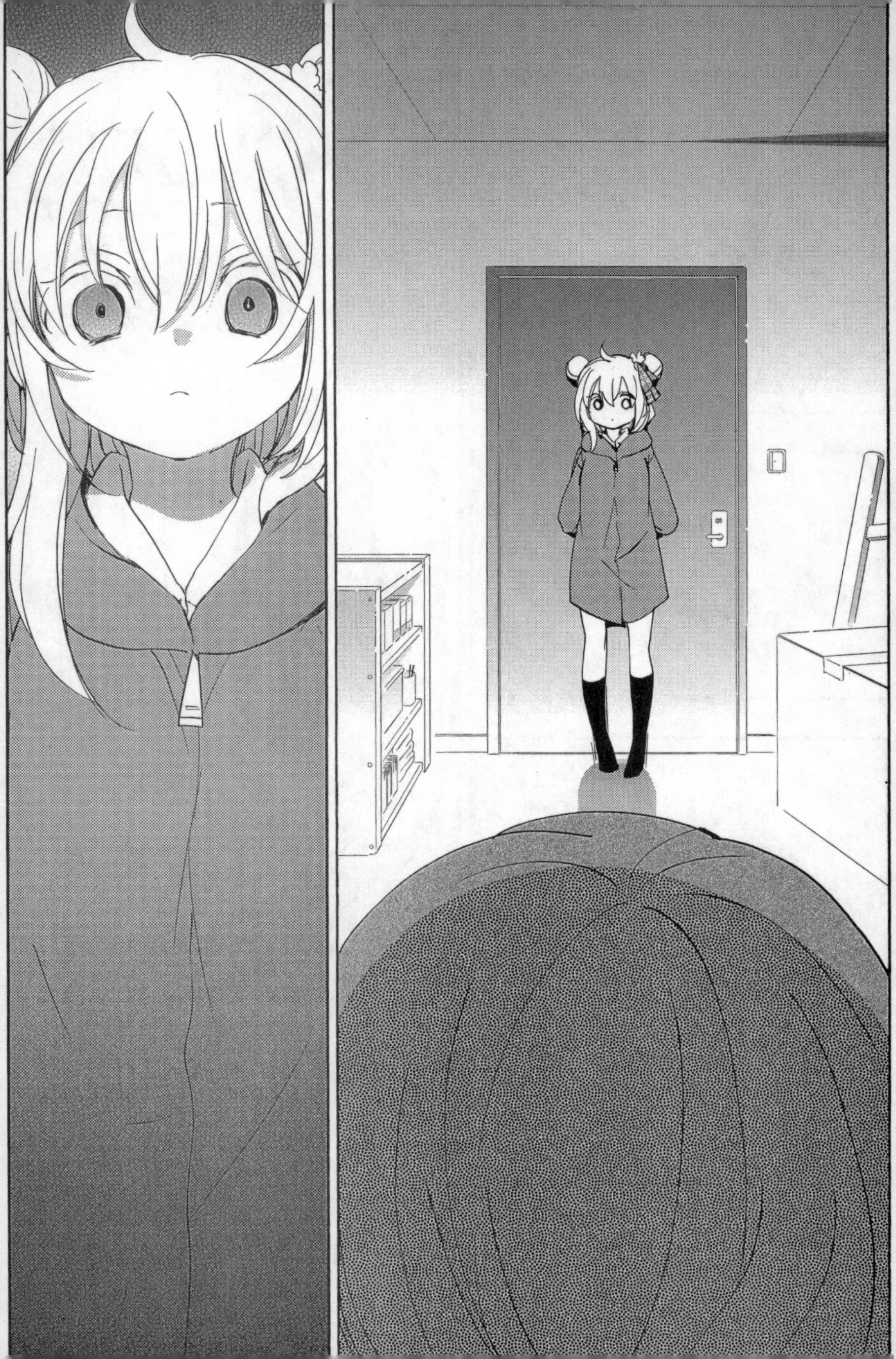

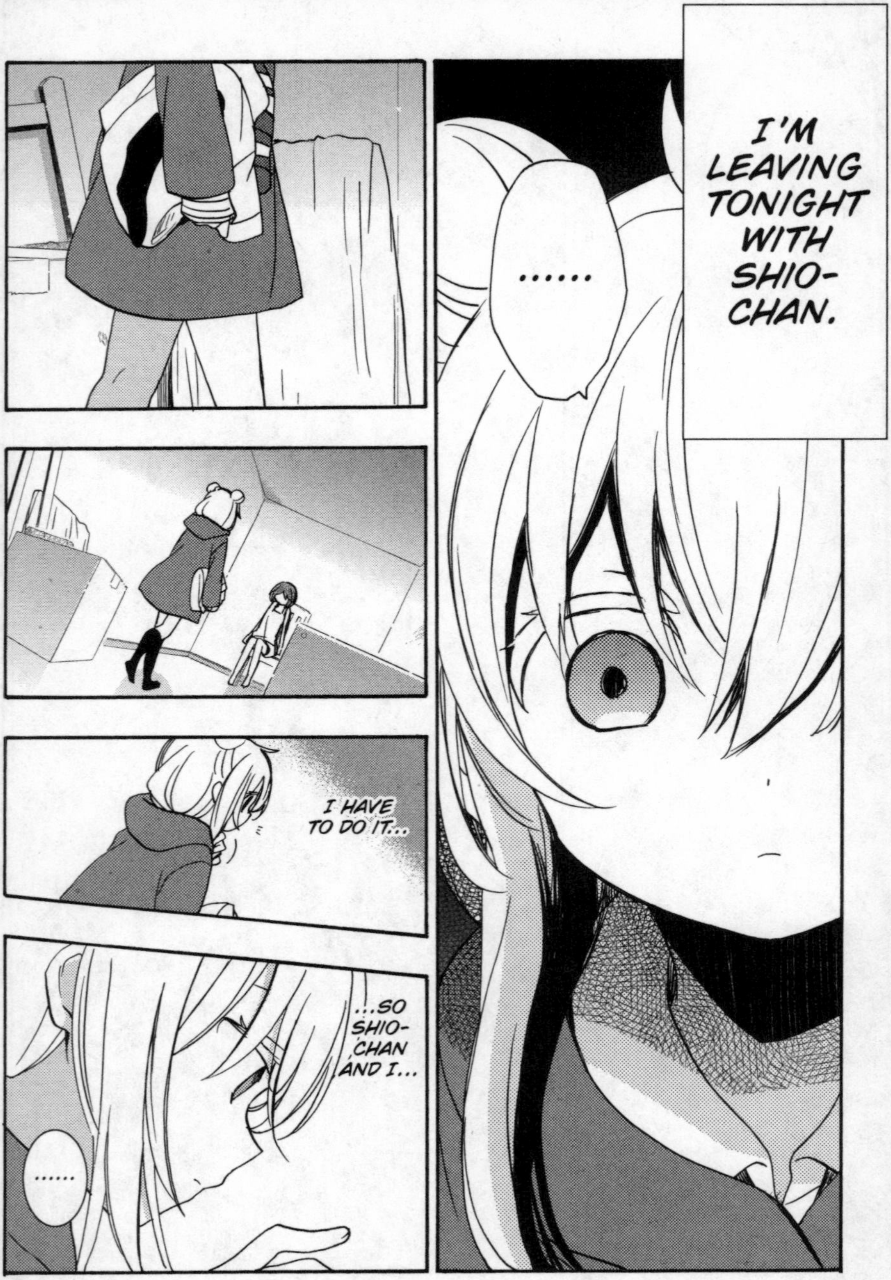
I'M LEAVING TONIGHT WITH SHIO-CHAN.
......
I HAVE TO DO IT...
...SO SHIO-CHAN AND I...
......

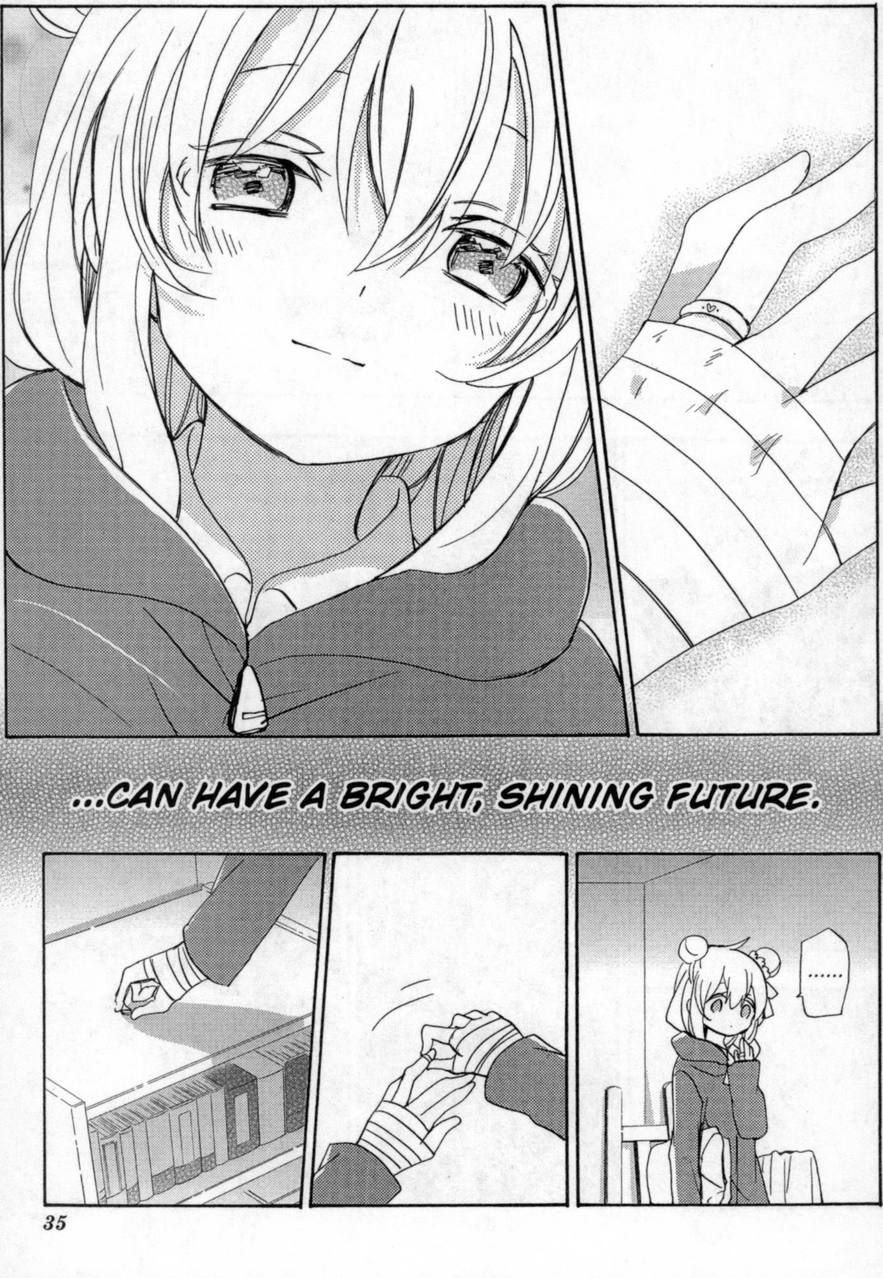
...CAN HAVE A BRIGHT, SHINING FUTURE.
......

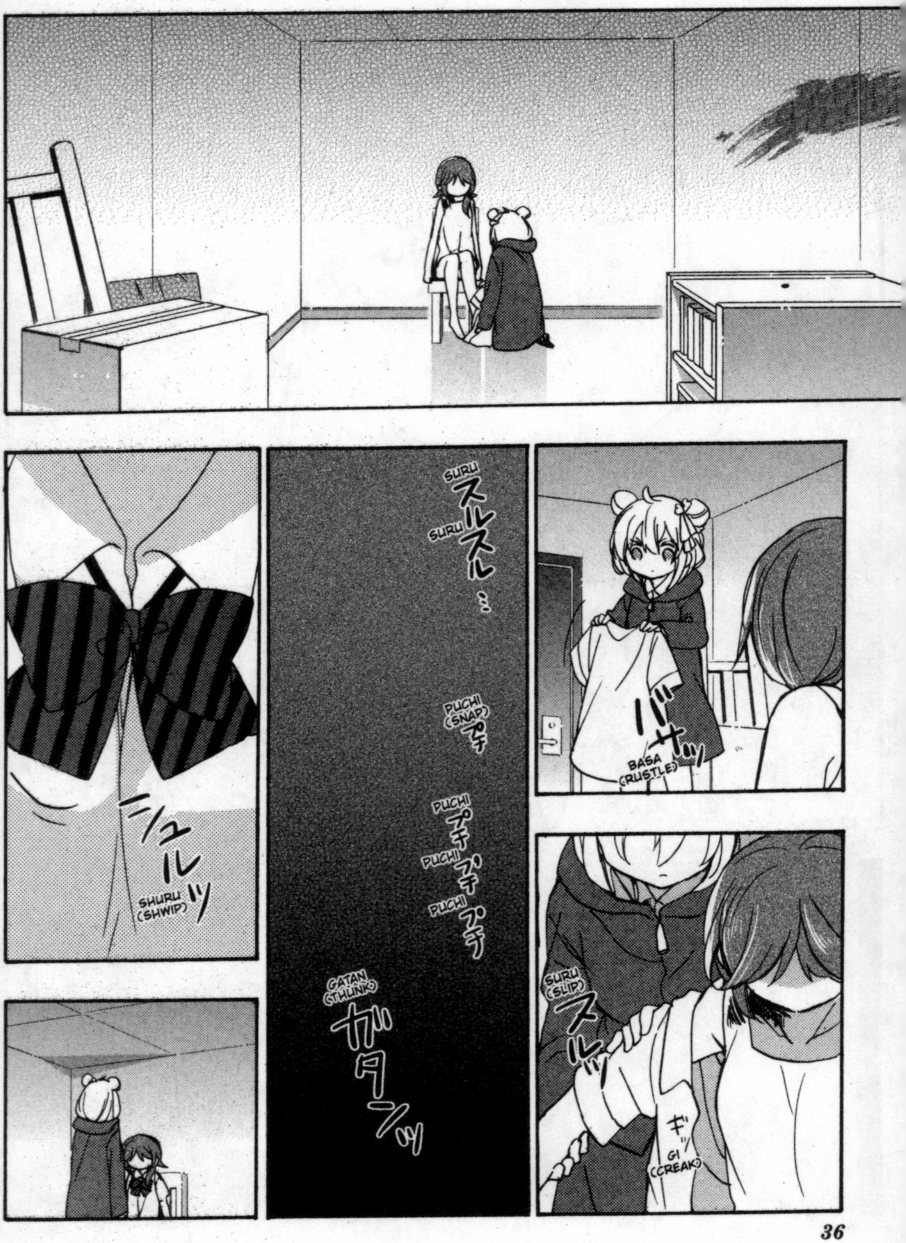
バサッ
BASA (RUSTLE)
スルッ
SURU (SLIP)
ギッ
GI (CREAK)
スルスル…
SURU SURU
プチ
PUCHI (SNAP)
プチ プチ プチ
PUCHI PUCHI PUCHI
ガタンッ
GATAN (THUNK)
シュルッ
SHURU (SHWIP)

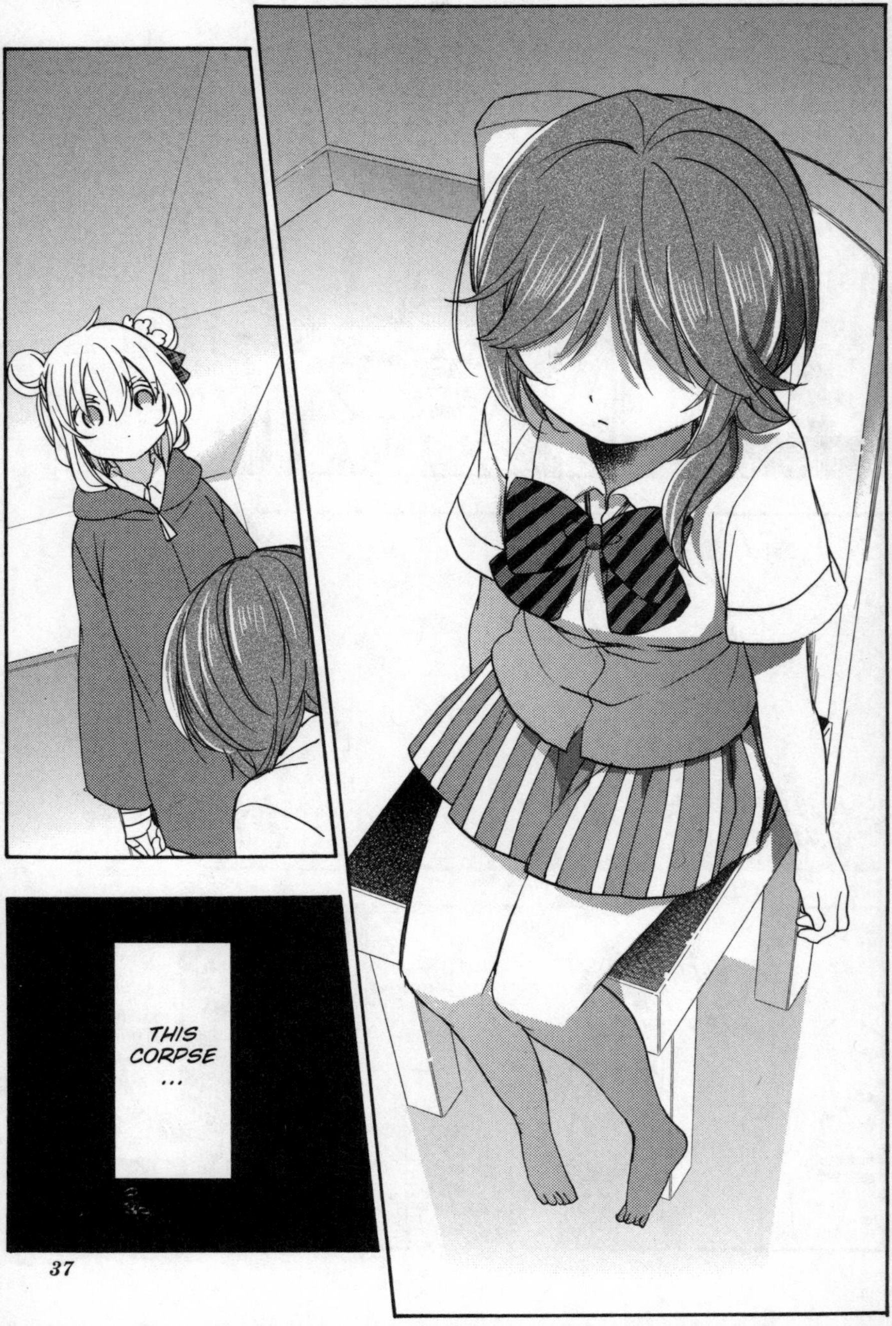
THIS CORPSE ...

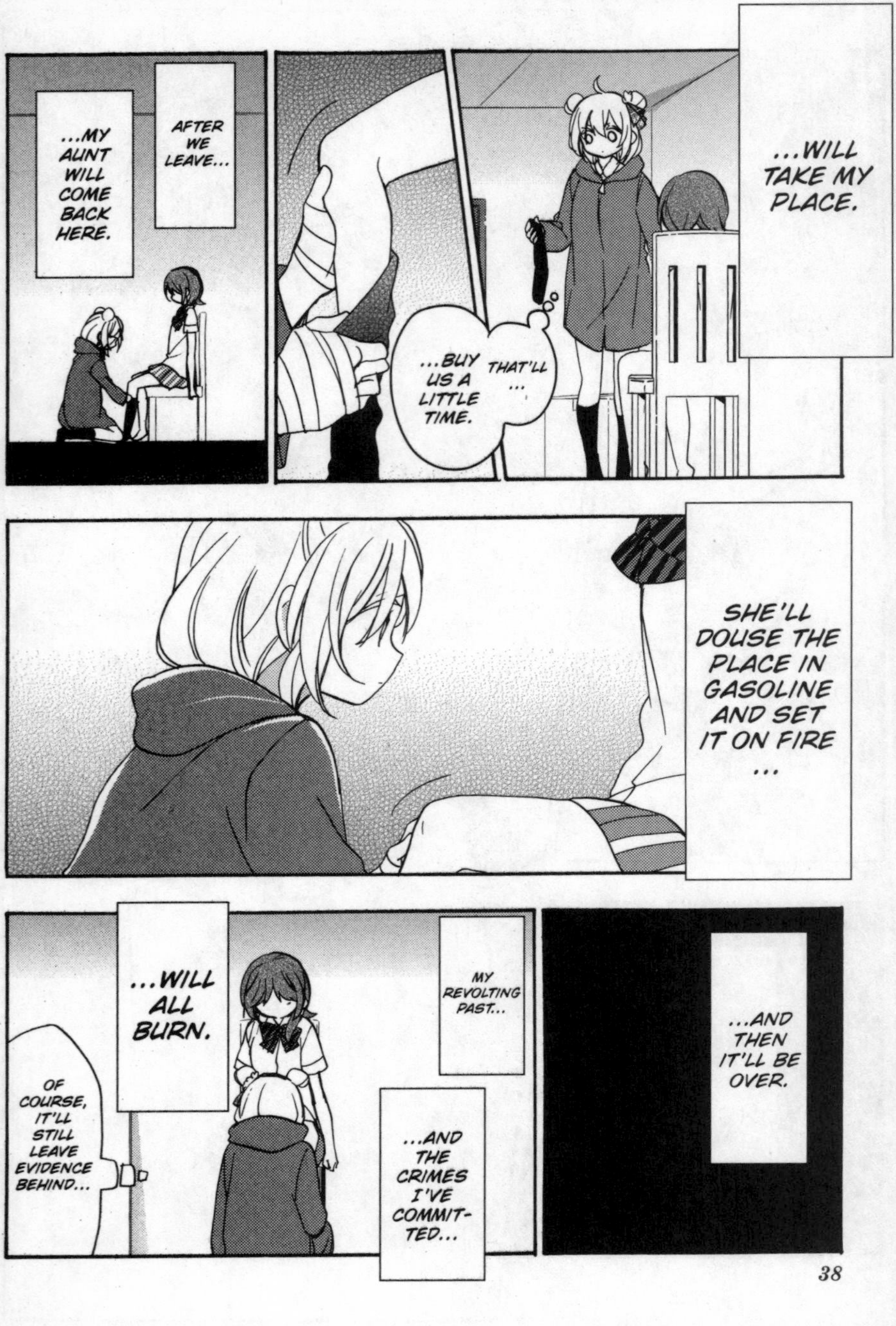
...WILL TAKE MY PLACE.
THAT'LL...
...BUY US A LITTLE TIME.
AFTER WE LEAVE...
...MY AUNT WILL COME BACK HERE.
SHE'LL DOUSE THE PLACE IN GASOLINE AND SET IT ON FIRE...
...AND THEN IT'LL BE OVER.
MY REVOLTING PAST...
...AND THE CRIMES I'VE COMMIT-TED...
...WILL ALL BURN.
OF COURSE, IT'LL STILL LEAVE EVIDENCE BEHIND...

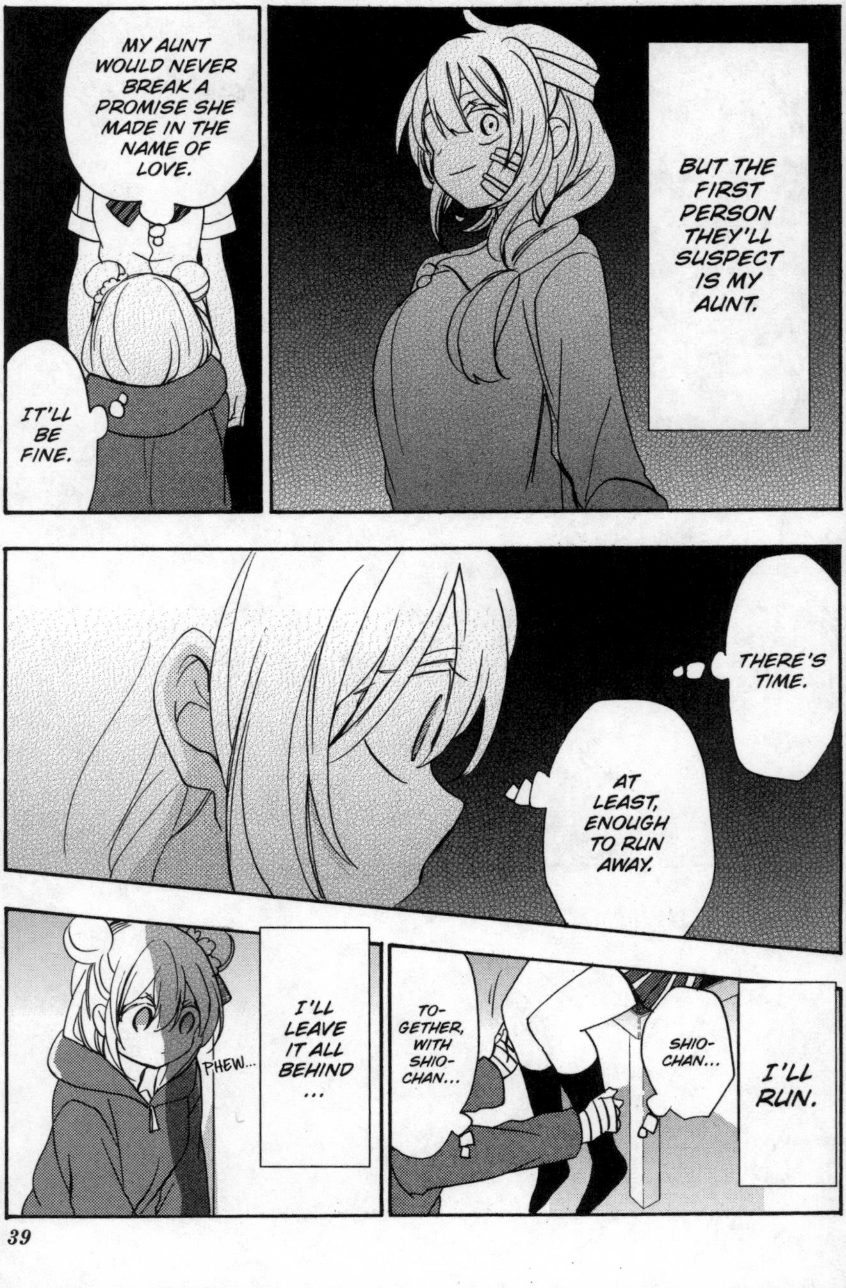
BUT THE FIRST PERSON THEY'LL SUSPECT IS MY AUNT.
MY AUNT WOULD NEVER BREAK A PROMISE SHE MADE IN THE NAME OF LOVE.
IT'LL BE FINE.
THERE'S TIME.
AT LEAST, ENOUGH TO RUN AWAY.
I'LL RUN.
SHIO-CHAN...
TO-GETHER, WITH SHIO-CHAN...
I'LL LEAVE IT ALL BEHIND ...
PHEW...

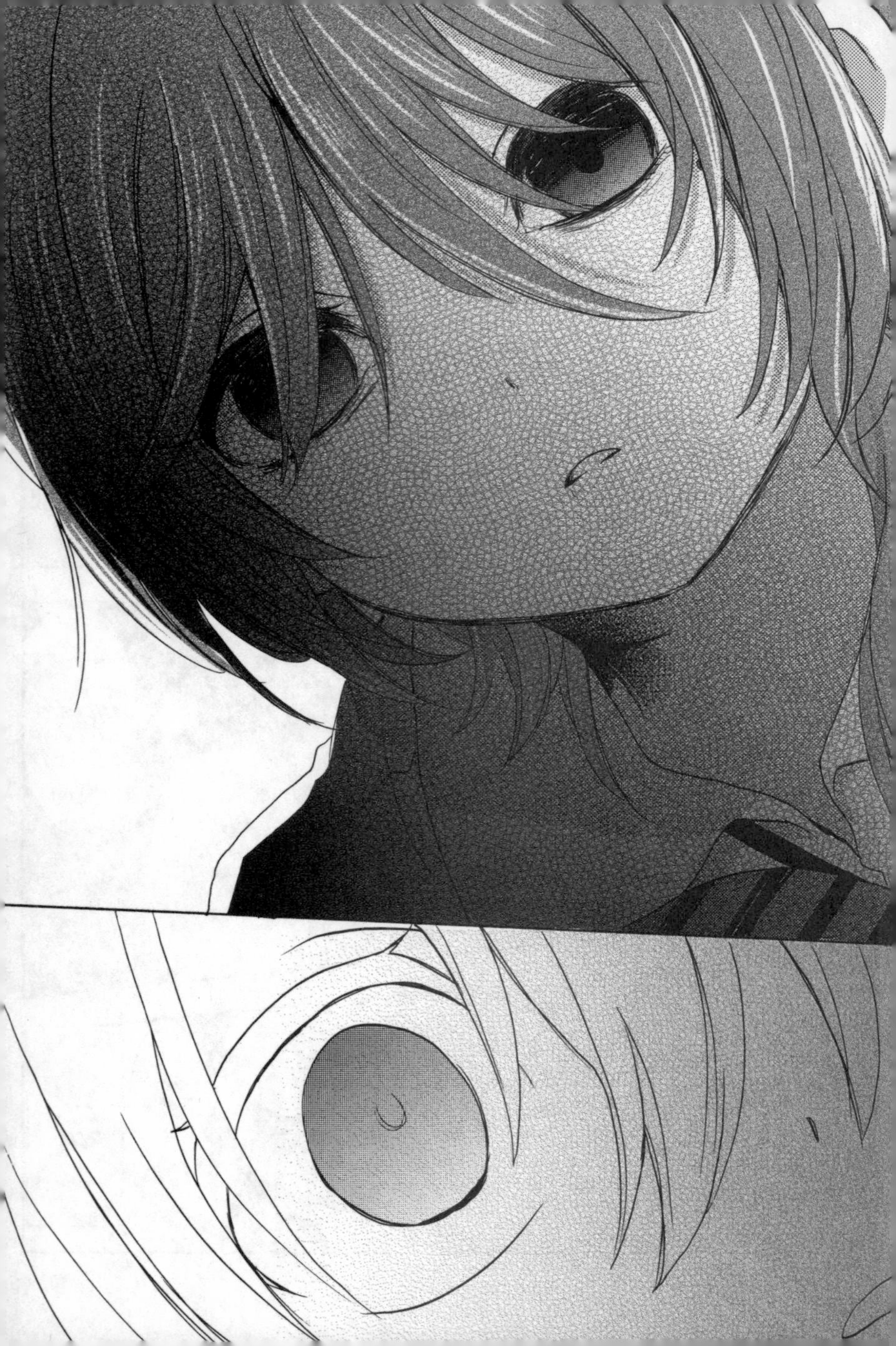

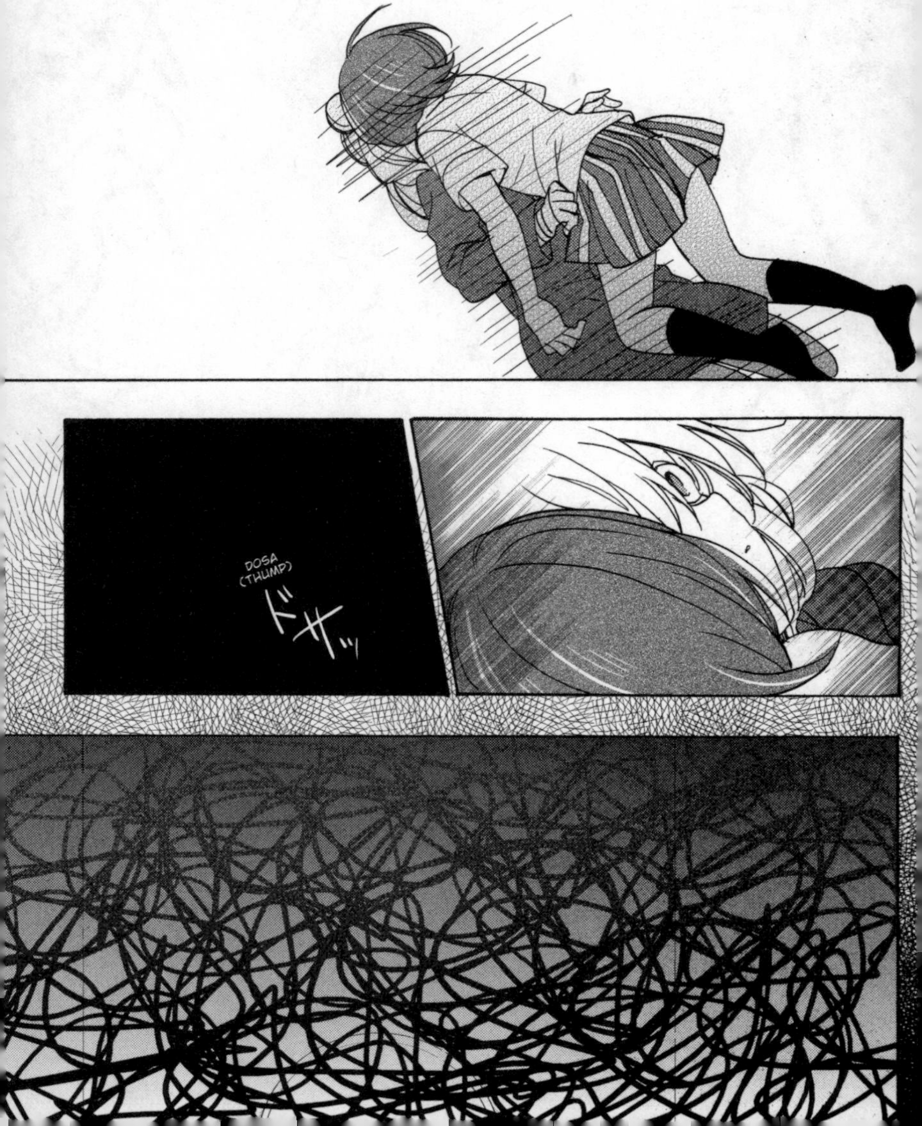
DOSA
(THUMP)
ドサッ

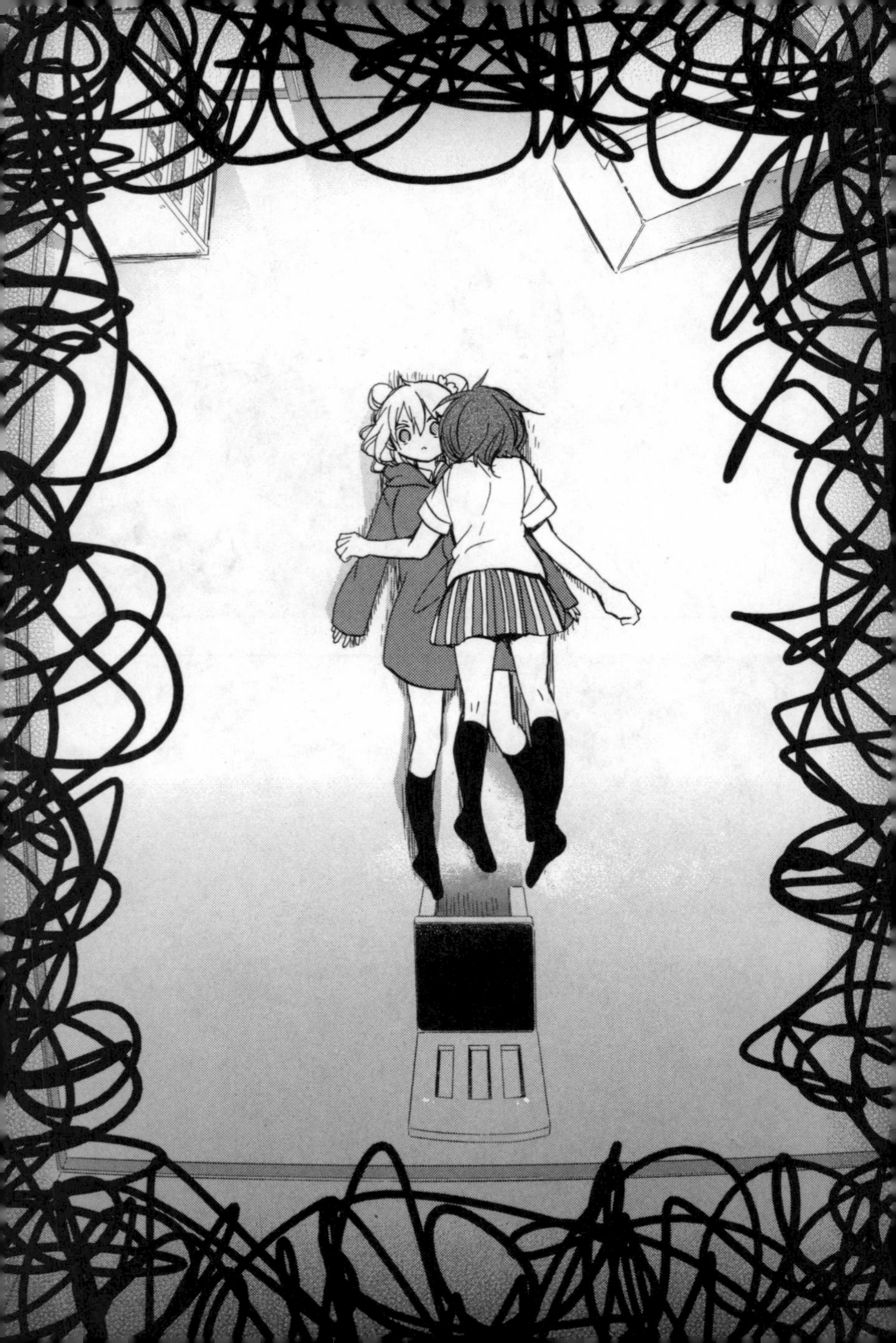

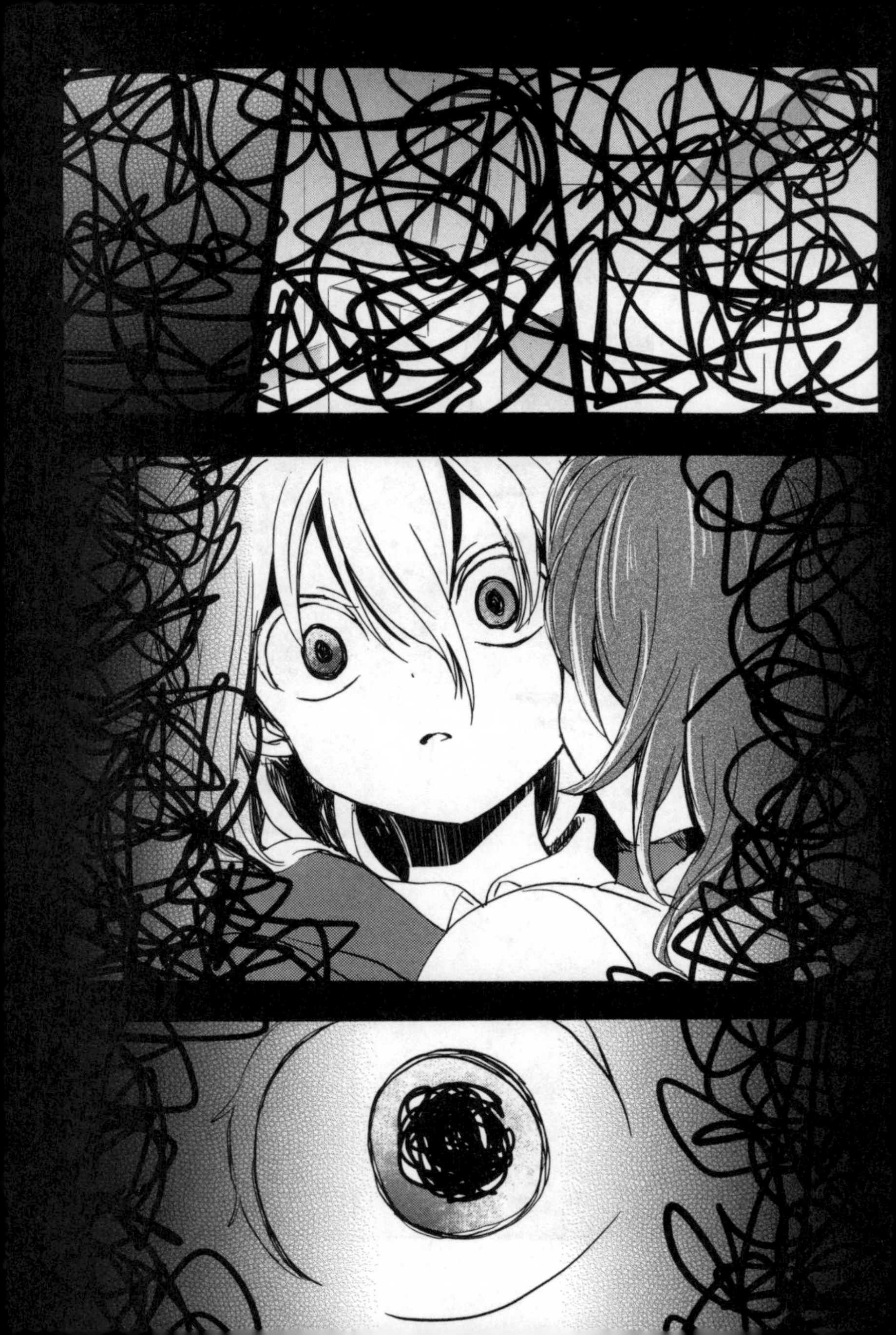

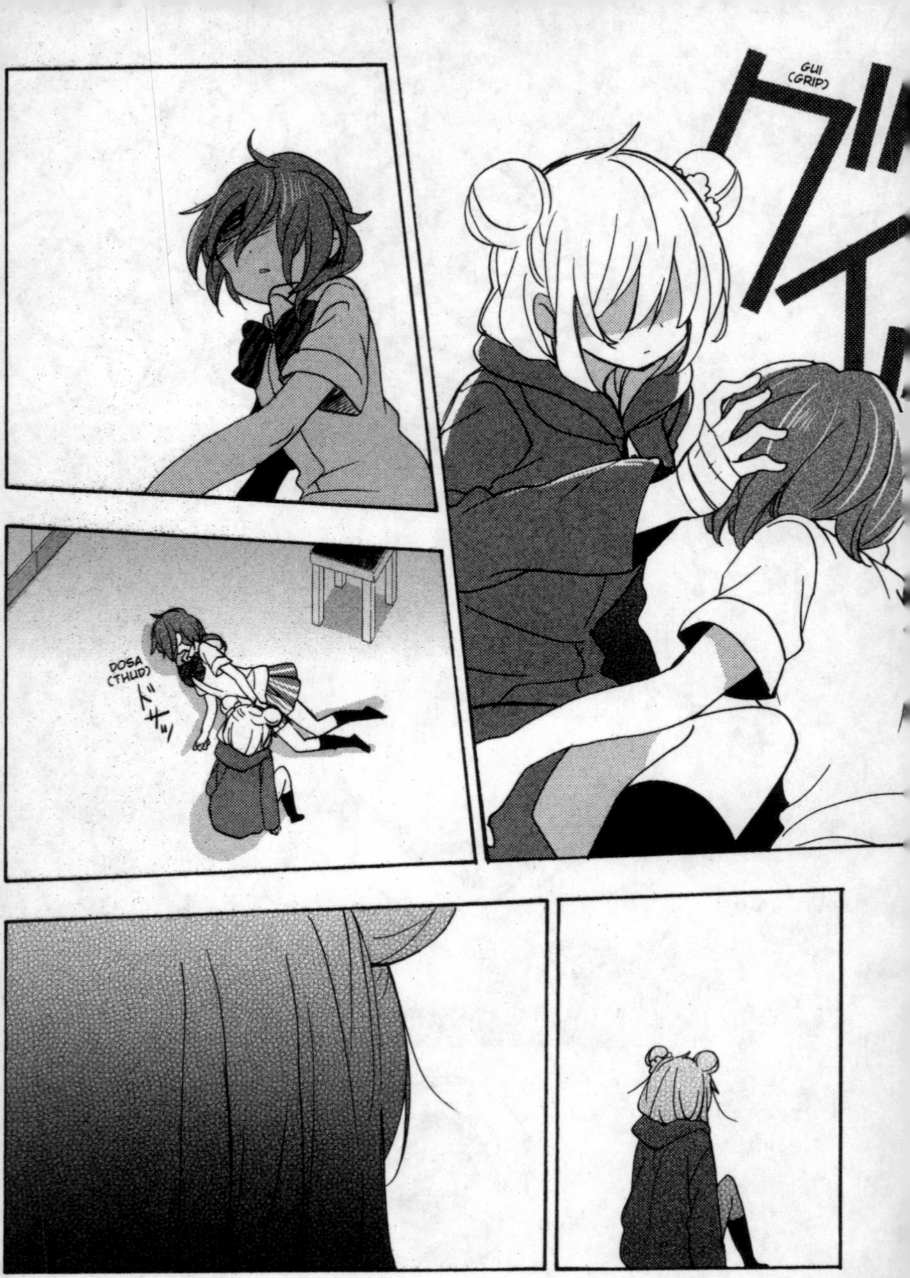
GUI (GRIP)
DOSA (THUD)
ドサッ

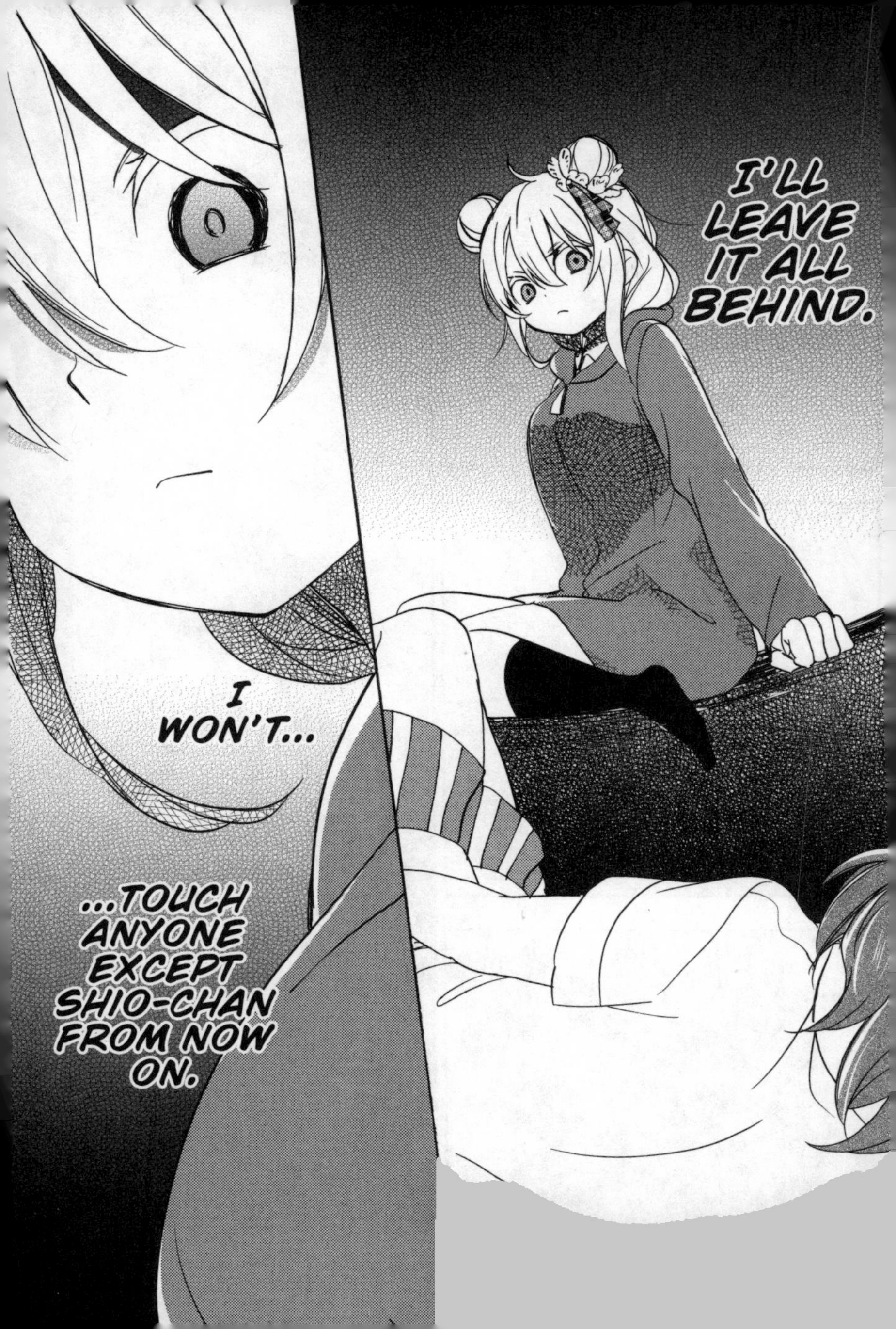
I'LL LEAVE IT ALL BEHIND.
I WON'T...
...TOUCH ANYONE EXCEPT SHIO-CHAN FROM NOW ON.

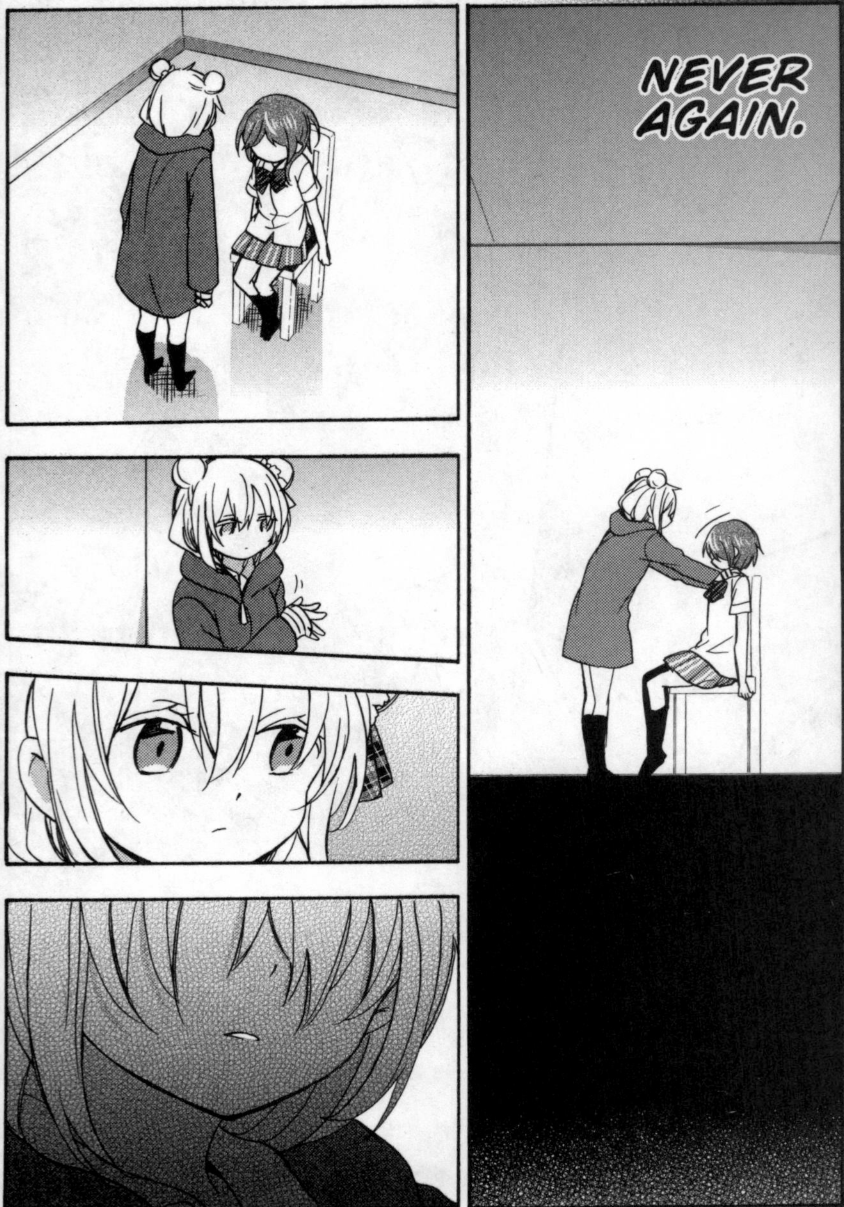
NEVER AGAIN.

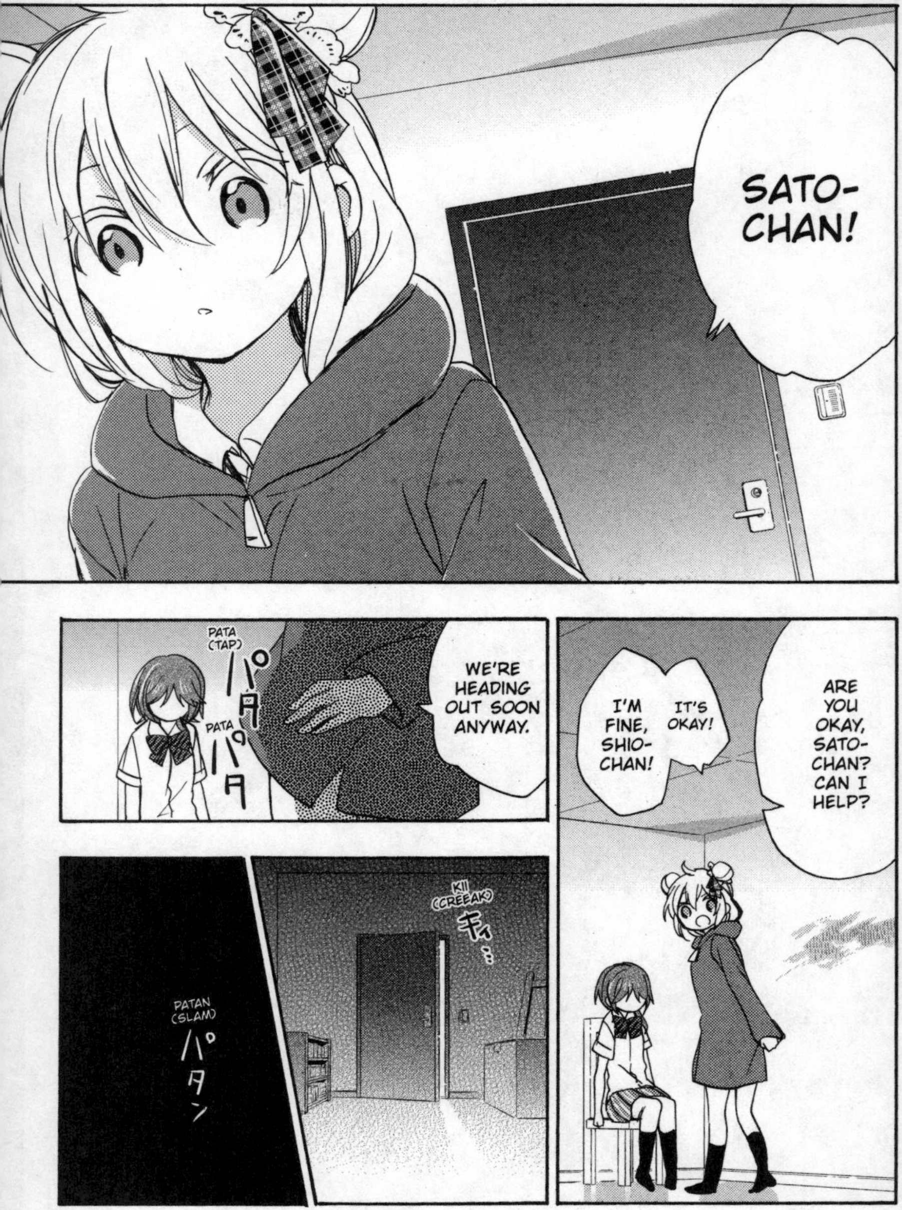
SATO-CHAN!
ARE YOU OKAY, SATO-CHAN? CAN I HELP?
IT'S OKAY!
I'M FINE, SHIO-CHAN!
WE'RE HEADING OUT SOON ANYWAY.
PATA (TAP)
パタ
PATA
パタ
KII (CREEAK)
キィ…
PATAN (SLAM)
パタン

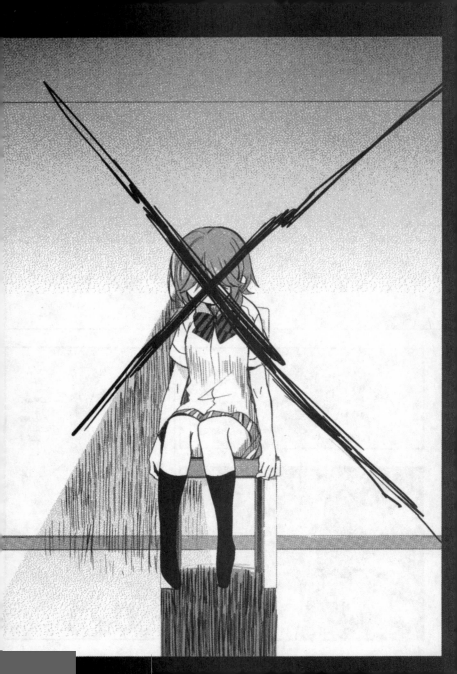

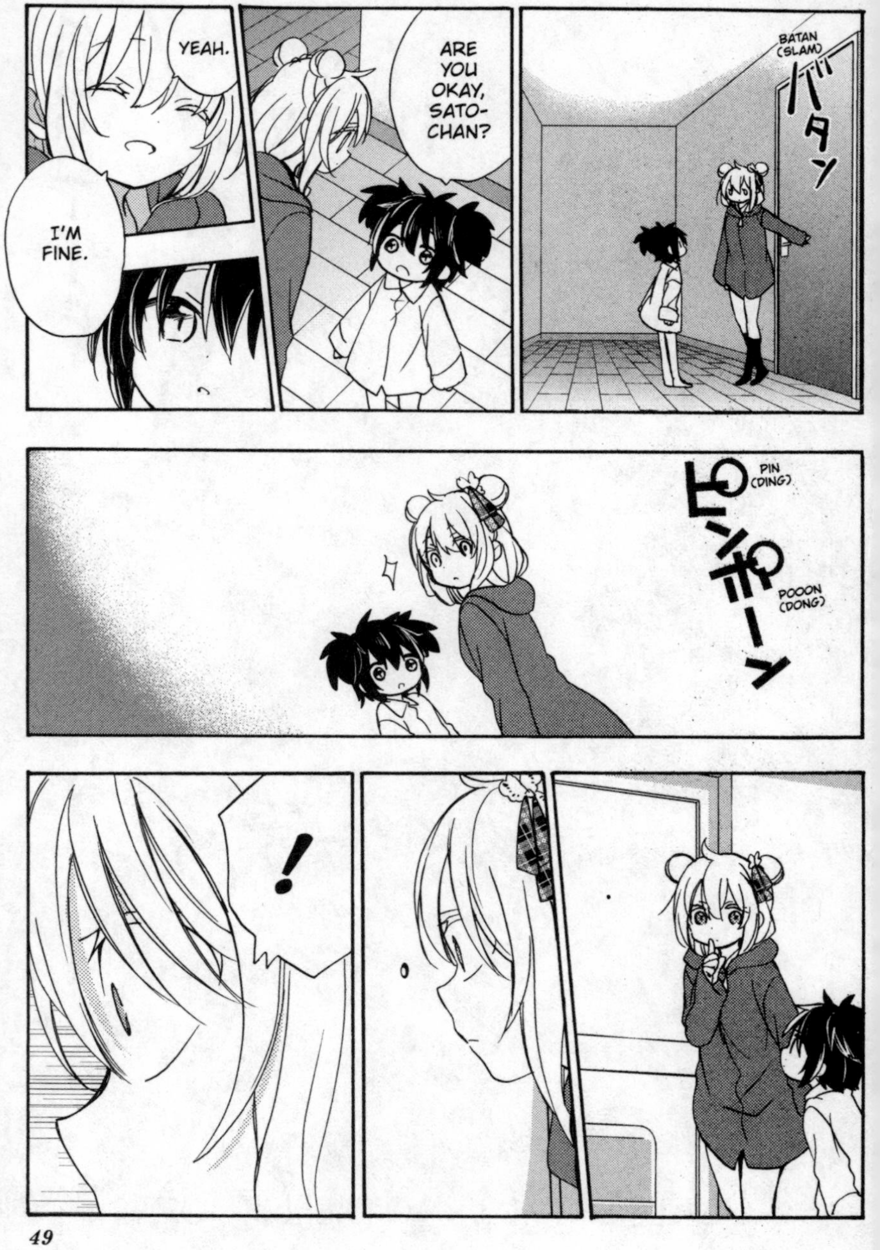
BATAN (SLAM)
バタン
ARE YOU OKAY, SATO-CHAN?
YEAH.
I'M FINE.
PIN (DING)
POOON (DONG)
ピンポーン
!

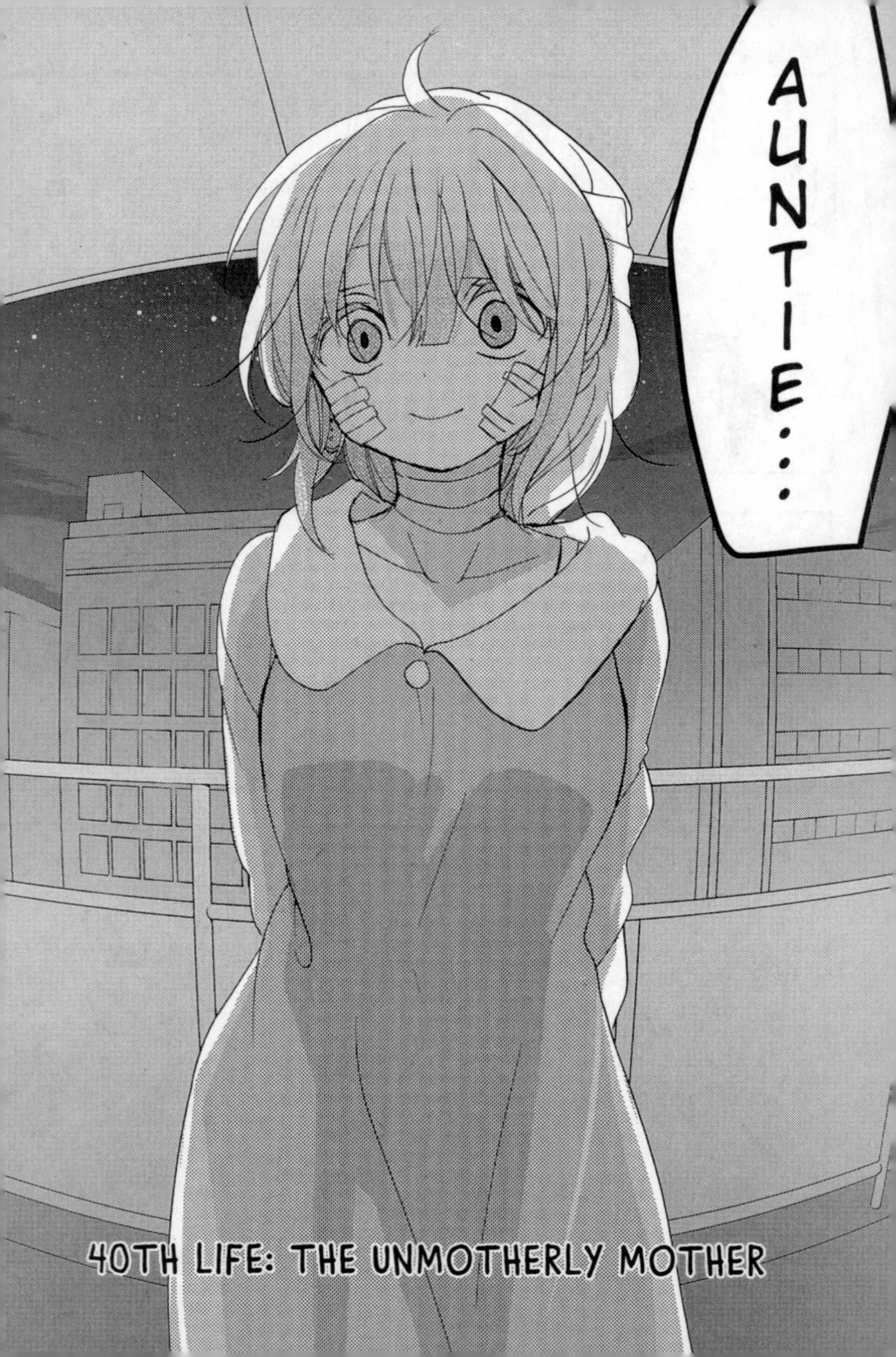
AUNTIE...
40TH LIFE: THE UNMOTHERLY MOTHER

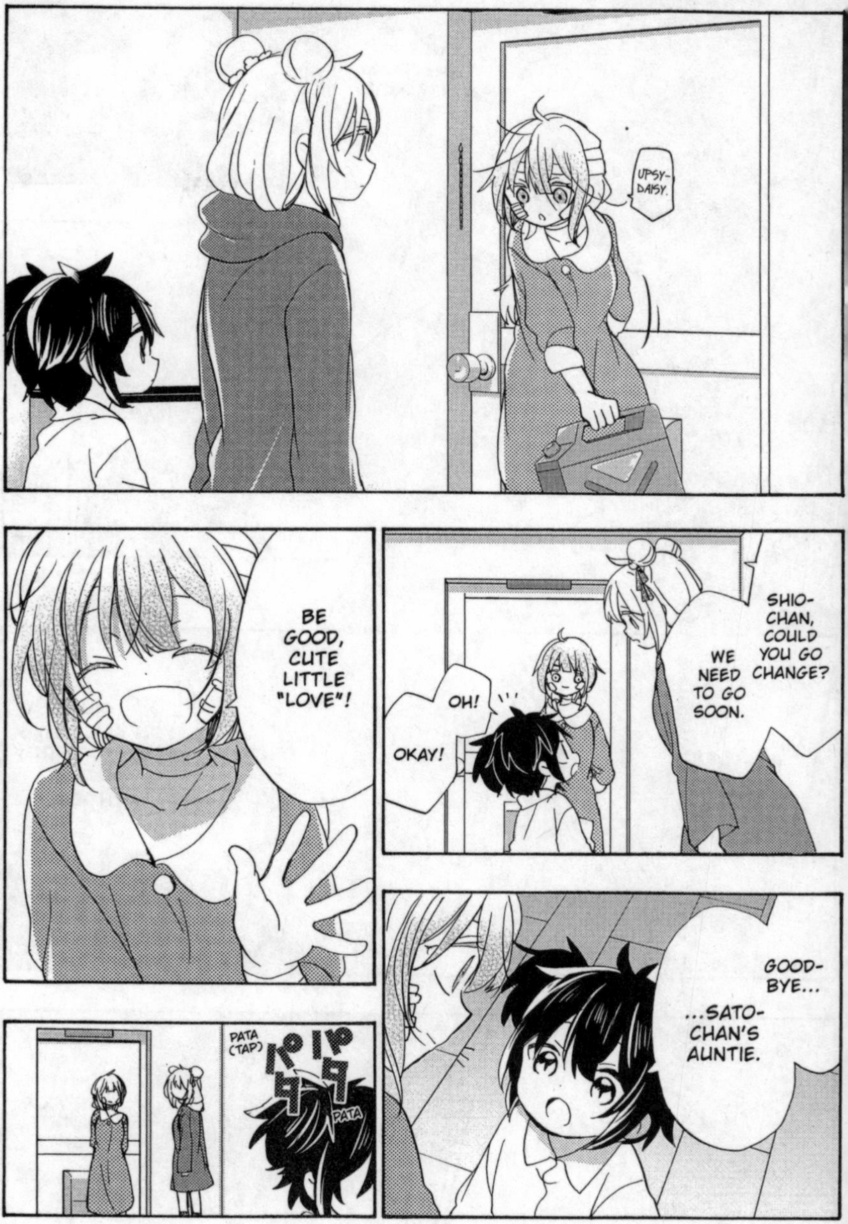
UPSY-DAISY.
SHIO-CHAN, COULD YOU GO CHANGE?
WE NEED TO GO SOON.
OH!
OKAY!
GOOD-BYE...
...SATO-CHAN'S AUNTIE.
BE GOOD, CUTE LITTLE "LOVE"!
PATA (TAP)
PATA

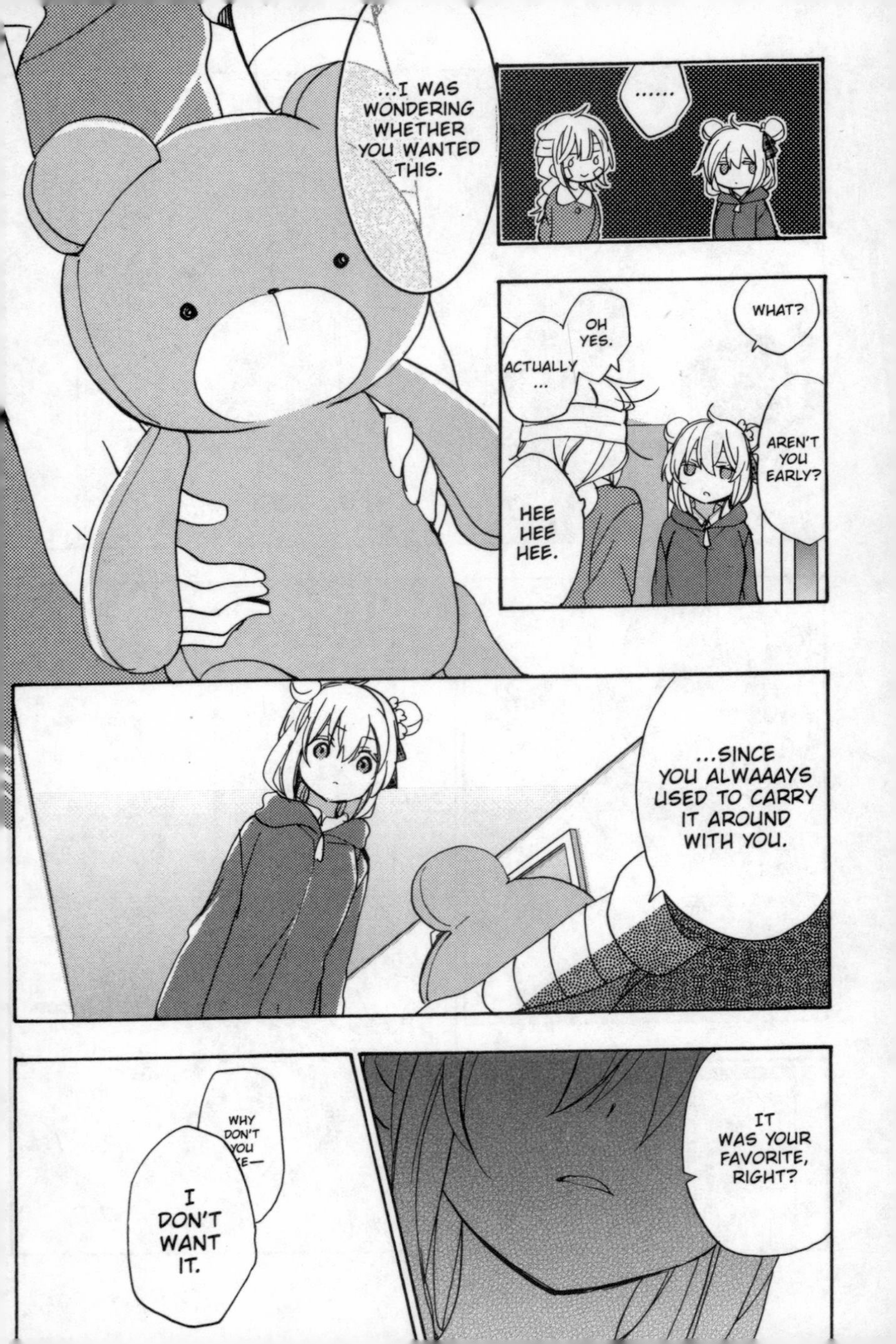
......
WHAT?
AREN'T YOU EARLY?
HEE HEE HEE.
OH YES. ACTUALLY...
...I WAS WONDERING WHETHER YOU WANTED THIS.
...SINCE YOU ALWAAAYS USED TO CARRY IT AROUND WITH YOU.
IT WAS YOUR FAVORITE, RIGHT?
WHY DON'T YOU
I DON'T WANT IT.

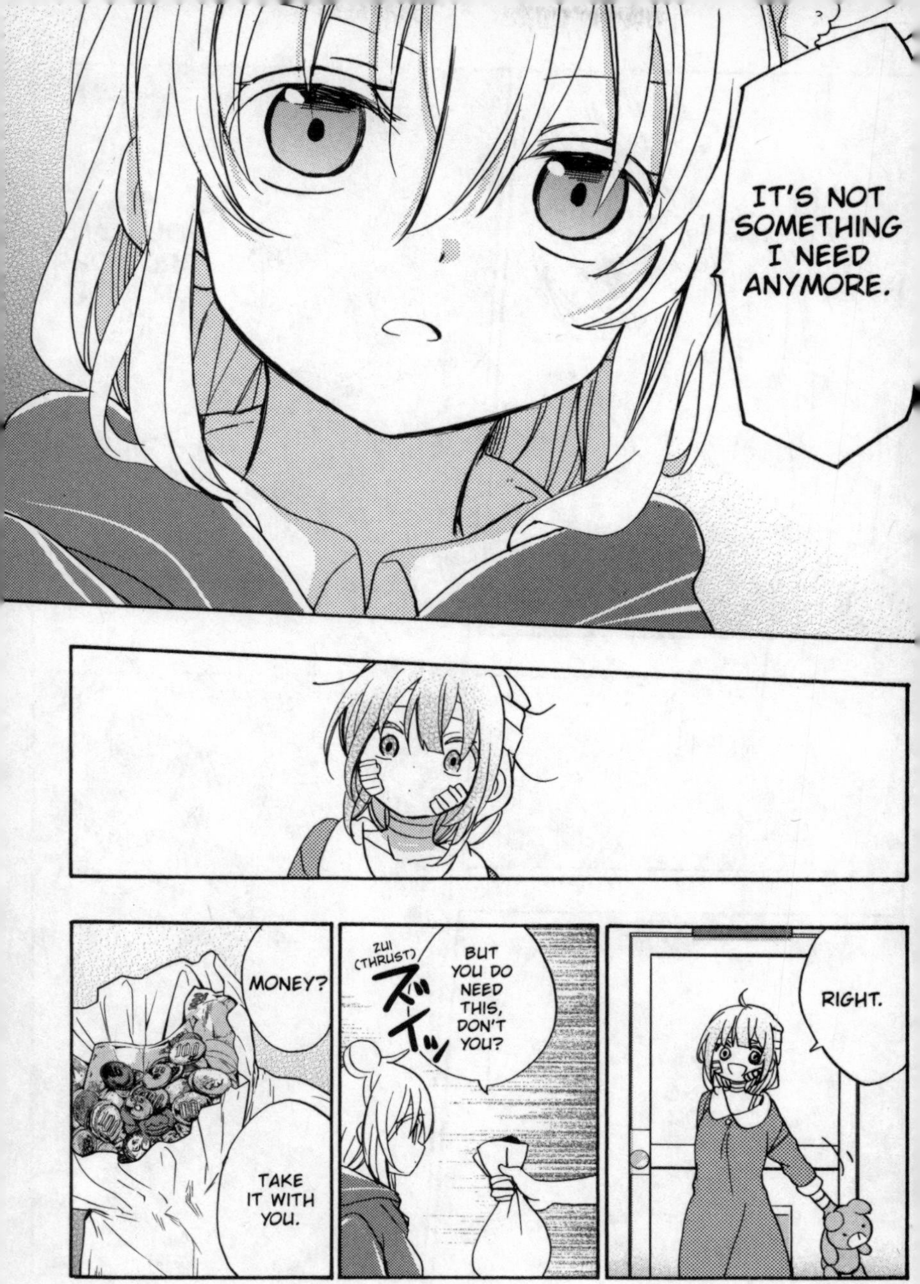
IT'S NOT SOMETHING I NEED ANYMORE.
RIGHT.
ZUI (THRUST)
ズイーイッ
BUT YOU DO NEED THIS, DON'T YOU?
MONEY?
TAKE IT WITH YOU.

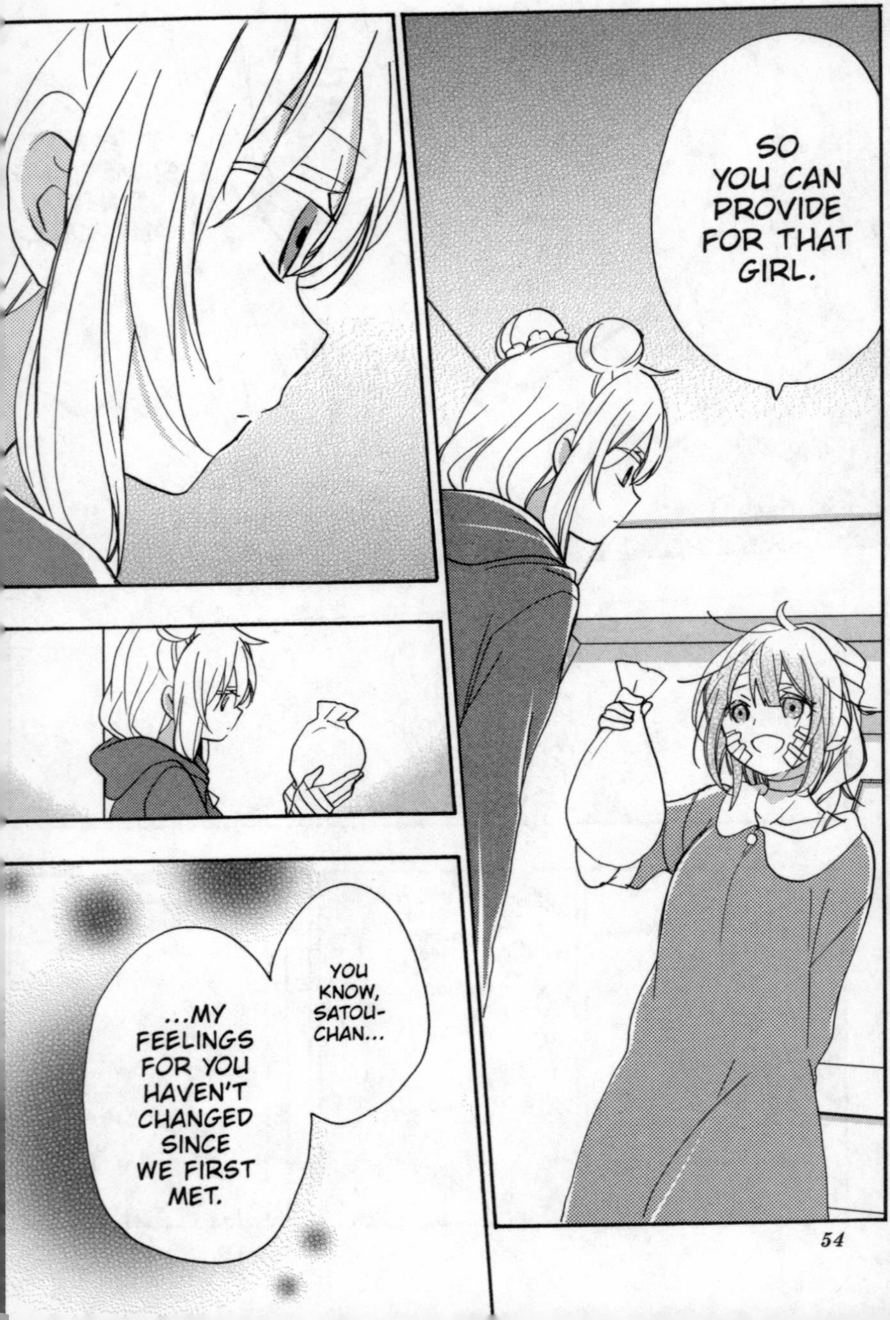
SO YOU CAN PROVIDE FOR THAT GIRL.
YOU KNOW, SATOU-CHAN...
...MY FEELINGS FOR YOU HAVEN'T CHANGED SINCE WE FIRST MET.

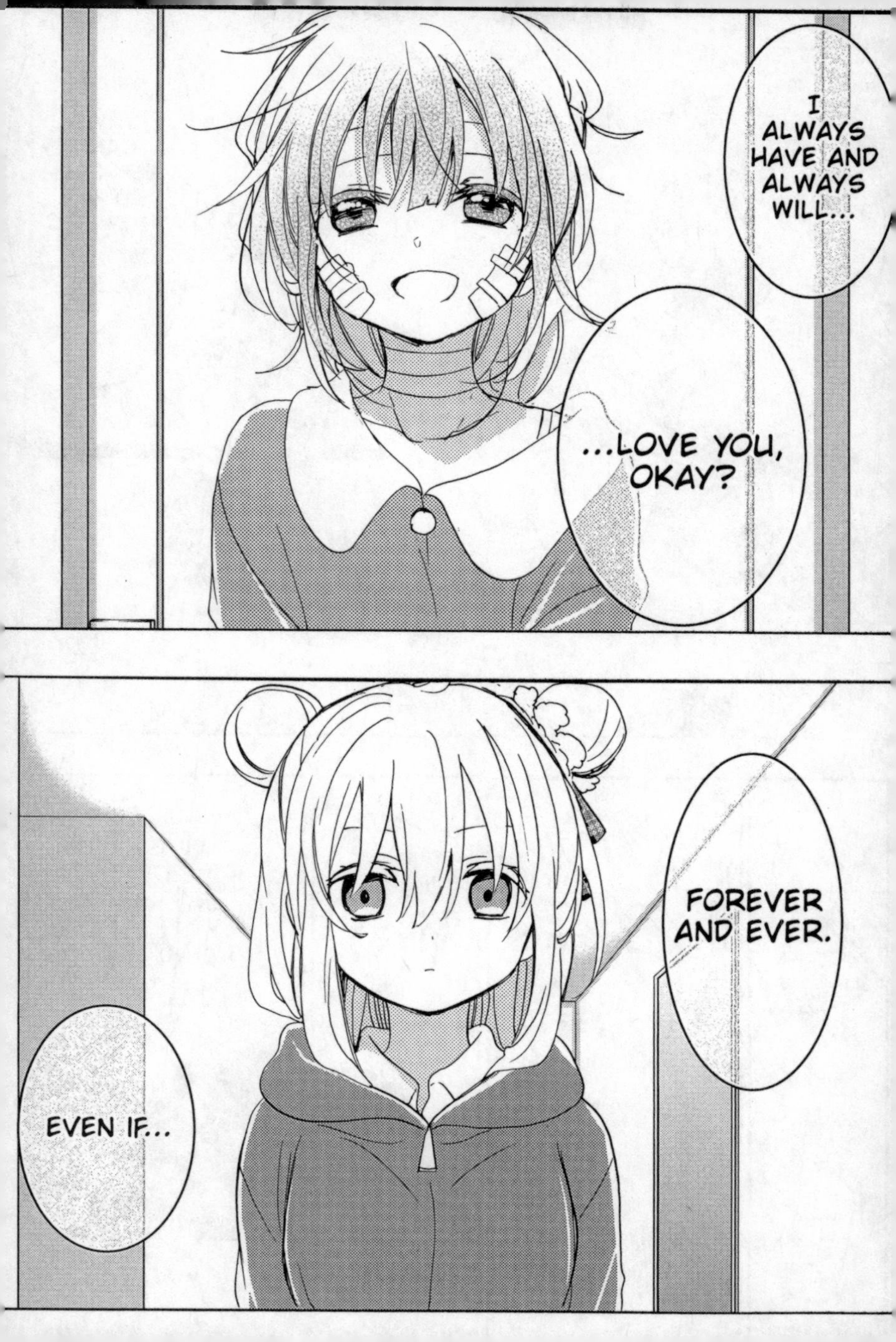
I ALWAYS HAVE AND ALWAYS WILL...
...LOVE YOU, OKAY?
FOREVER AND EVER.
EVEN IF...

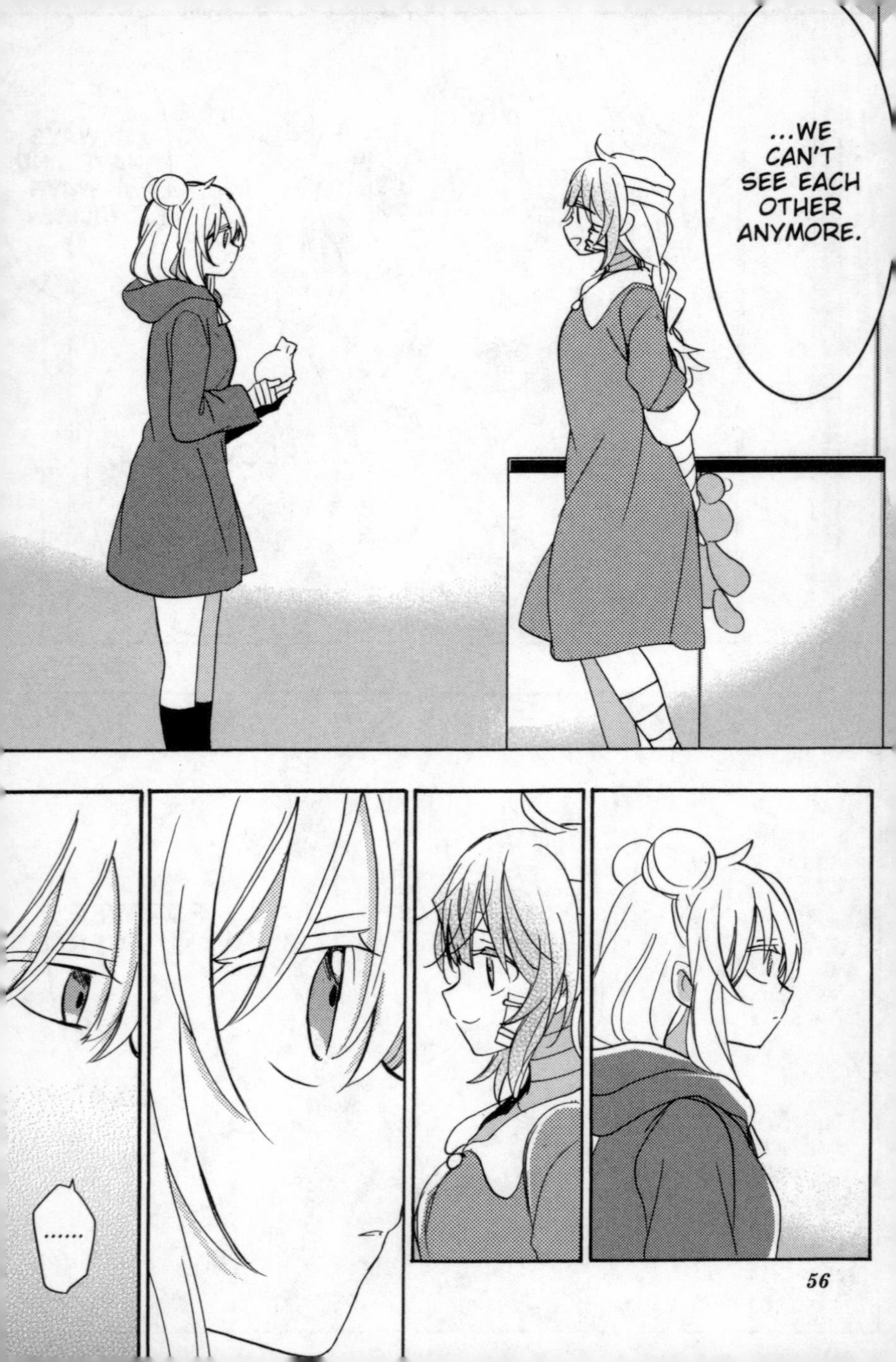
...WE CAN'T SEE EACH OTHER ANYMORE.
....

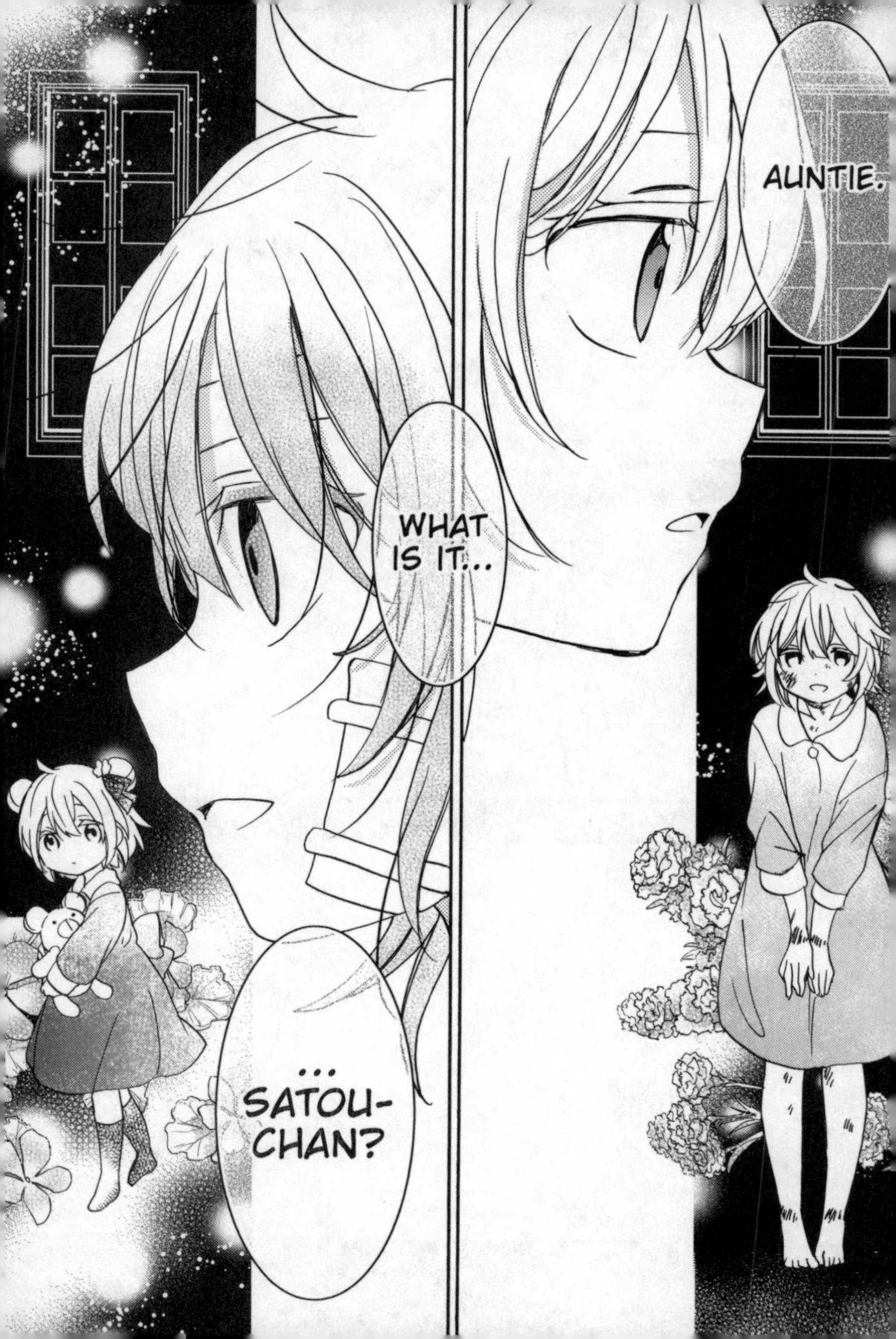
AUNTIE.
WHAT IS IT...
... SATOU-CHAN?

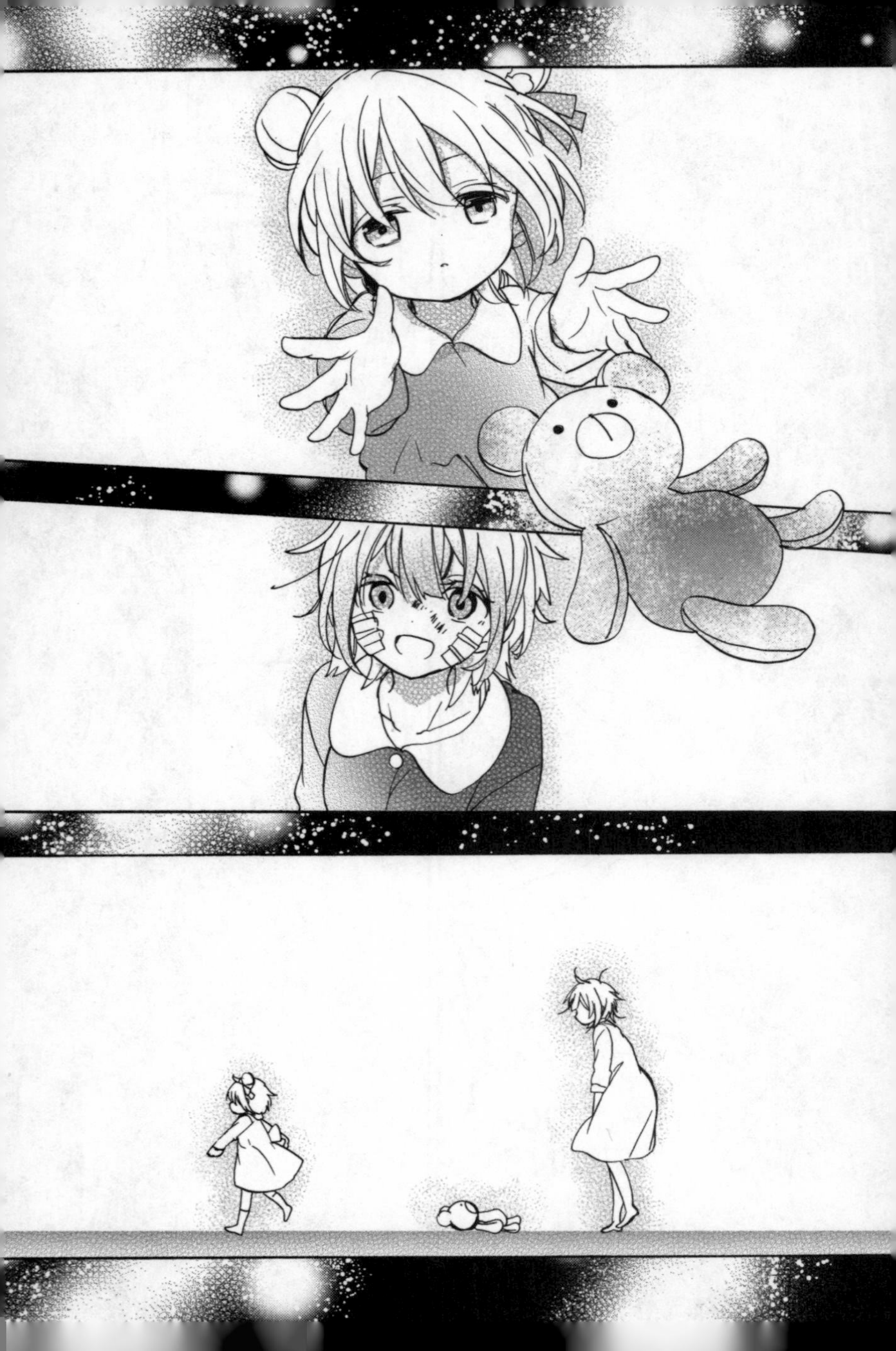

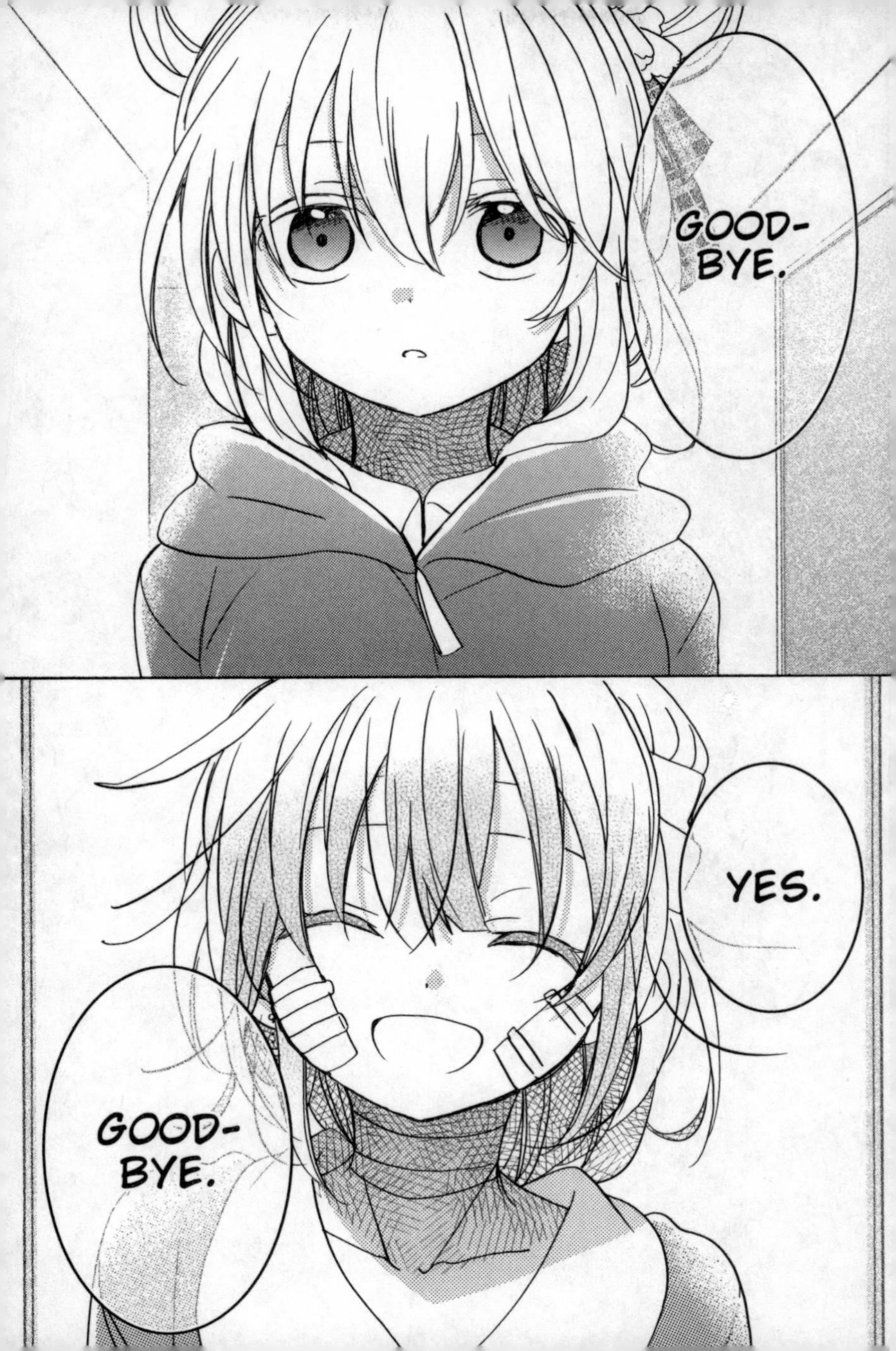
GOOD-BYE.
YES.
GOOD-BYE.

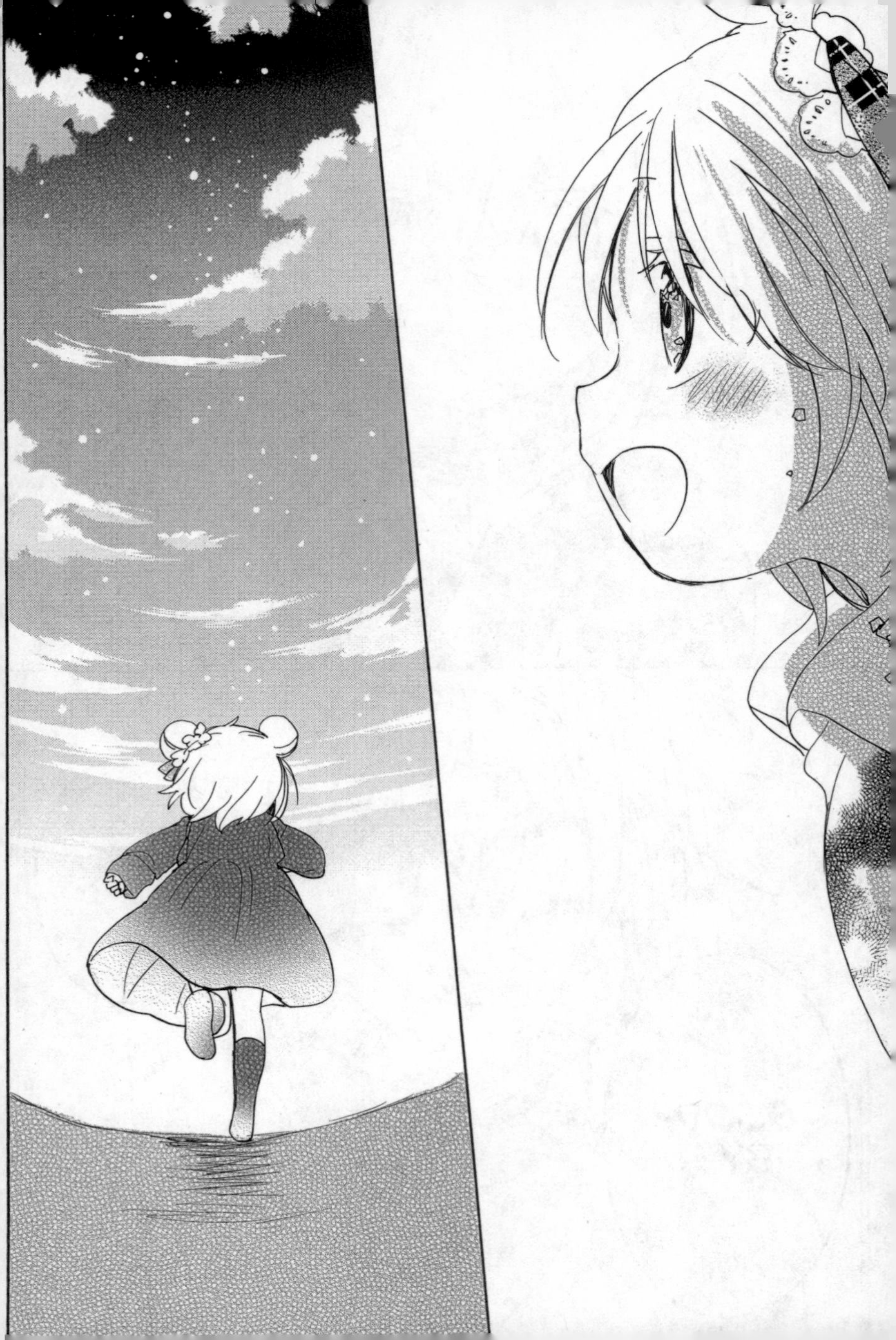

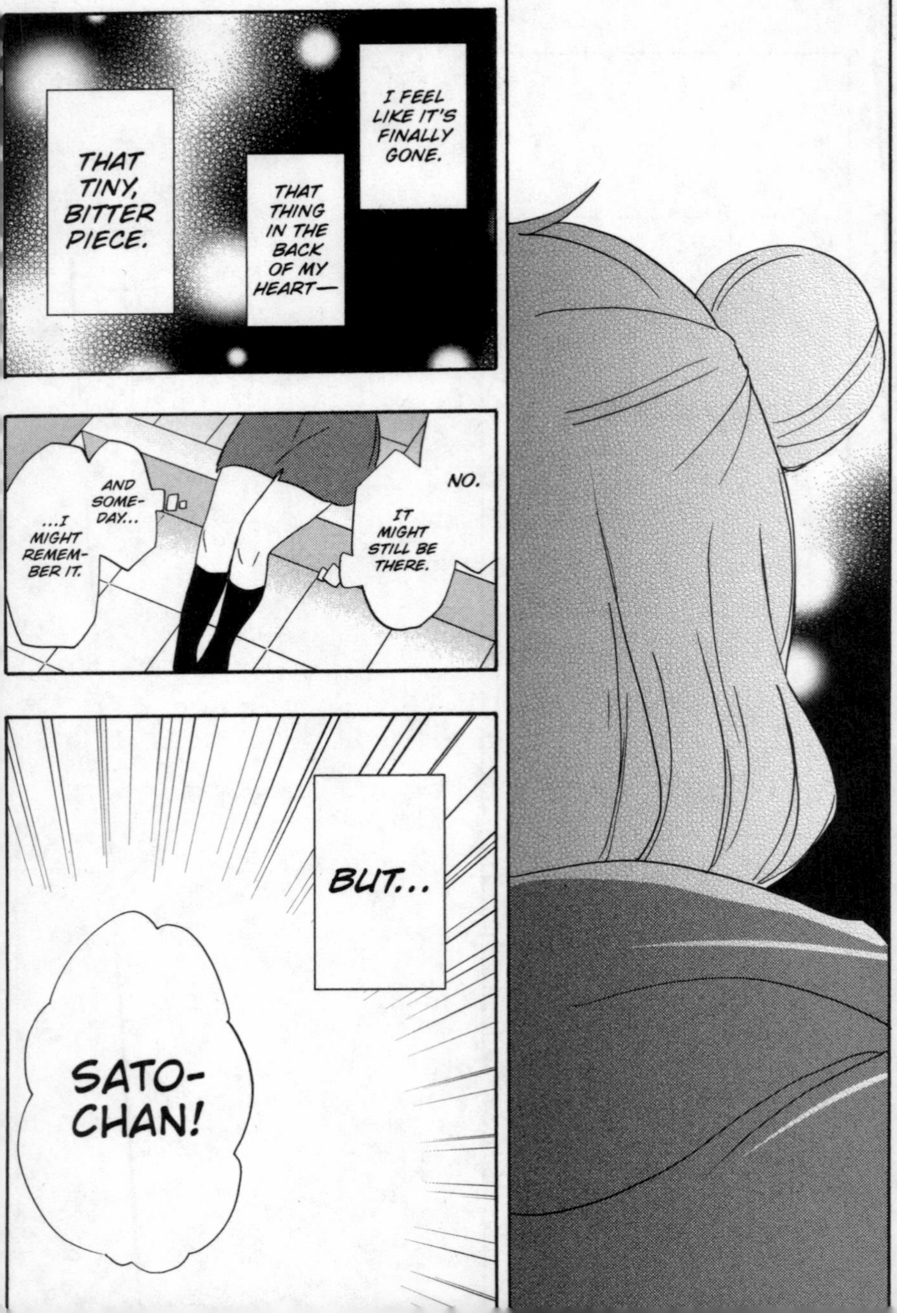
I FEEL LIKE IT'S FINALLY GONE.
THAT THING IN THE BACK OF MY HEART—
THAT TINY, BITTER PIECE.
NO.
IT MIGHT STILL BE THERE.
AND SOME-DAY...
...I MIGHT REMEM-BER IT.
BUT...
SATO-CHAN!

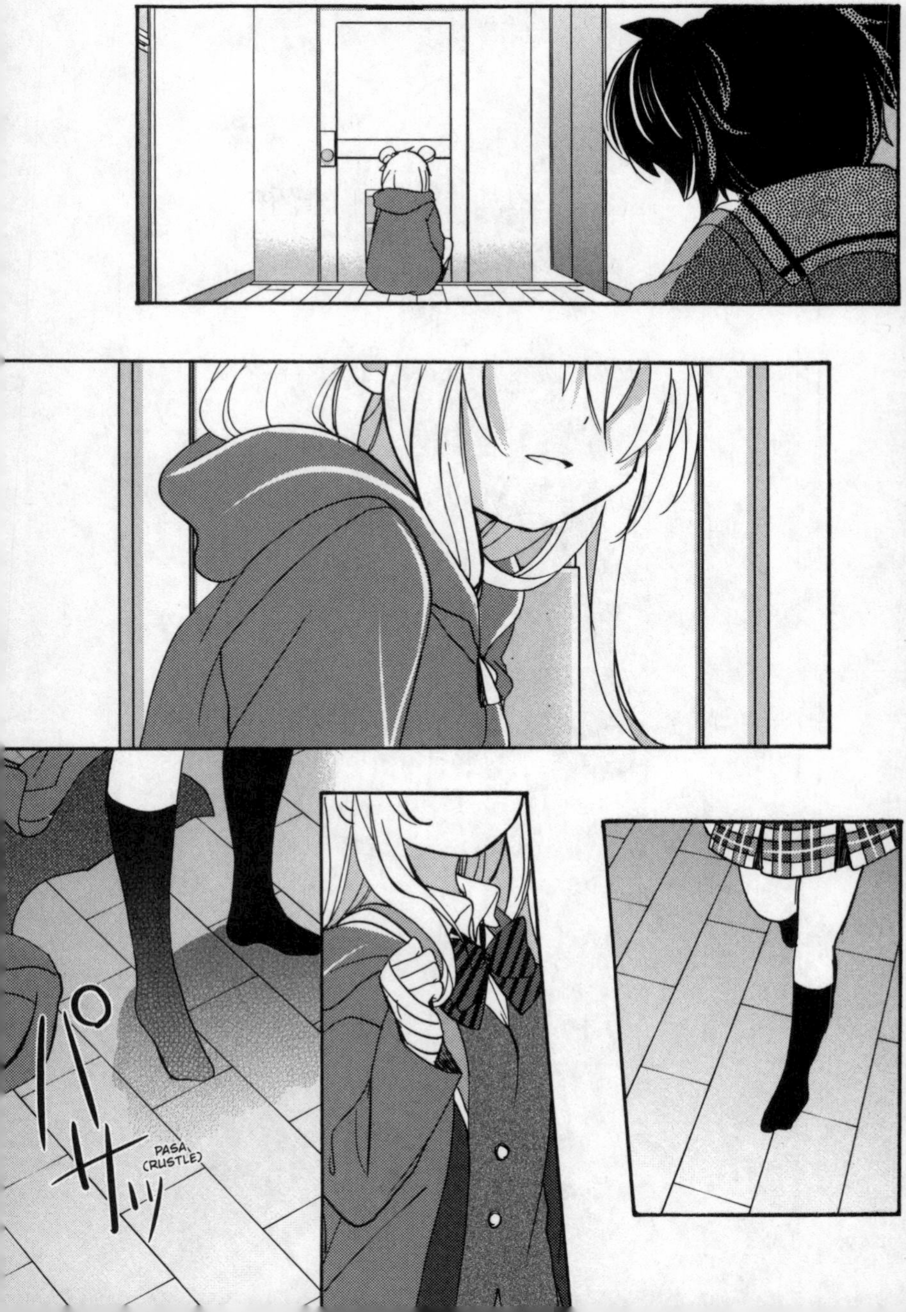
パサッ
PASA (RUSTLE)

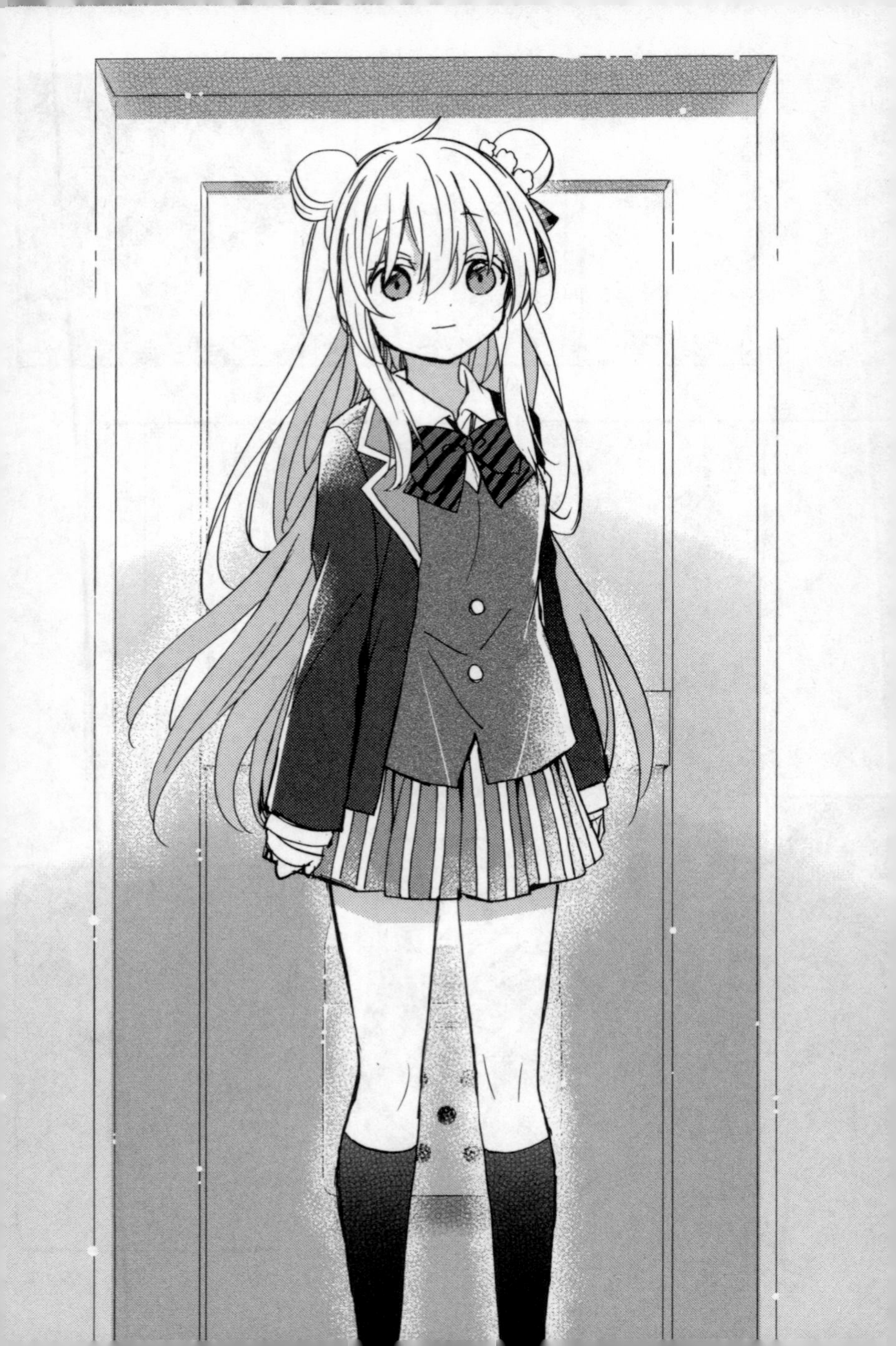

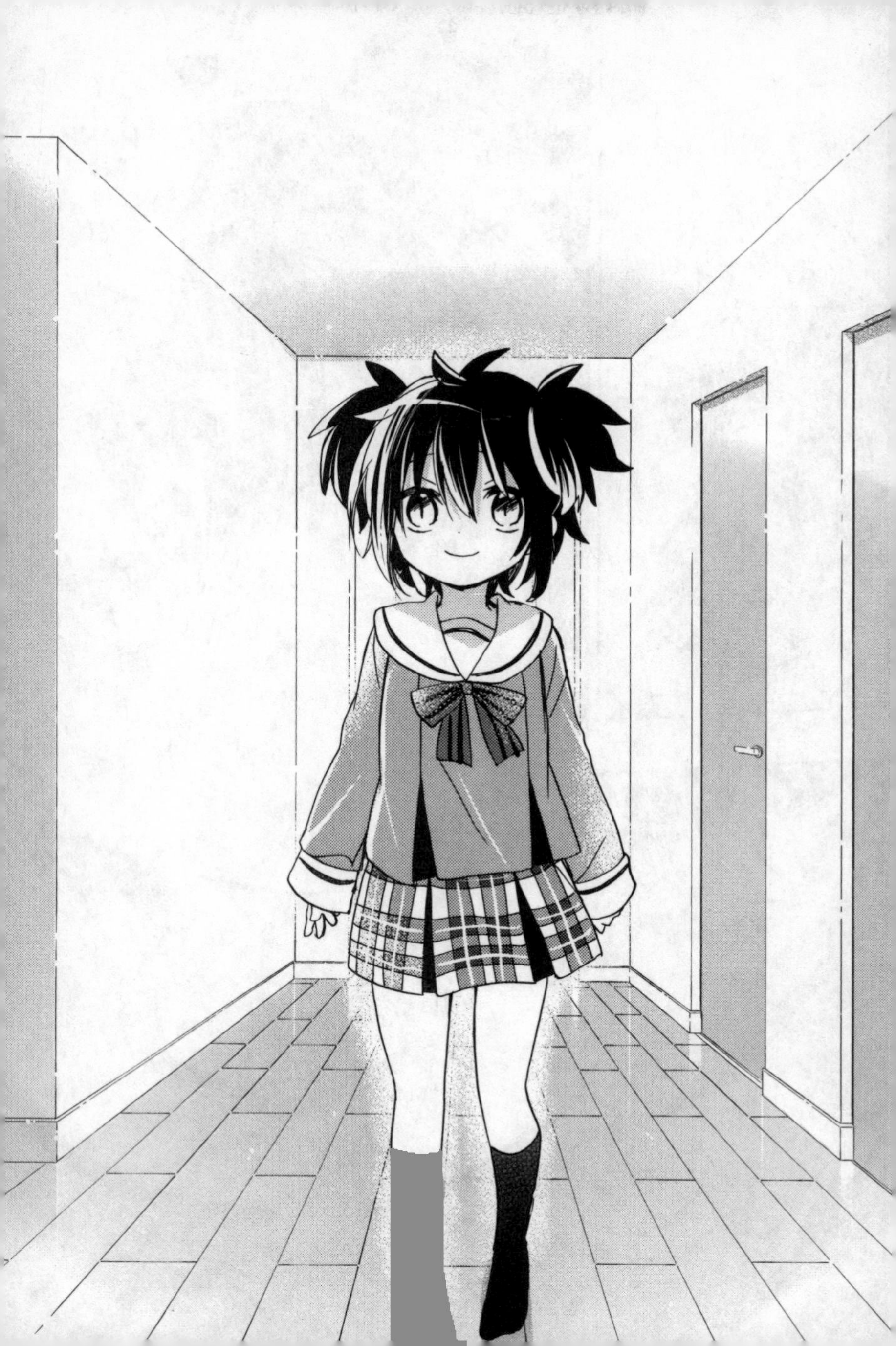

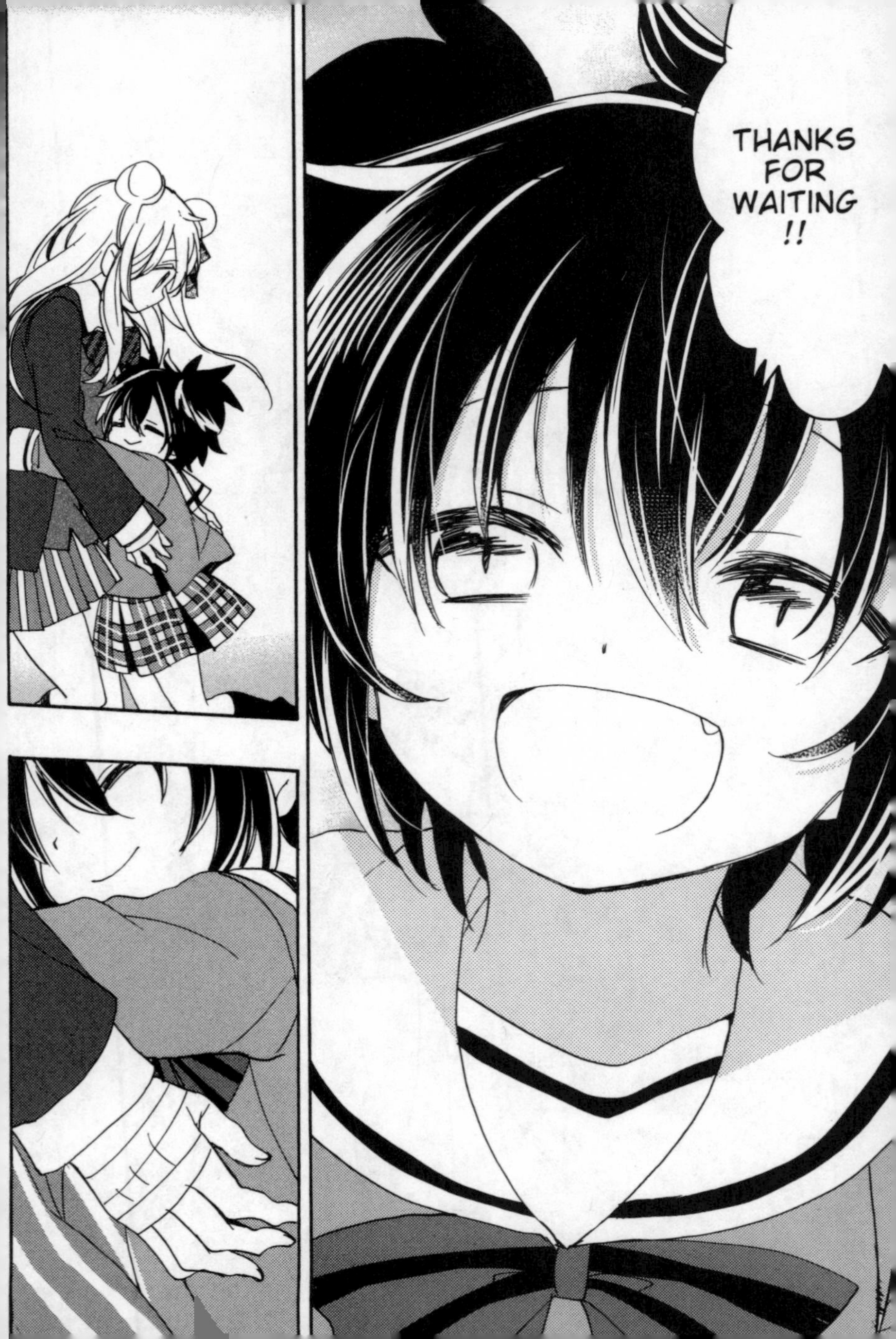
THANKS FOR WAITING !!

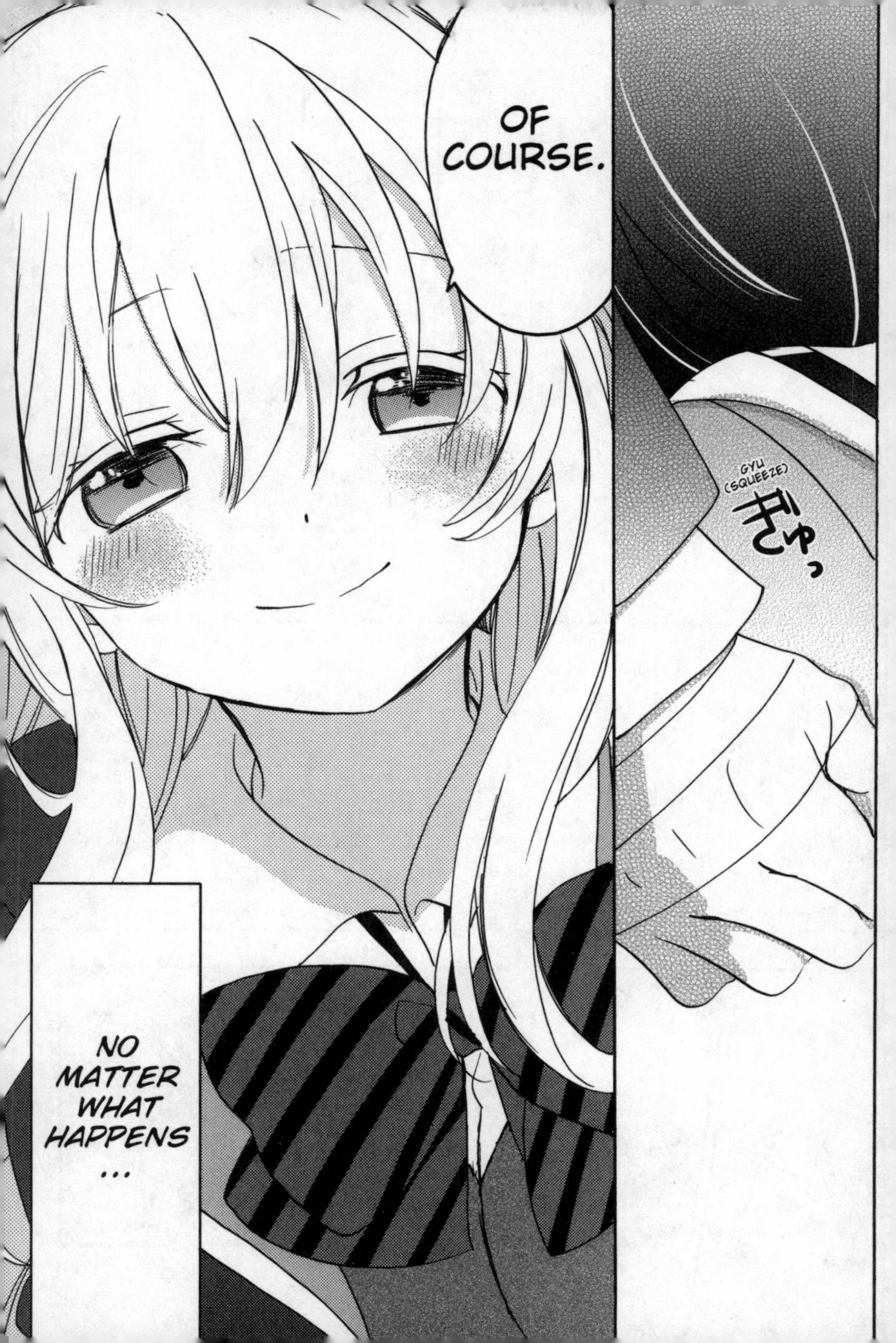
GYU (SQUEEZE)
ぎゅっ
OF COURSE.
NO MATTER WHAT HAPPENS ...

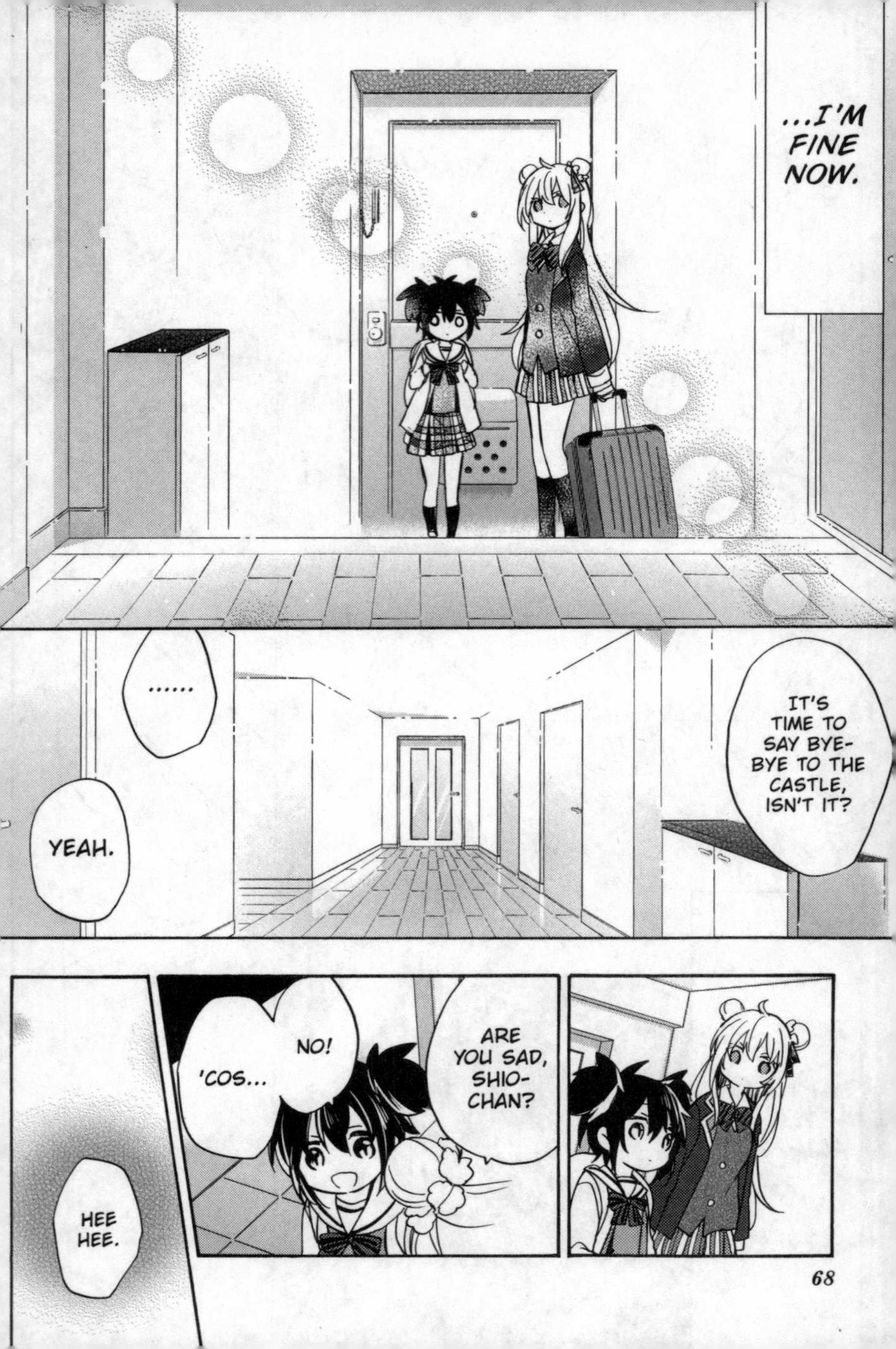
...I'M FINE NOW.
IT'S TIME TO SAY BYE-BYE TO THE CASTLE, ISN'T IT?
......
YEAH.
ARE YOU SAD, SHIO-CHAN?
NO!
'COS...
HEE HEE.

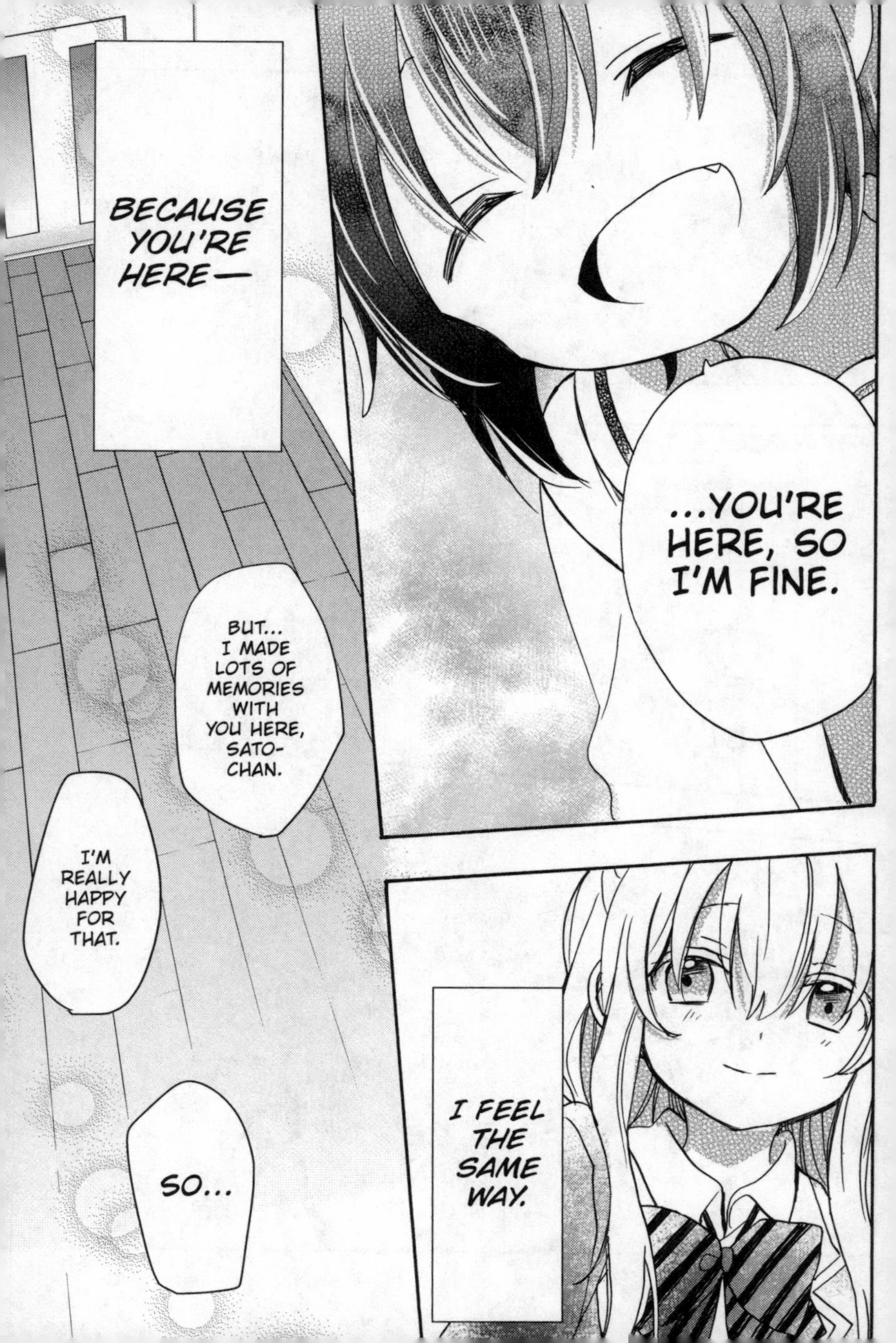
BUT... I MADE LOTS OF MEMORIES WITH YOU HERE, SATO-CHAN.
I'M REALLY HAPPY FOR THAT.
SO...
...YOU'RE HERE, SO I'M FINE.
BECAUSE YOU'RE HERE—
I FEEL THE SAME WAY.

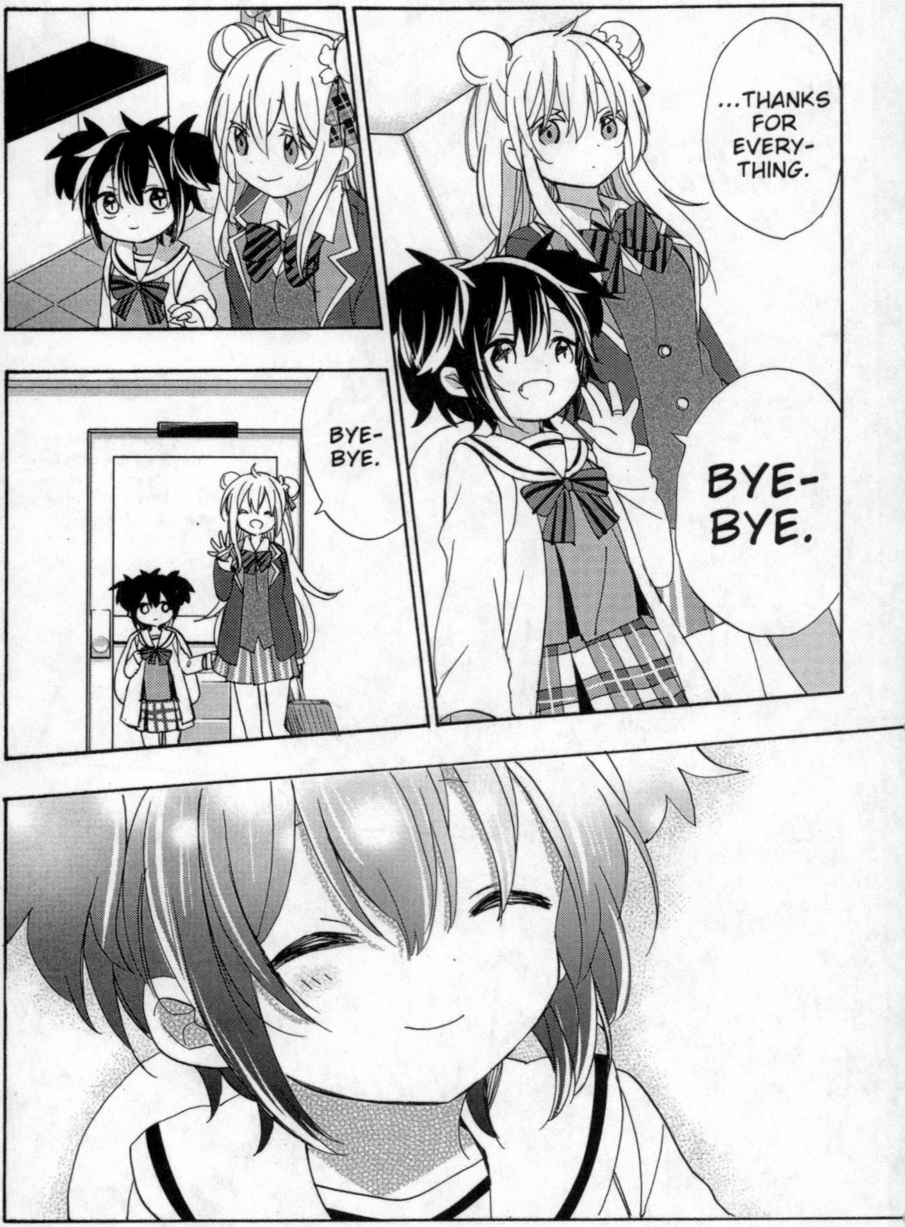
...THANKS FOR EVERY-THING.
BYE-BYE.
BYE-BYE.

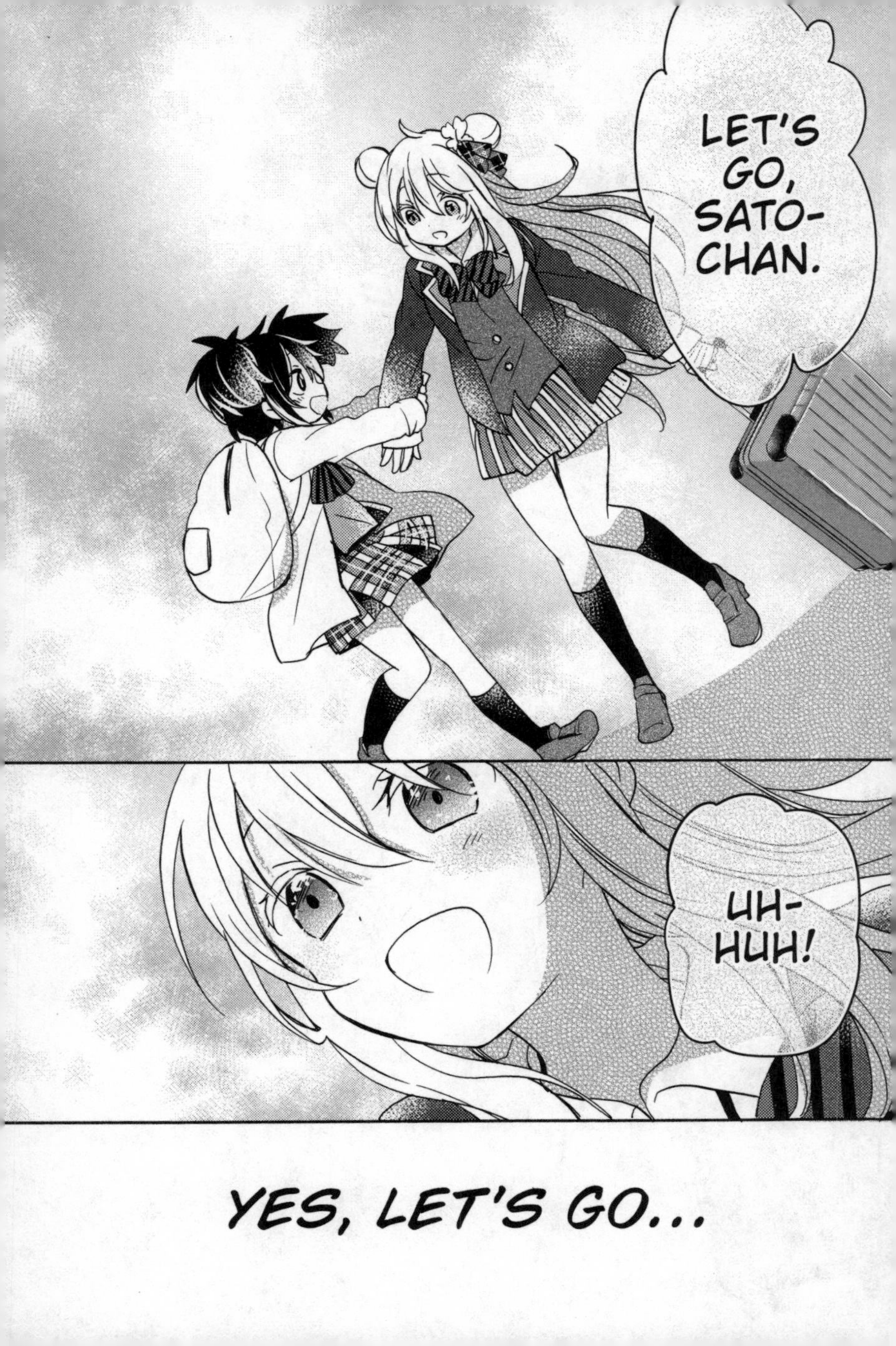
LET'S GO, SATO-CHAN.
UH-HUH!
YES, LET'S GO...

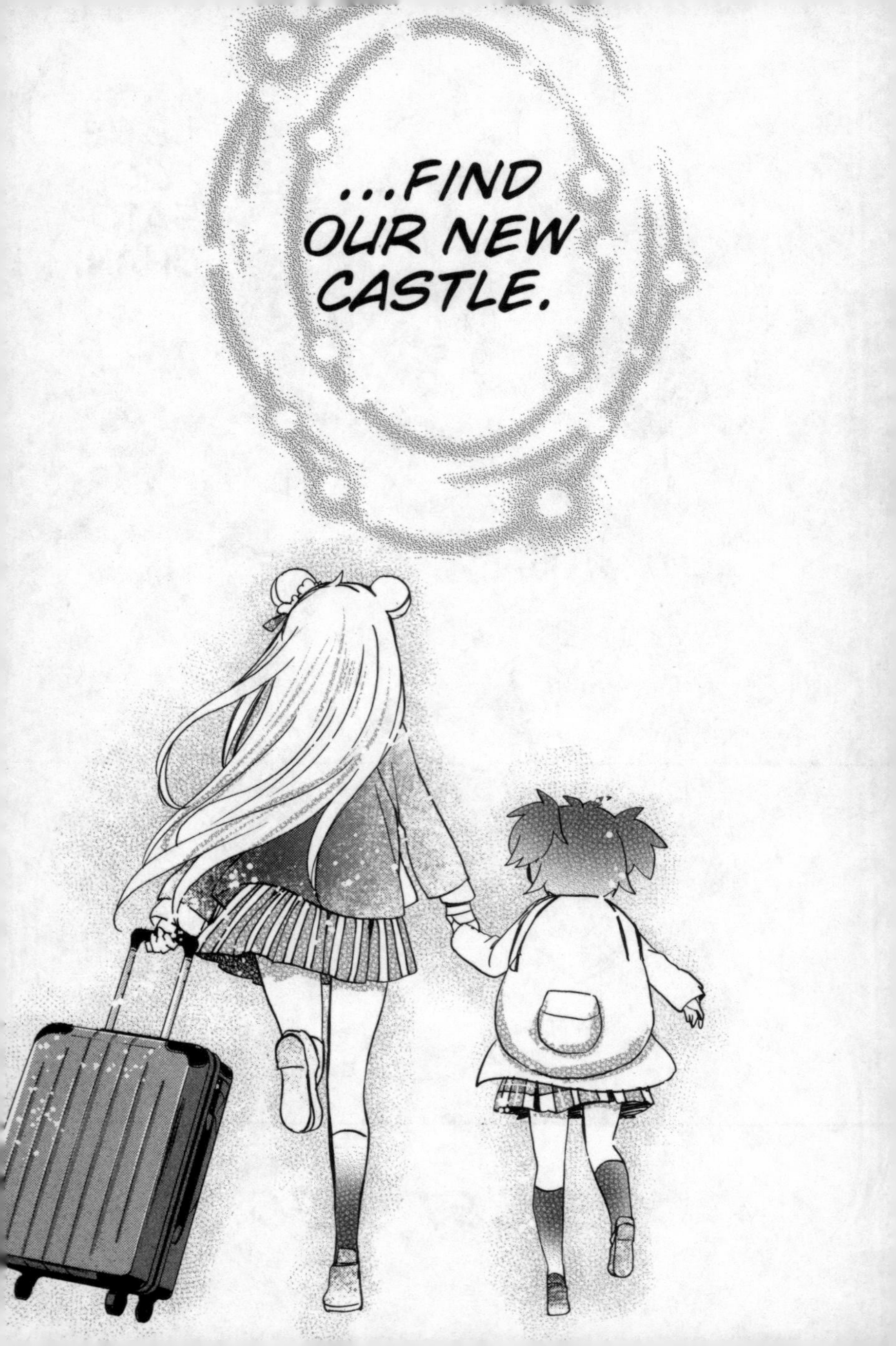
...FIND OUR NEW CASTLE.

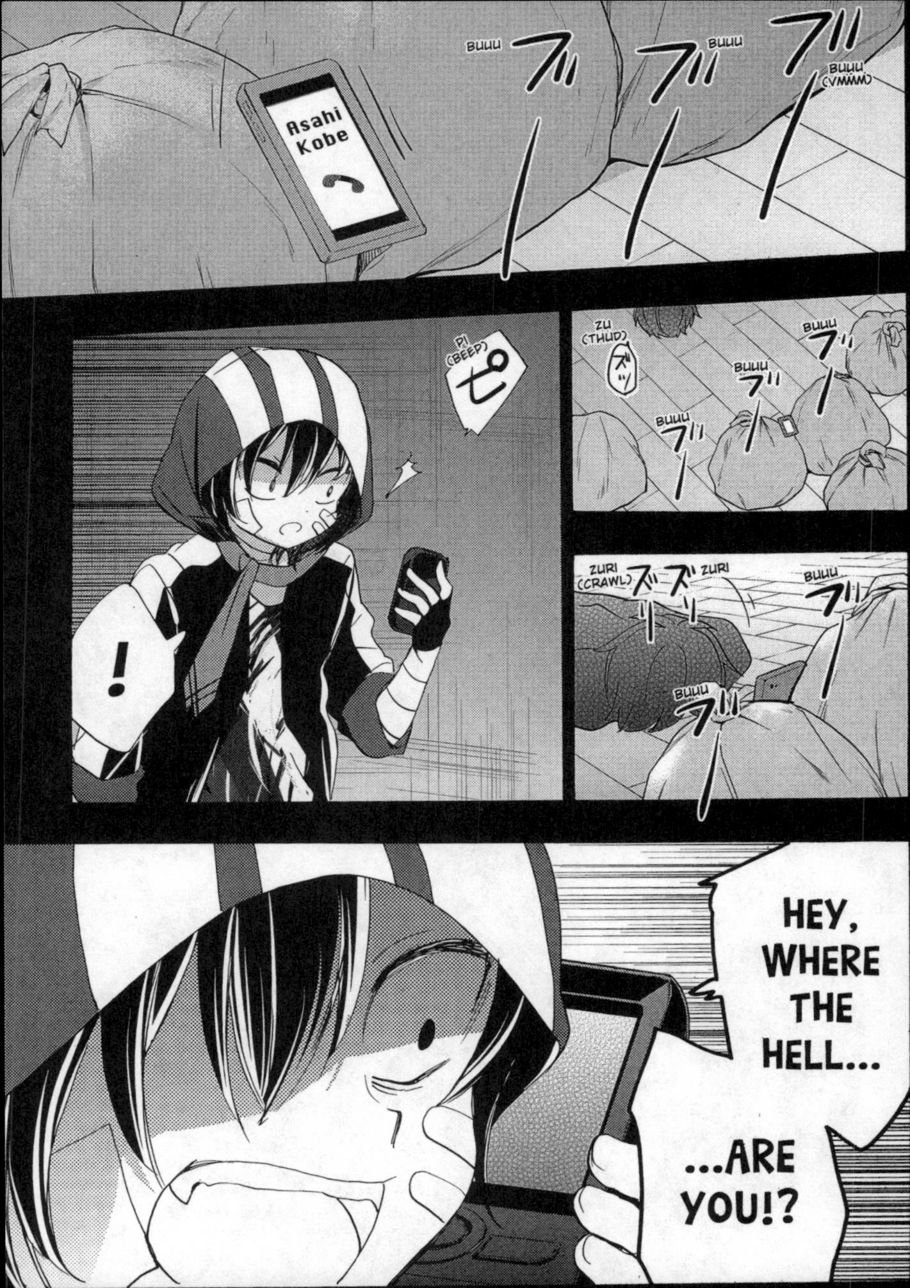
BUUU (VMMM)
ブ
BUUU
ブ
Asahi Kobe
BUUU
ブ
BUUU
ブ
BUUU
ブ
ZU (THUD)
ズッ
BUUU
ブ
BUUU
ブ
BUUU
ブ
ZURI
ズリ
ZURI (CRAWL)
ズリ
BUUU
ブ
PI (BEEP)
ピ
!
HEY, WHERE THE HELL...
...ARE YOU!?

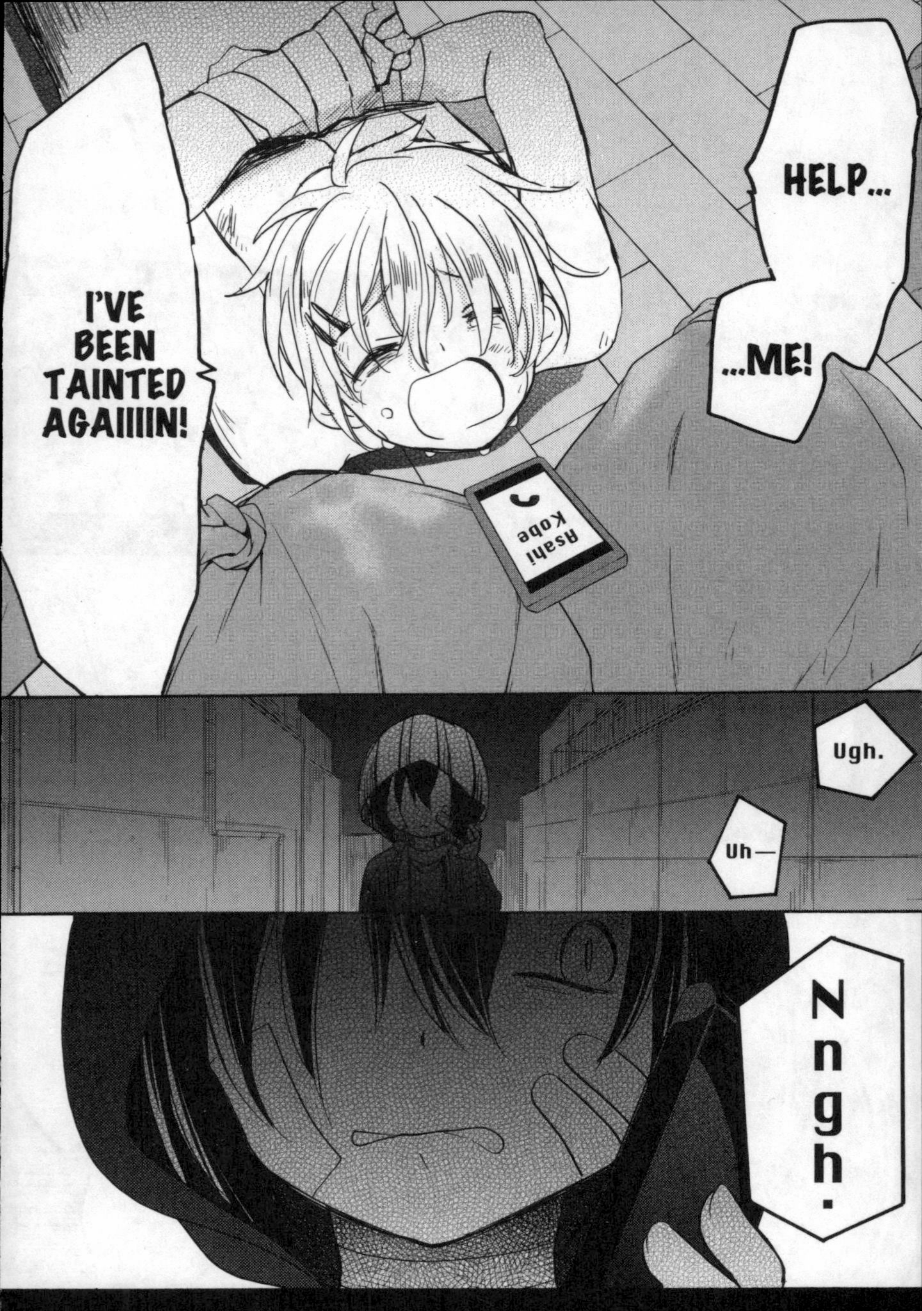
HELP...
...ME!
I'VE BEEN TAINTED AGAIIIIIN!
Asahi Kobe
Ugh.
Uh—
Nngh.

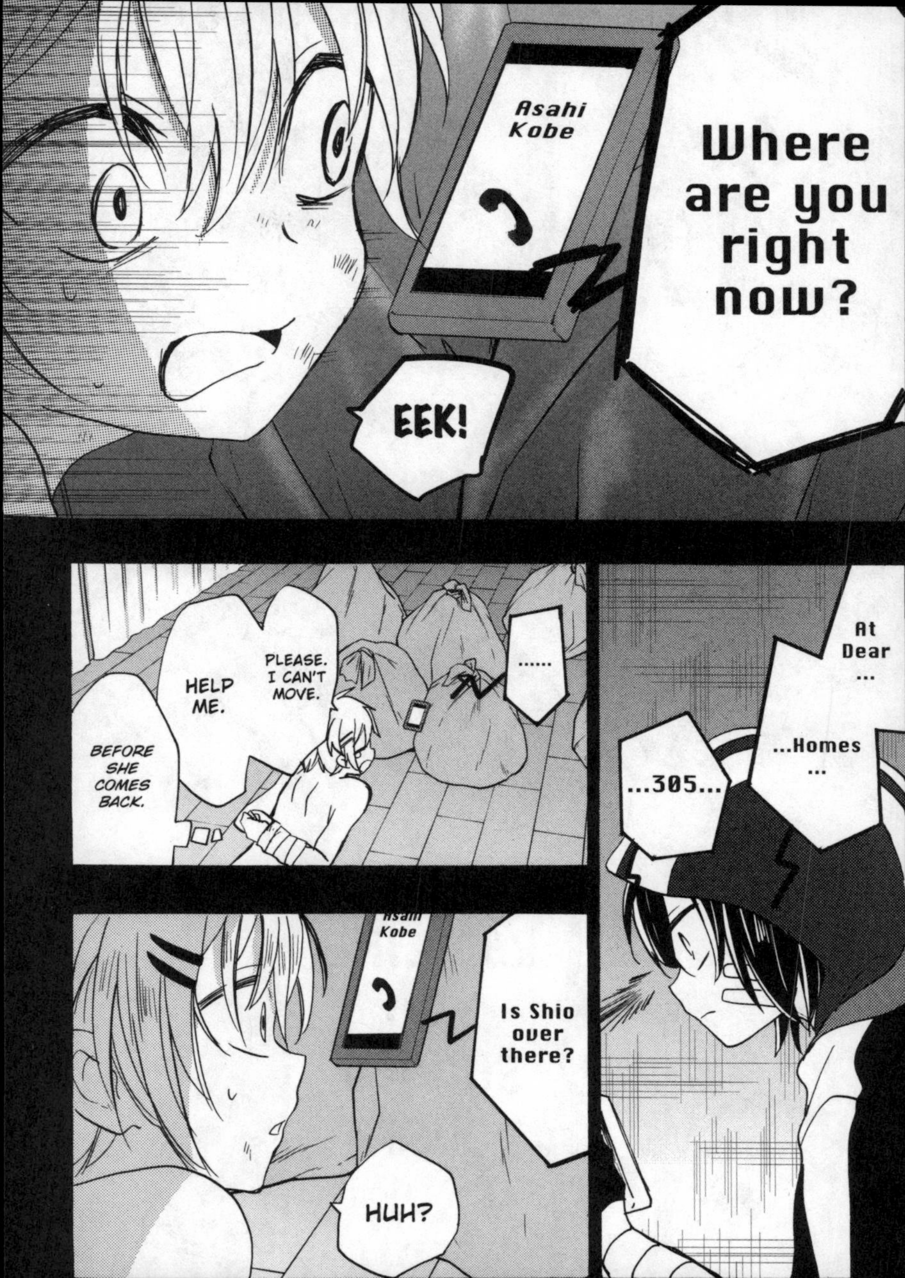
Asahi Kobe
Where are you right now?
EEK!
At Dear ...
...Homes ...
...305...
......
PLEASE. I CAN'T MOVE.
HELP ME.
BEFORE SHE COMES BACK.
Kobe
Is Shio over there?
HUH?

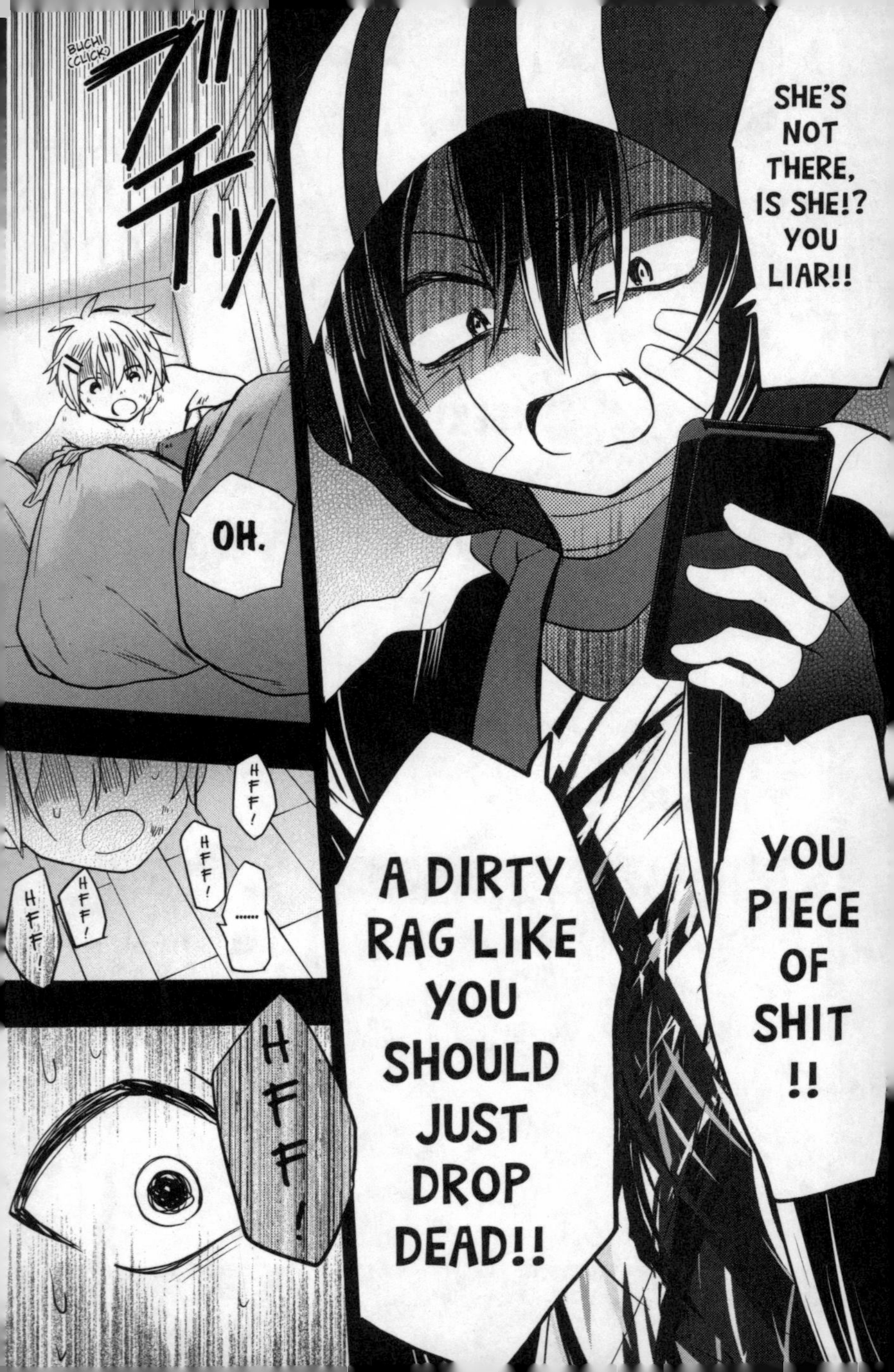

SHE'S NOT THERE, IS SHE!? YOU LIAR!!
YOU PIECE OF SHIT!!
A DIRTY RAG LIKE YOU SHOULD JUST DROP DEAD!!
BUCHI (CLICK)
OH.
HFF!
HFF!
HFF!
HFF!
......
HFF!

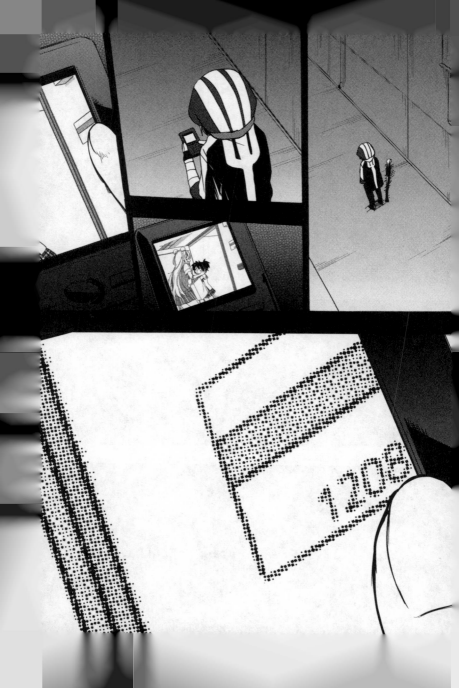

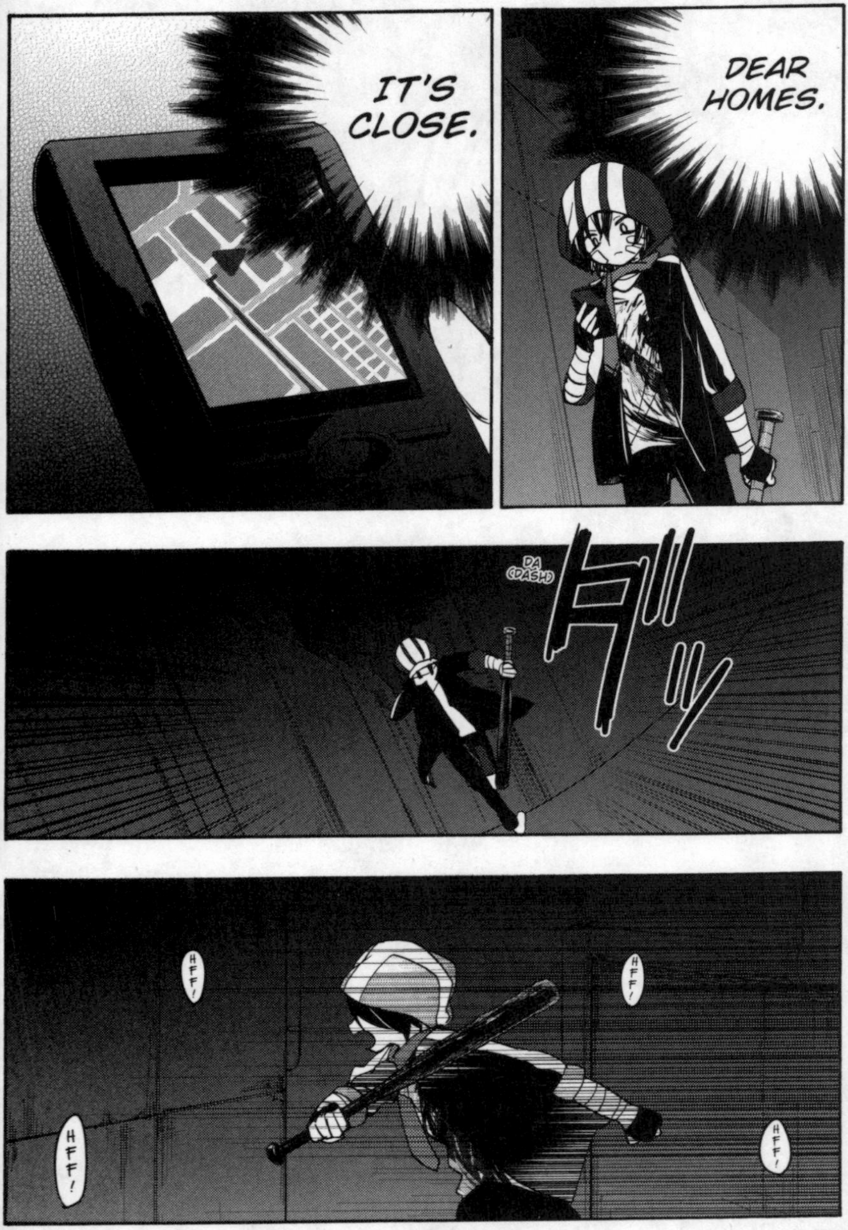
DEAR HOMES.
IT'S CLOSE.
DA (DASH)
ダッ
HFF!
HFF!
HFF!
HFF!

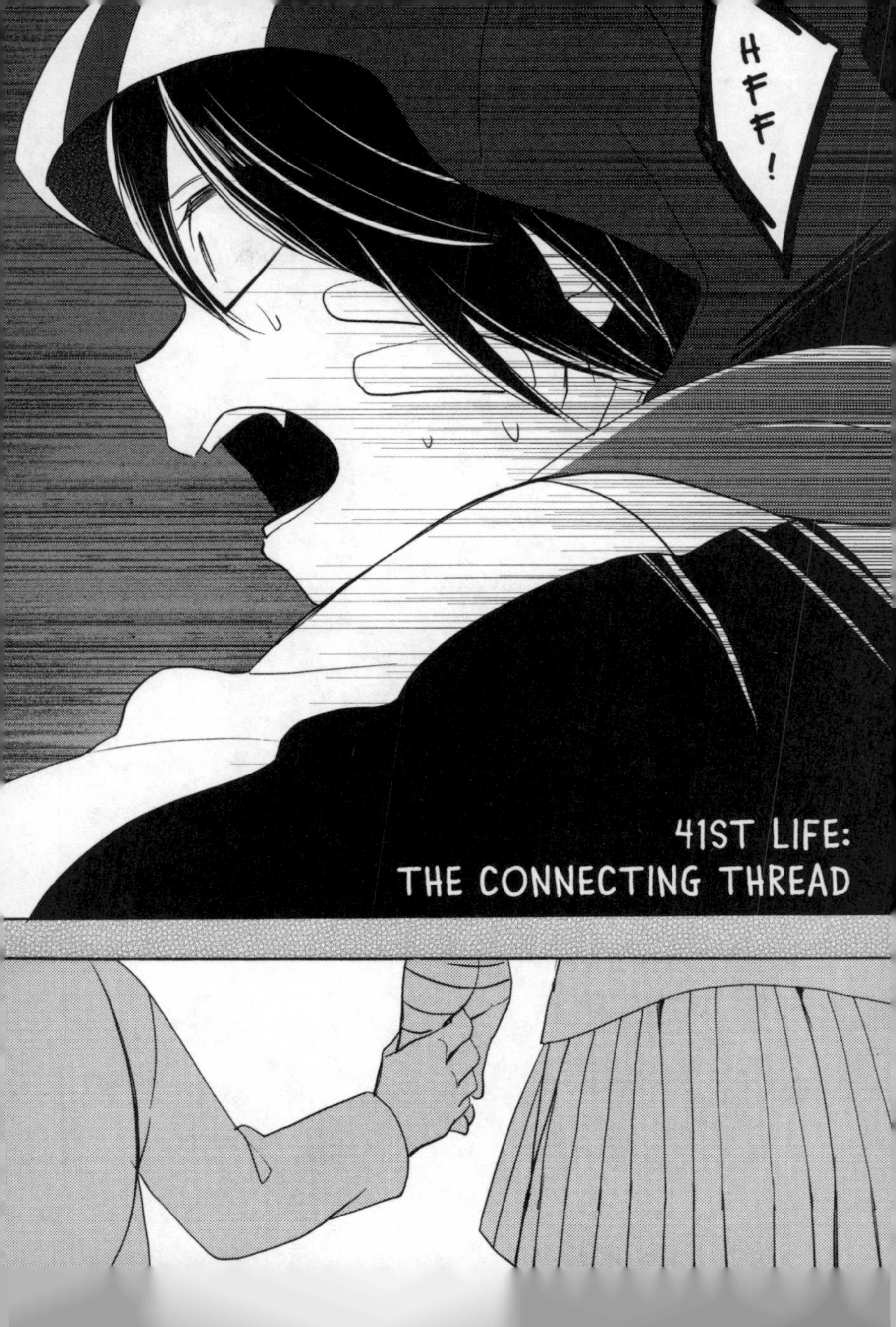
HFF!
41ST LIFE:
THE CONNECTING THREAD

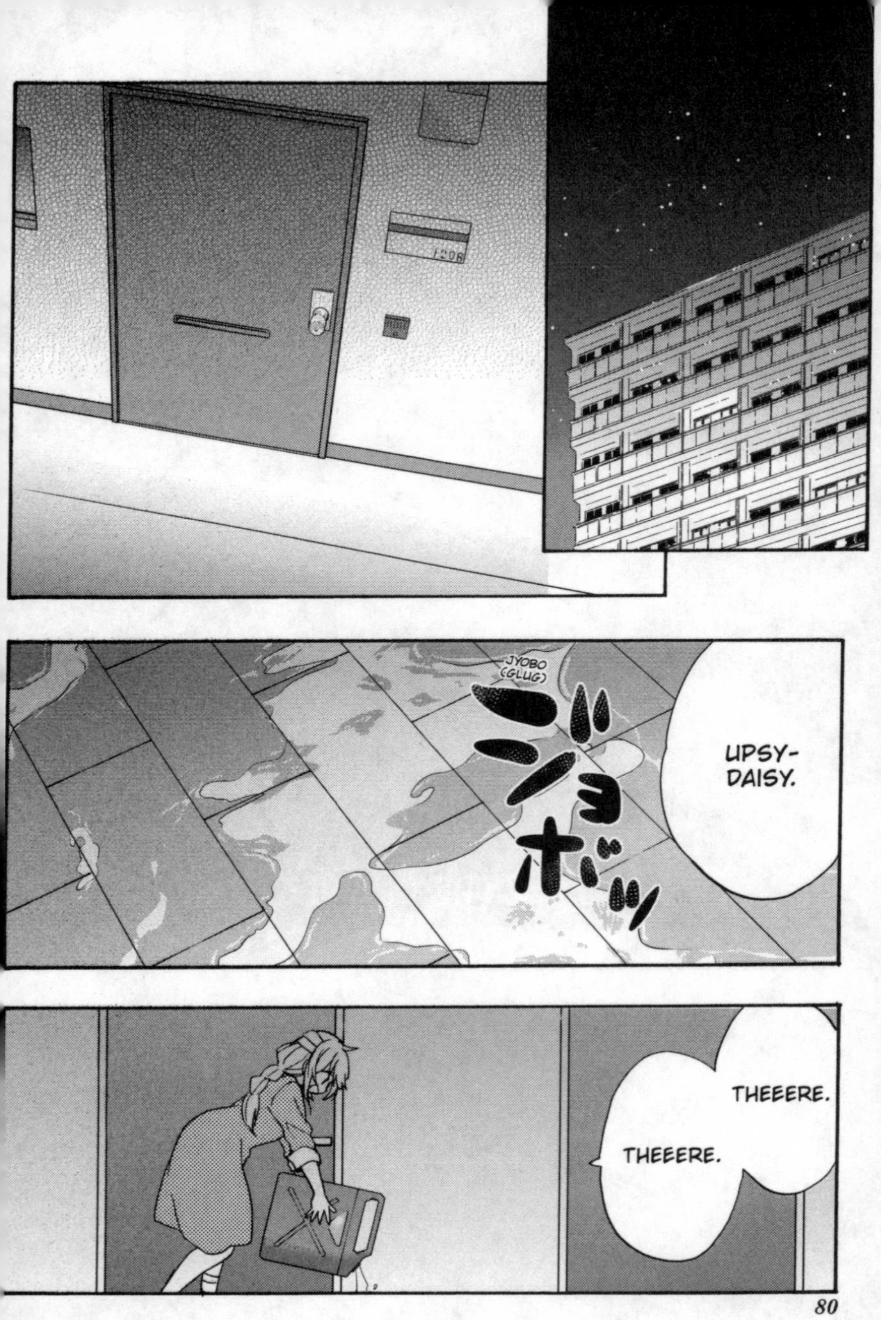
1208
UPSY-DAISY.
JYOBO (GLUG)
THEEERE.
THEEERE.

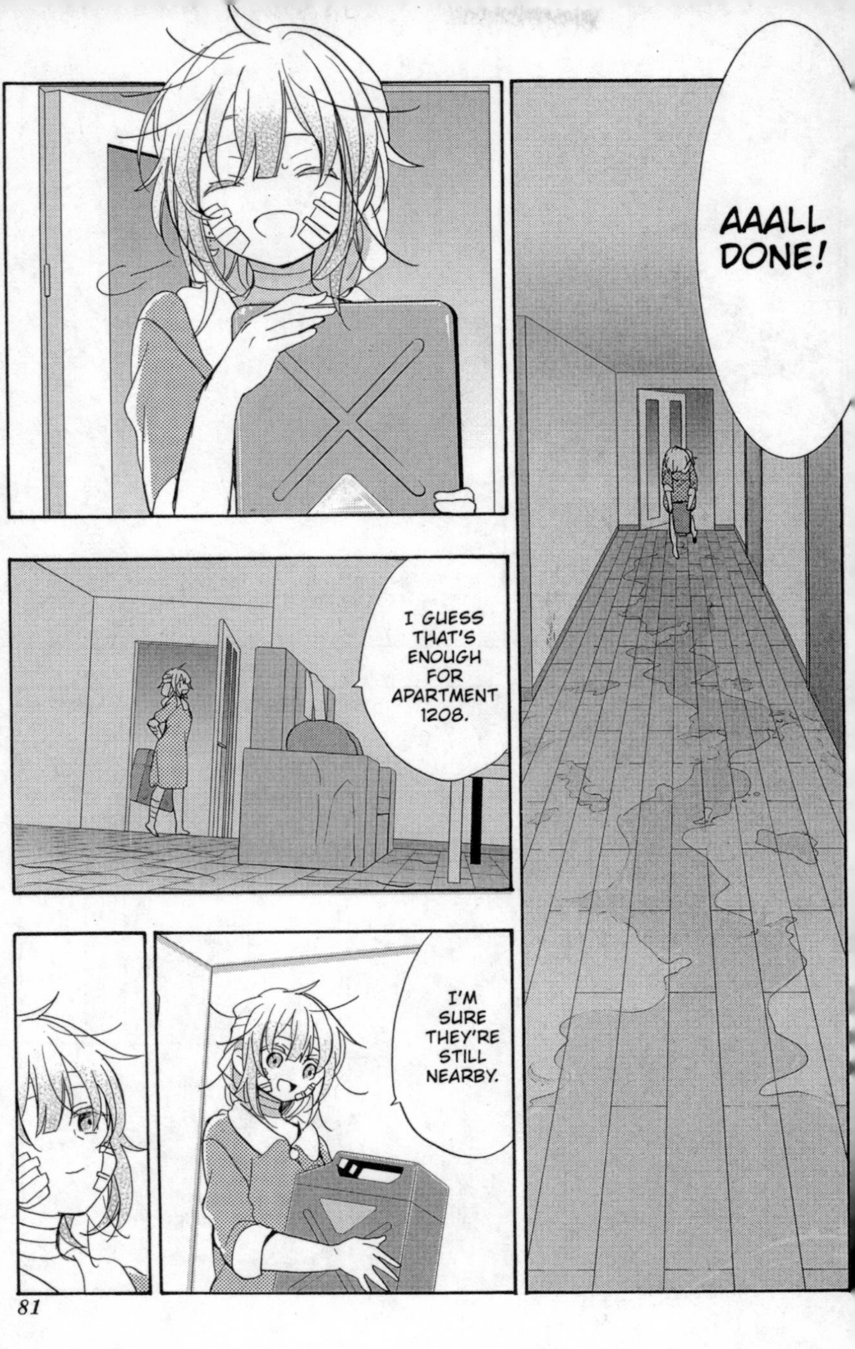
AAALL DONE!
I GUESS THAT'S ENOUGH FOR APARTMENT 1208.
I'M SURE THEY'RE STILL NEARBY.

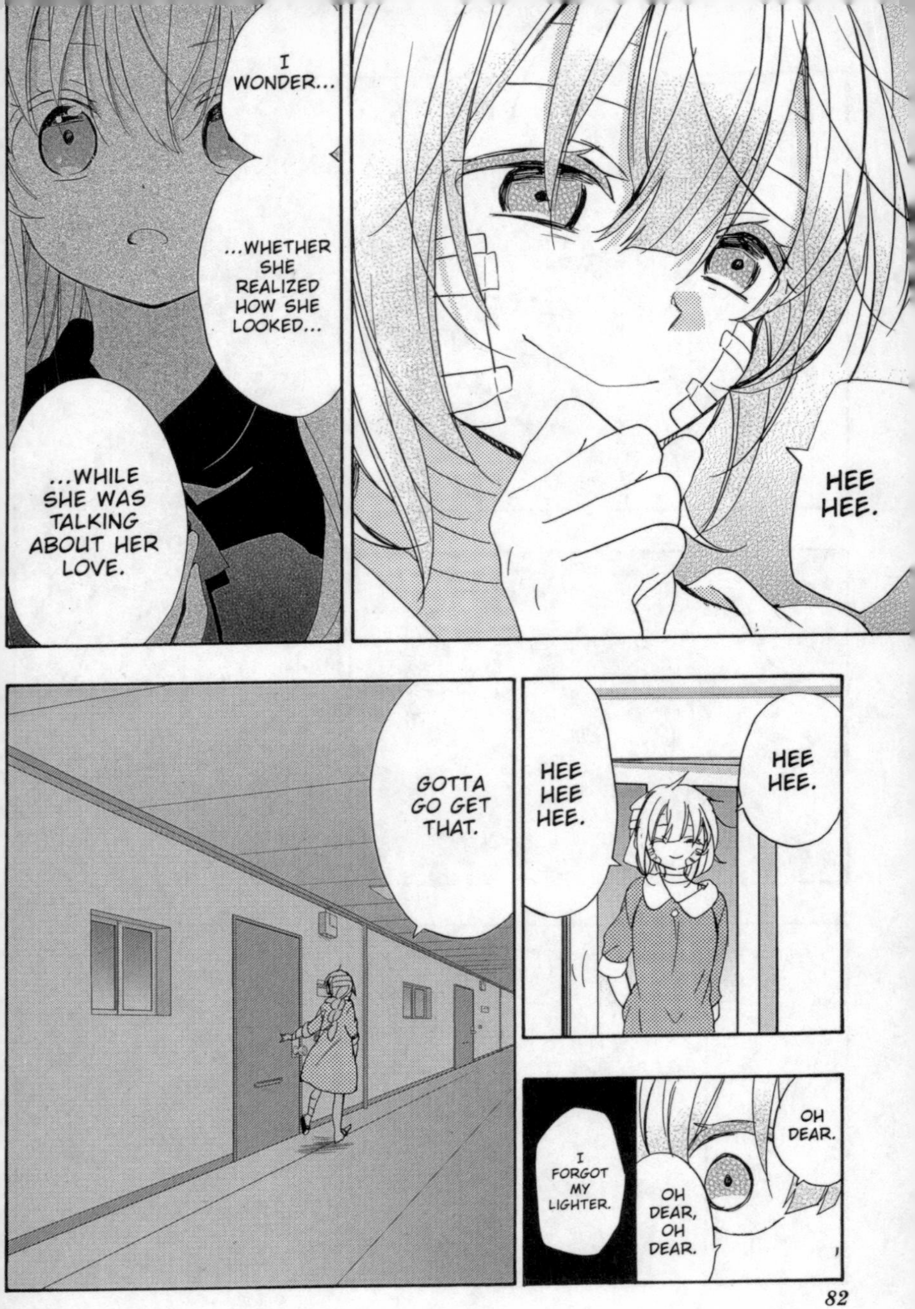
HEE HEE.
I WONDER...
...WHETHER SHE REALIZED HOW SHE LOOKED...
...WHILE SHE WAS TALKING ABOUT HER LOVE.
HEE HEE.
HEE HEE HEE.
OH DEAR.
OH DEAR, OH DEAR.
I FORGOT MY LIGHTER.
GOTTA GO GET THAT.

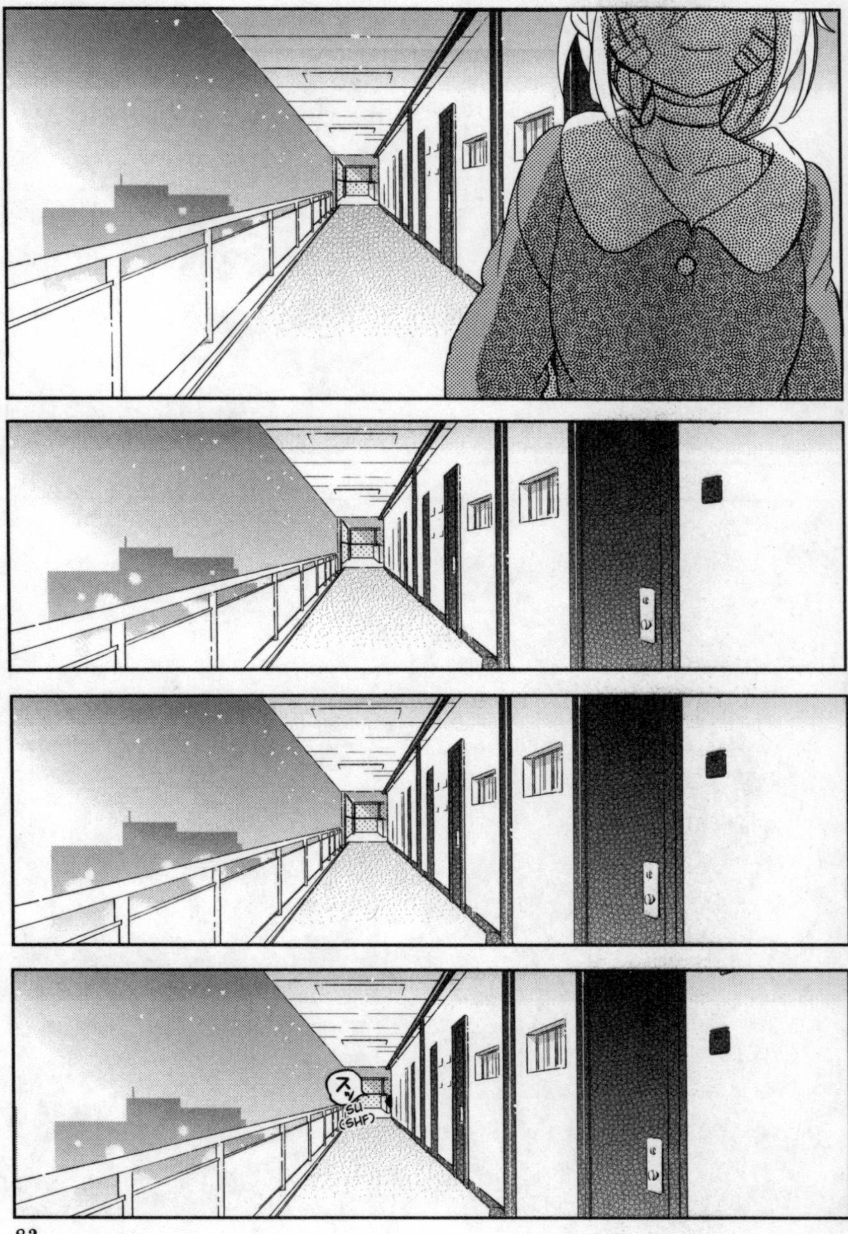
スッ
SU
(SHF)

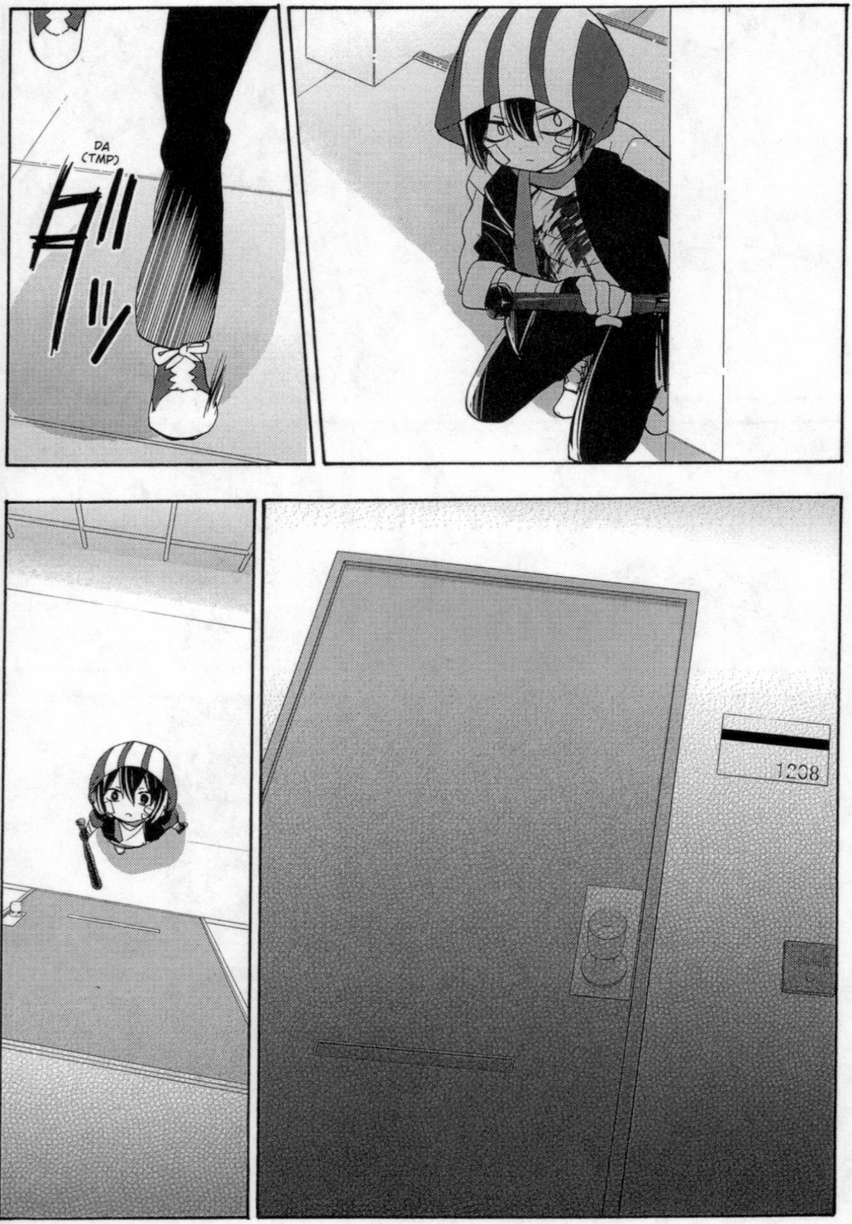
ダッ
DA
(TMP)
1208

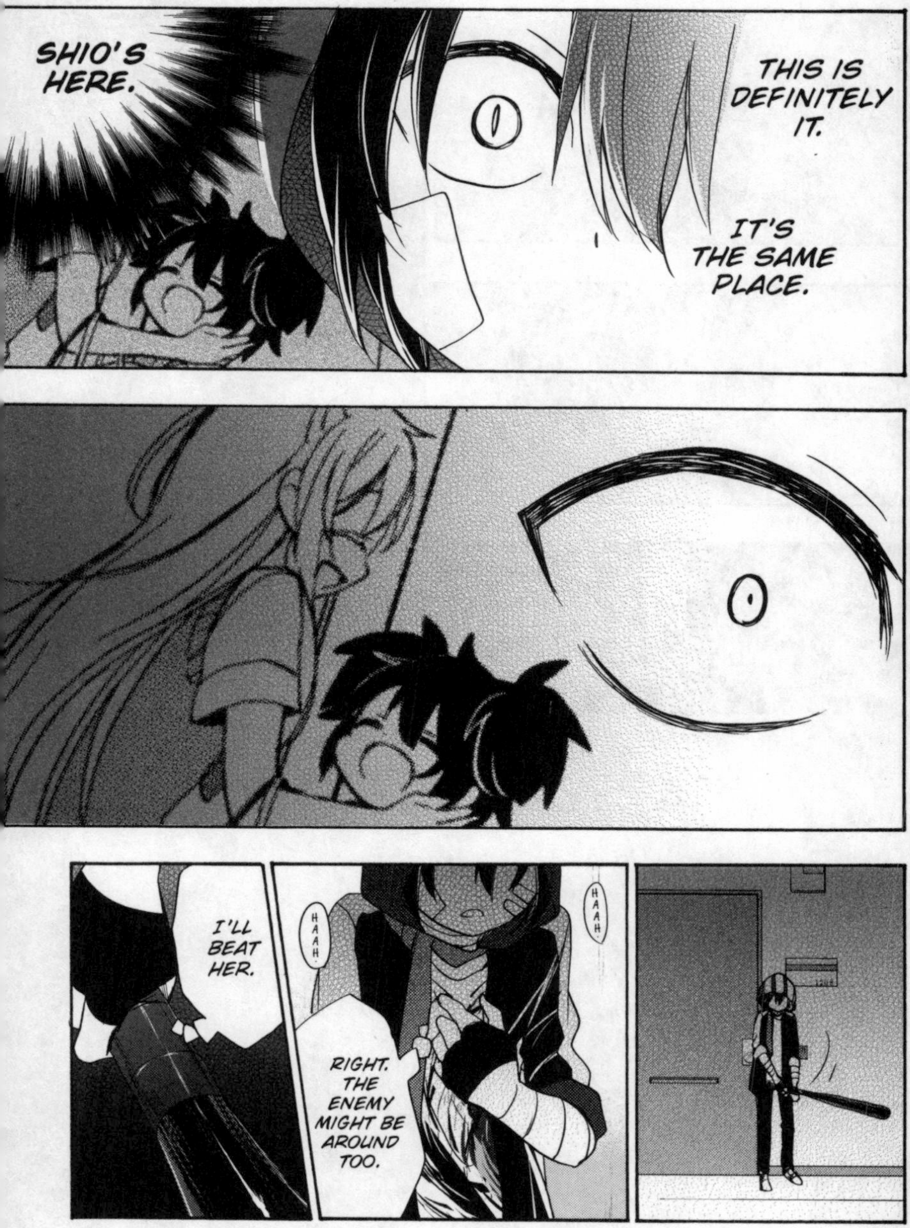
THIS IS DEFINITELY IT.
IT'S THE SAME PLACE.
SHIO'S HERE.
HAAAH.
RIGHT. THE ENEMY MIGHT BE AROUND TOO.
HAAAH.
I'LL BEAT HER.

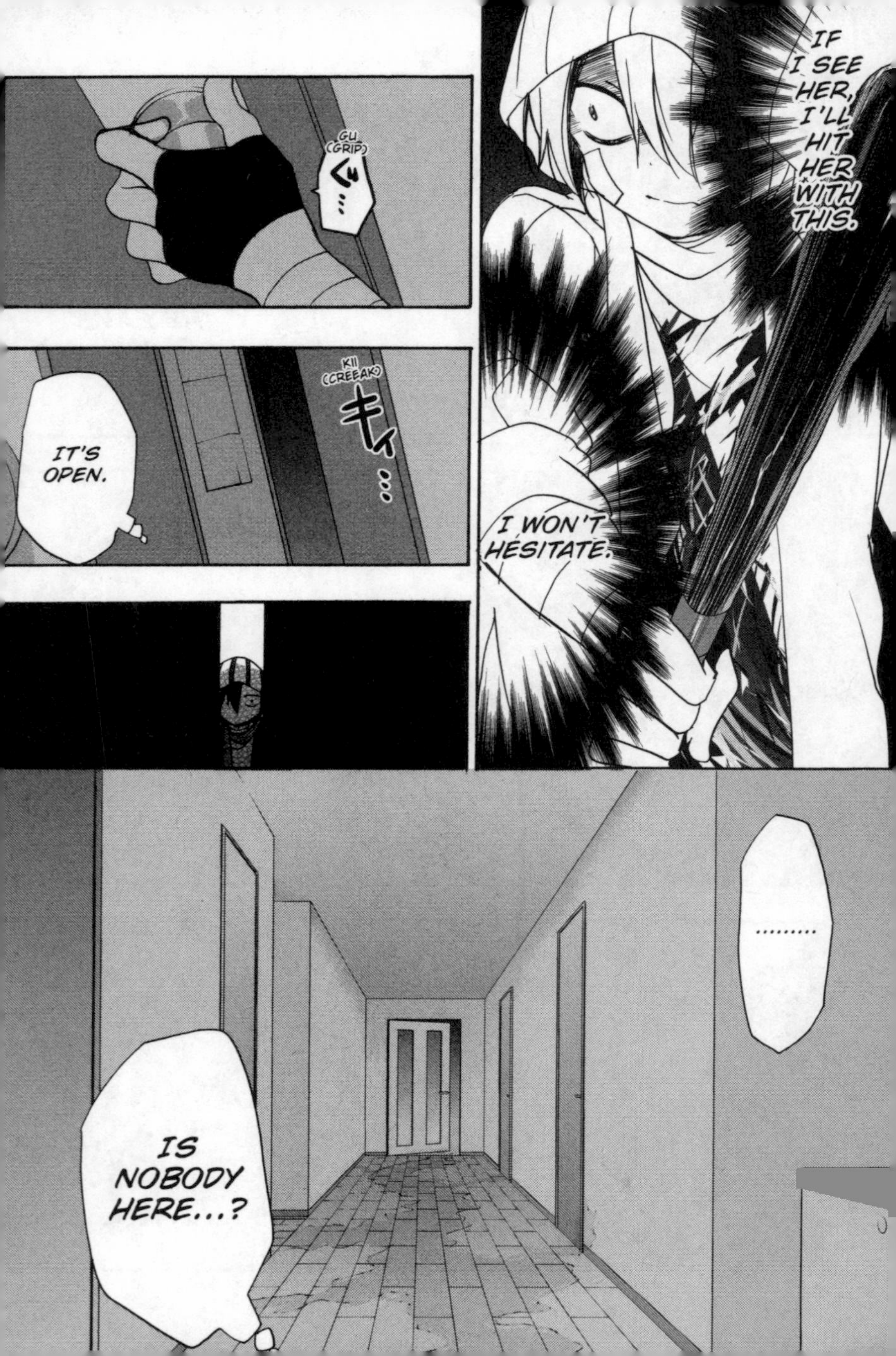
IF I SEE HER, I'LL HIT HER WITH THIS.
I WON'T HESITATE.
GU (GRIP)
ぐ…
KII (CREEAK)
キィ…
IT'S OPEN.
....
IS NOBODY HERE...?

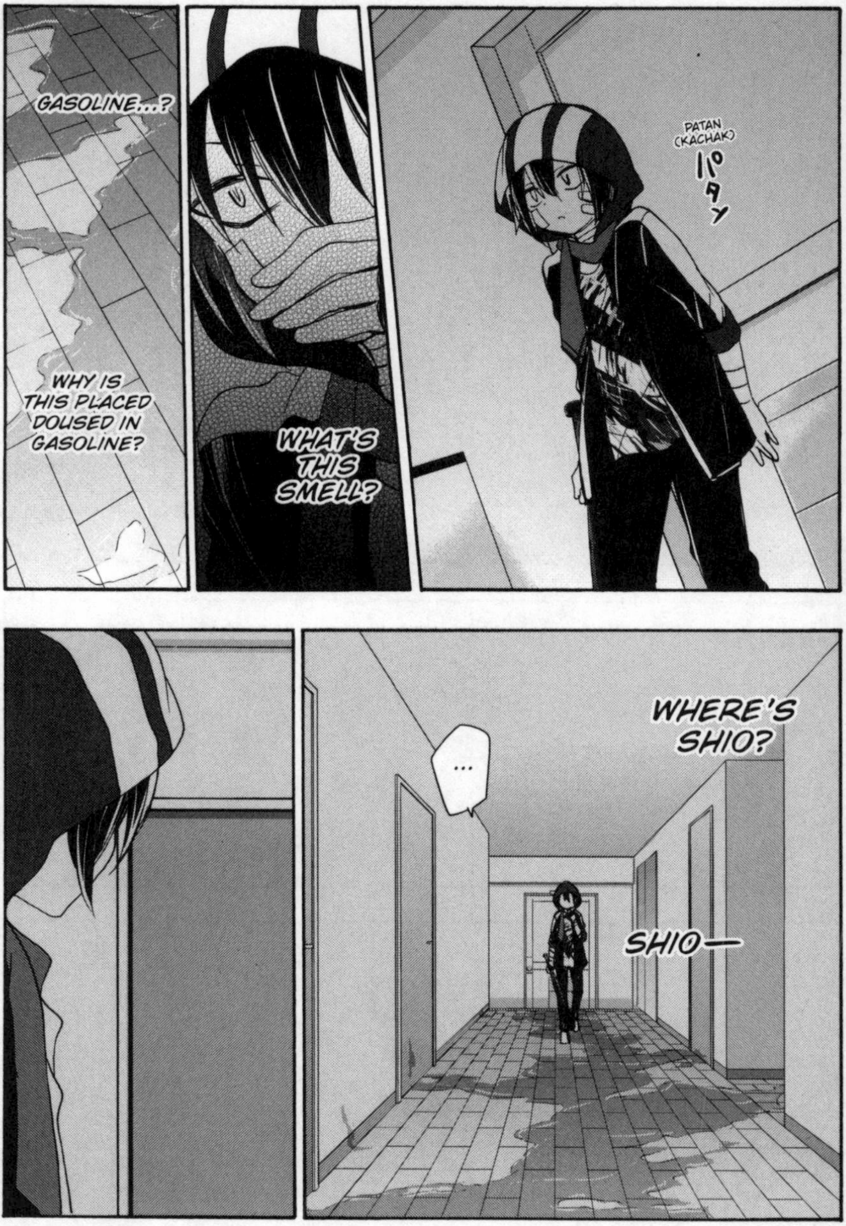
PATAN (KACHAK)
パタン
WHAT'S THIS SMELL?
GASOLINE...?
WHY IS THIS PLACED DOUSED IN GASOLINE?
WHERE'S SHIO?
...
SHIO—

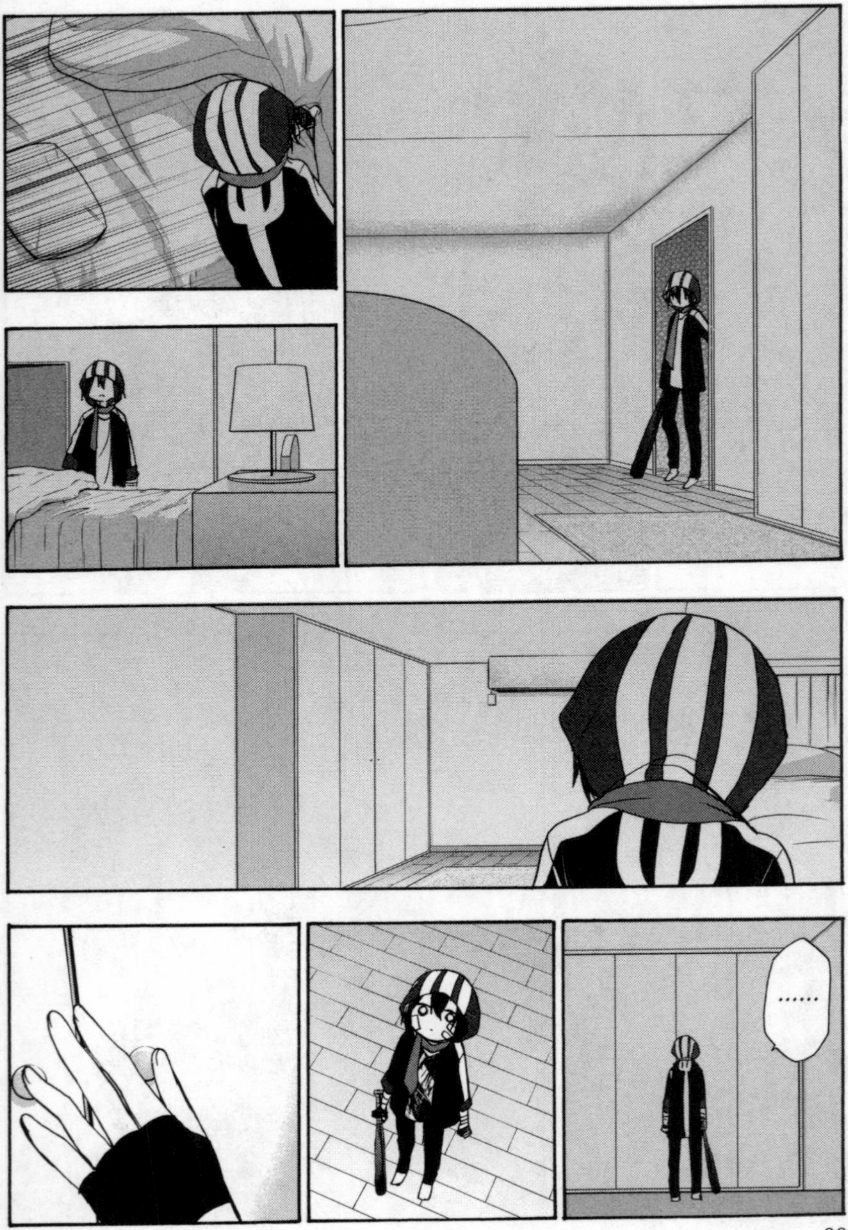
......

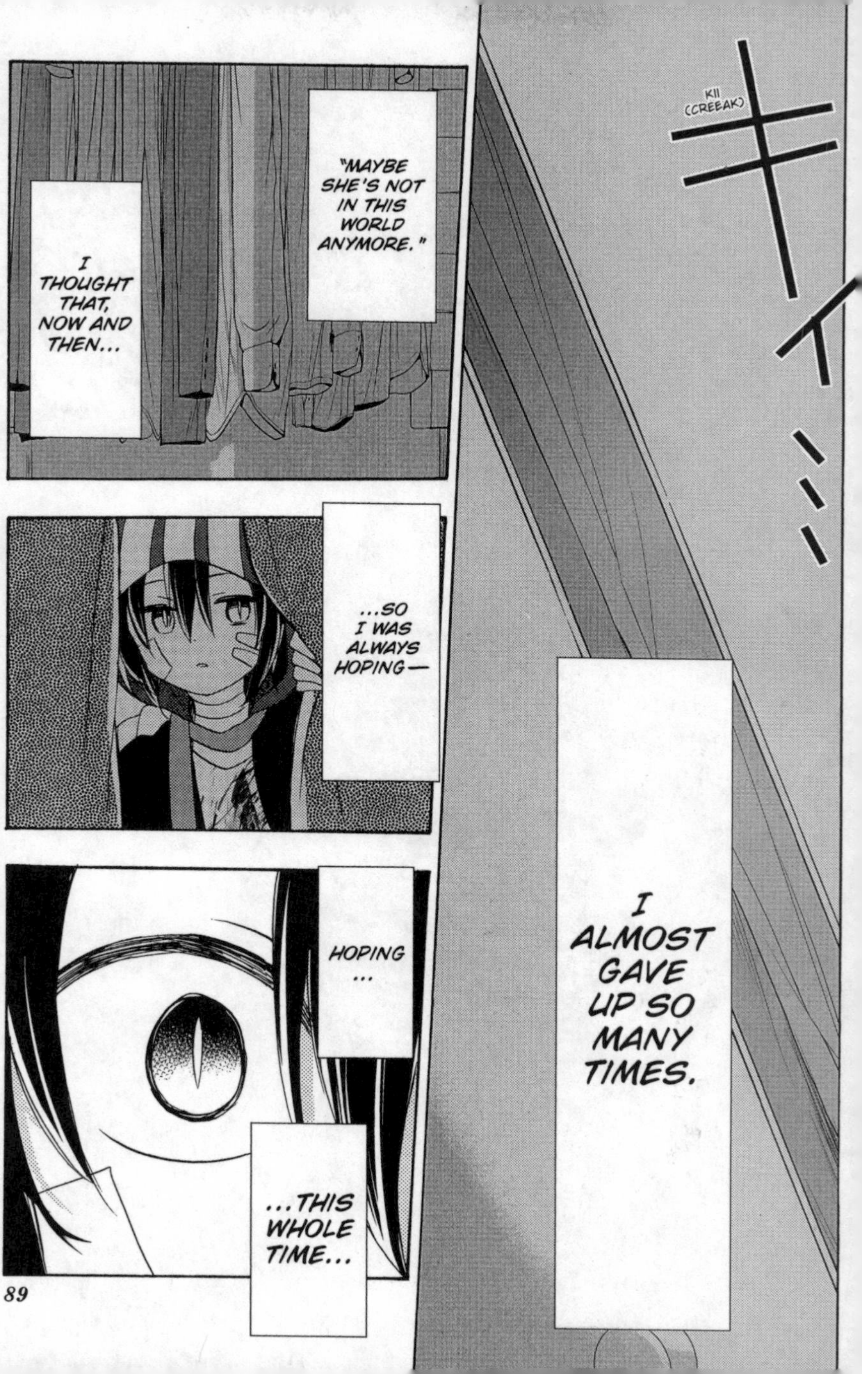
KII (CREEAK)
I ALMOST GAVE UP SO MANY TIMES.
"MAYBE SHE'S NOT IN THIS WORLD ANYMORE."
I THOUGHT THAT, NOW AND THEN...
...SO I WAS ALWAYS HOPING—
HOPING...
...THIS WHOLE TIME...

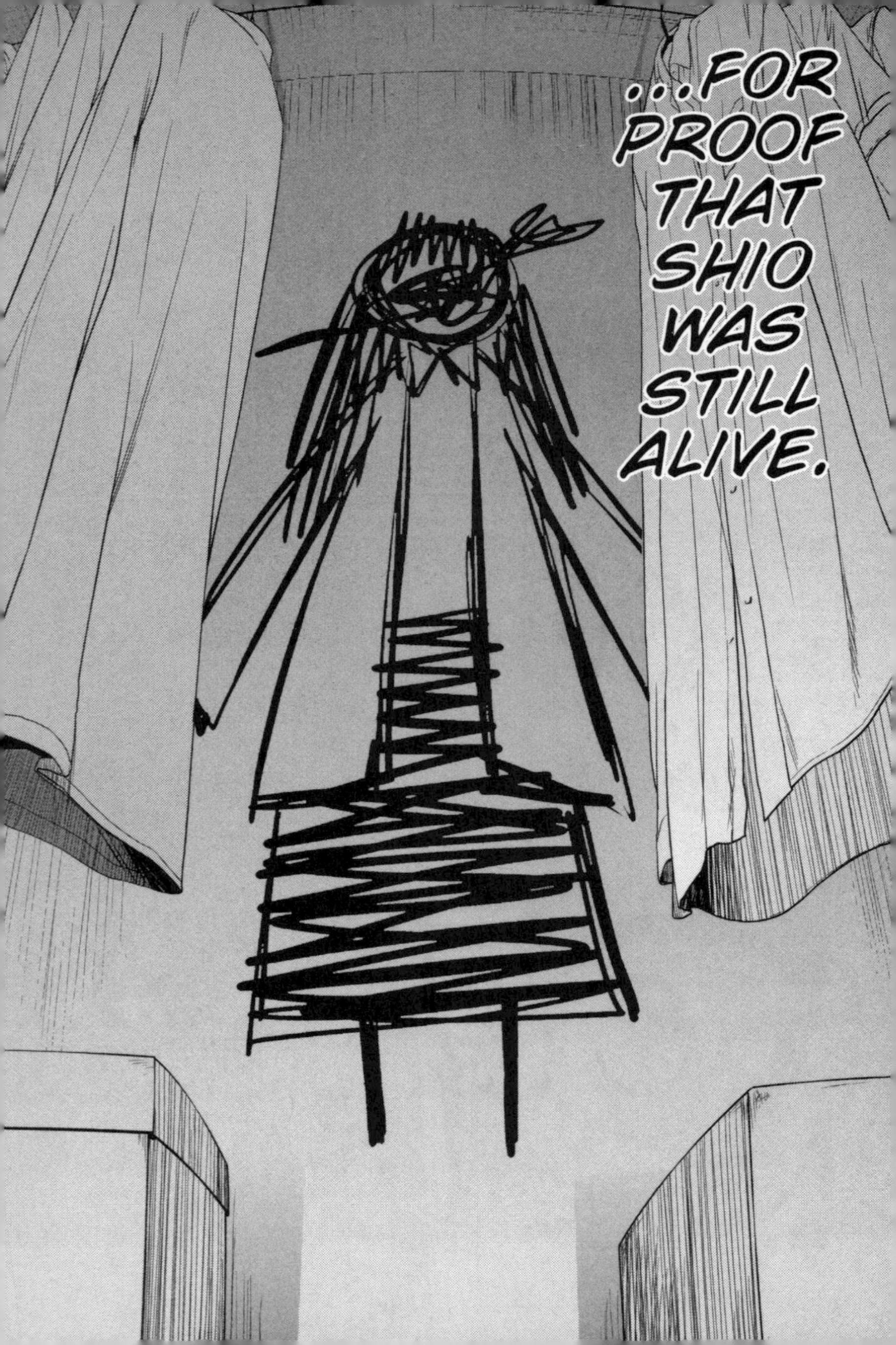
...FOR PROOF THAT SHIO WAS STILL ALIVE.

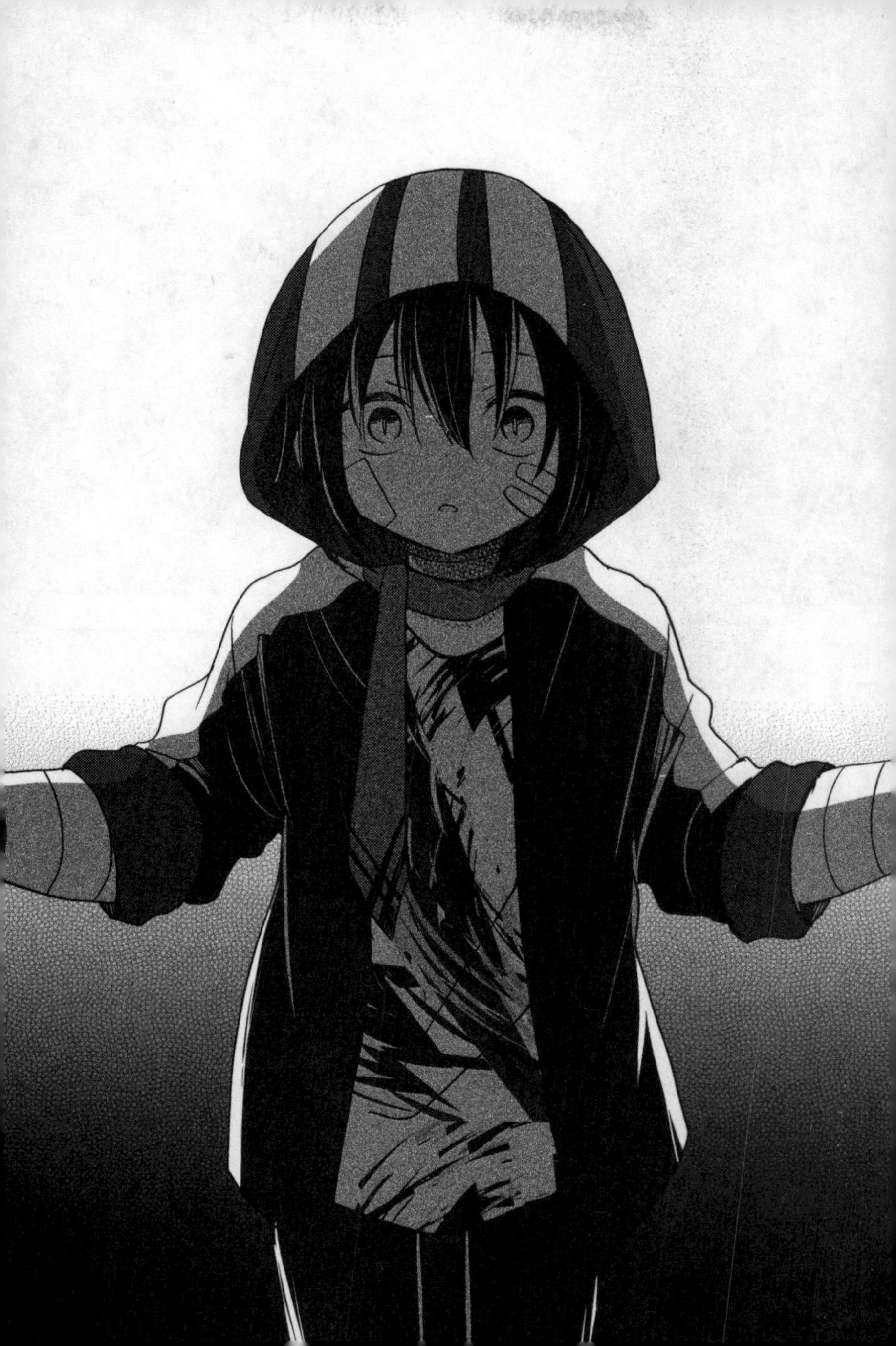

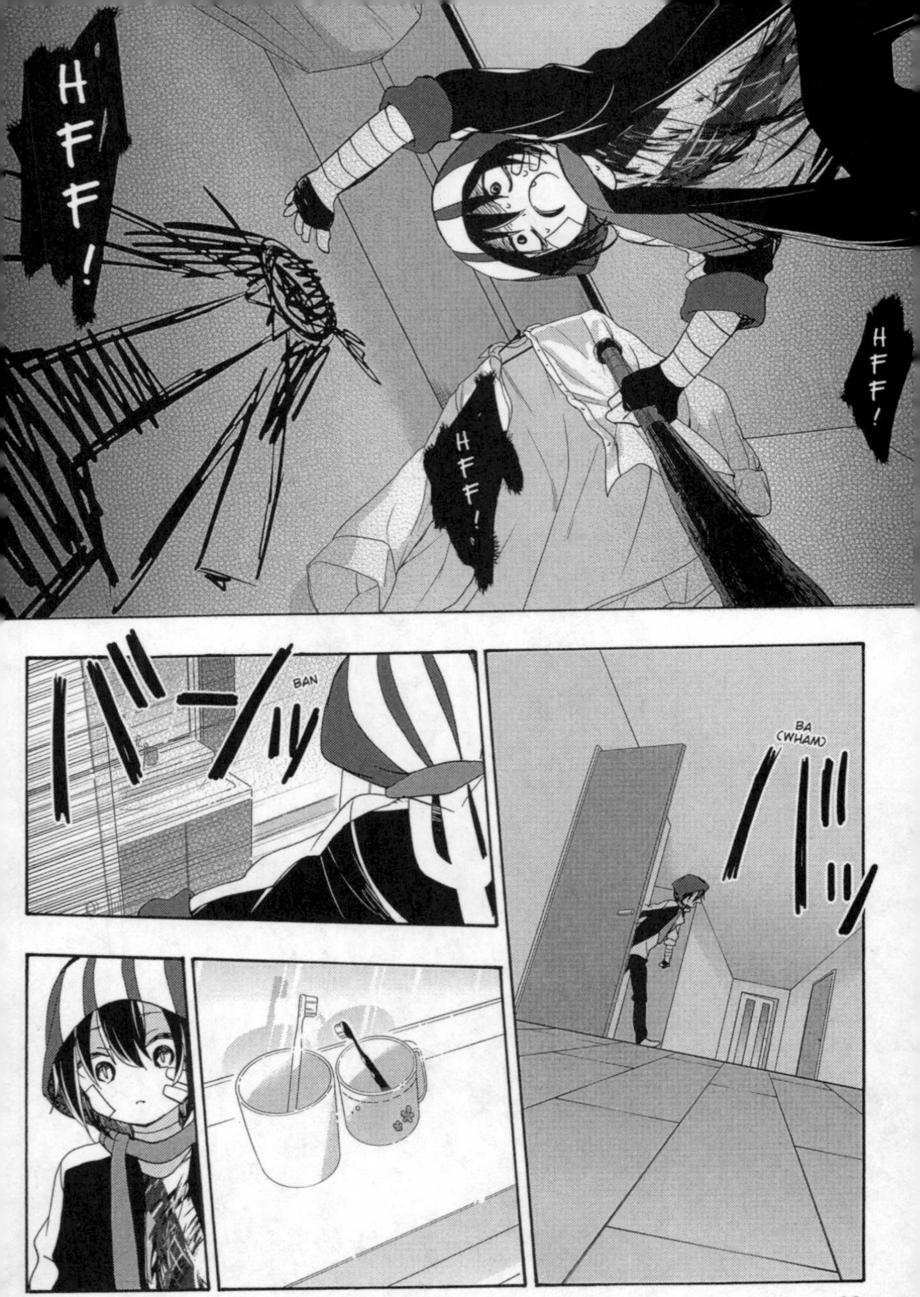
HFF!
HFF!
HFF!
BA (WHAM)
BAN

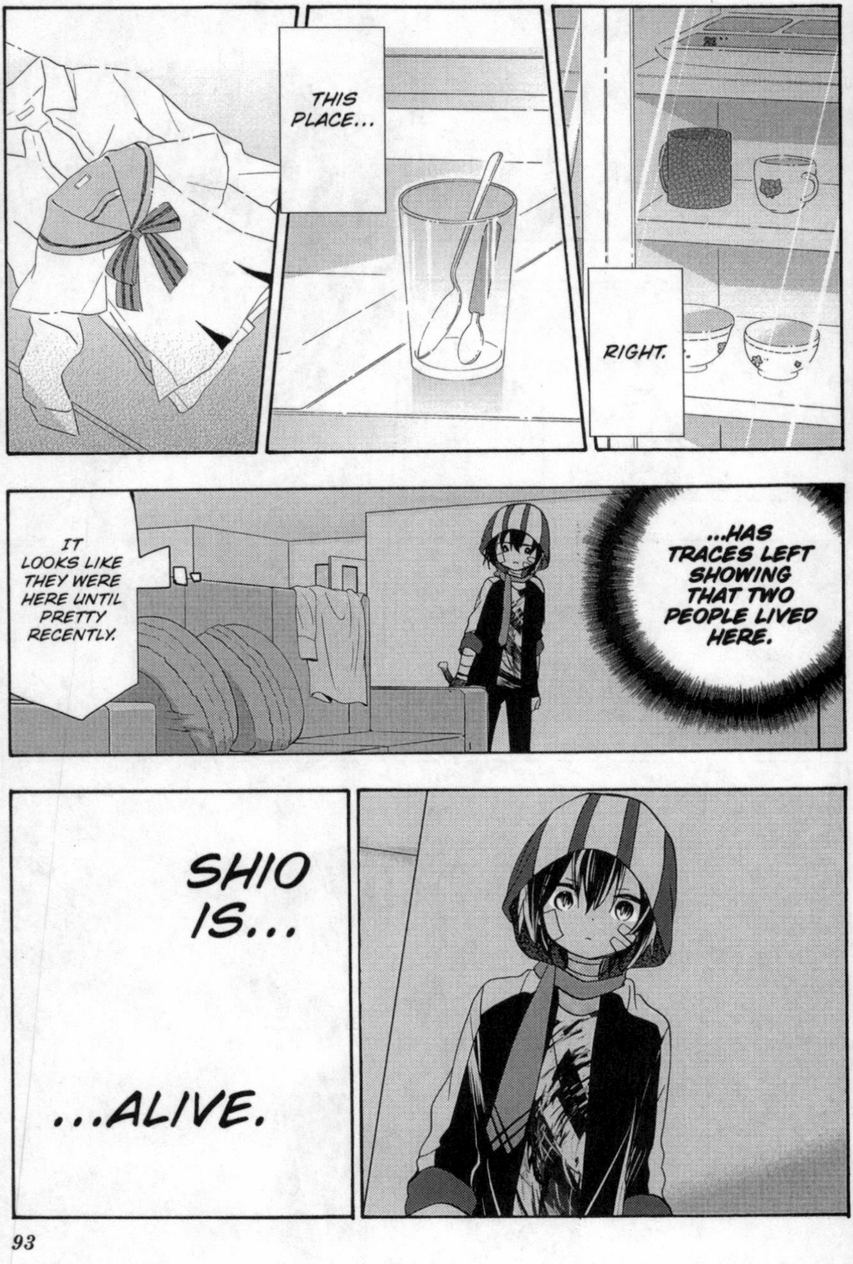
RIGHT.
THIS PLACE...
...HAS TRACES LEFT SHOWING THAT TWO PEOPLE LIVED HERE.
IT LOOKS LIKE THEY WERE HERE UNTIL PRETTY RECENTLY.
SHIO IS...
...ALIVE.

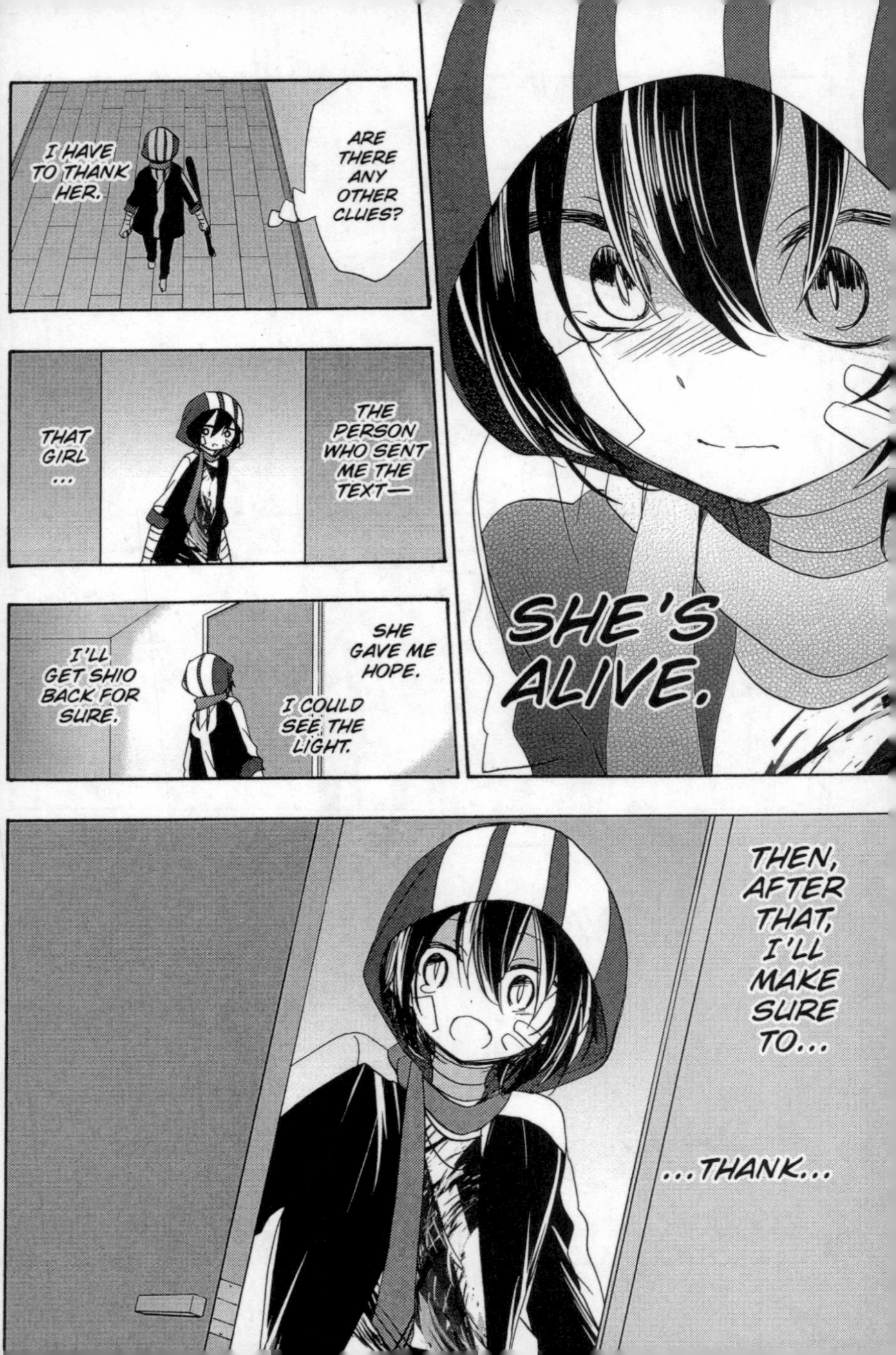
SHE'S ALIVE.
ARE THERE ANY OTHER CLUES?
I HAVE TO THANK HER.
THE PERSON WHO SENT ME THE TEXT—
THAT GIRL...
SHE GAVE ME HOPE.
I COULD SEE THE LIGHT.
I'LL GET SHIO BACK FOR SURE.
THEN, AFTER THAT, I'LL MAKE SURE TO...
...THANK...

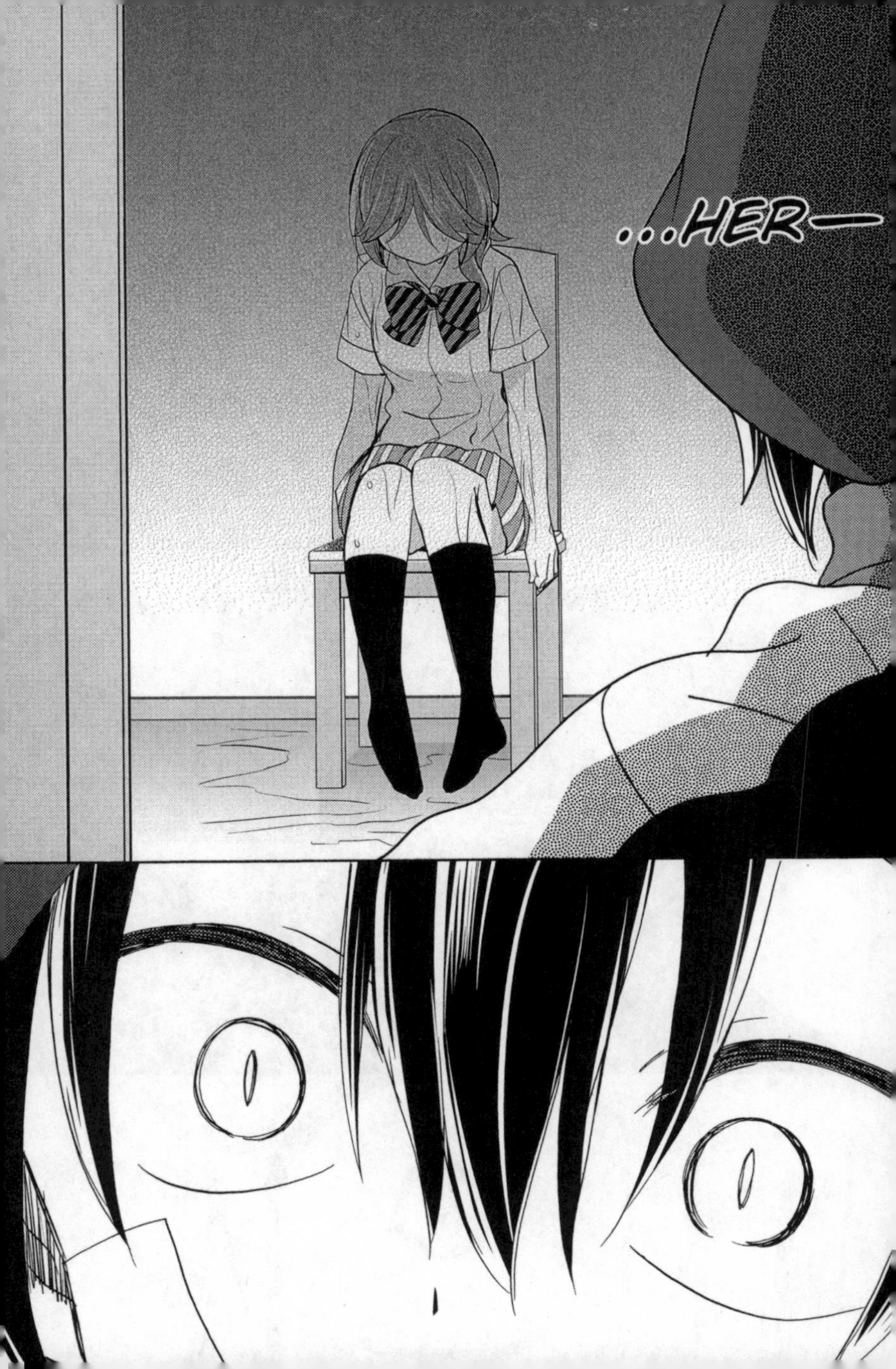
...HER—

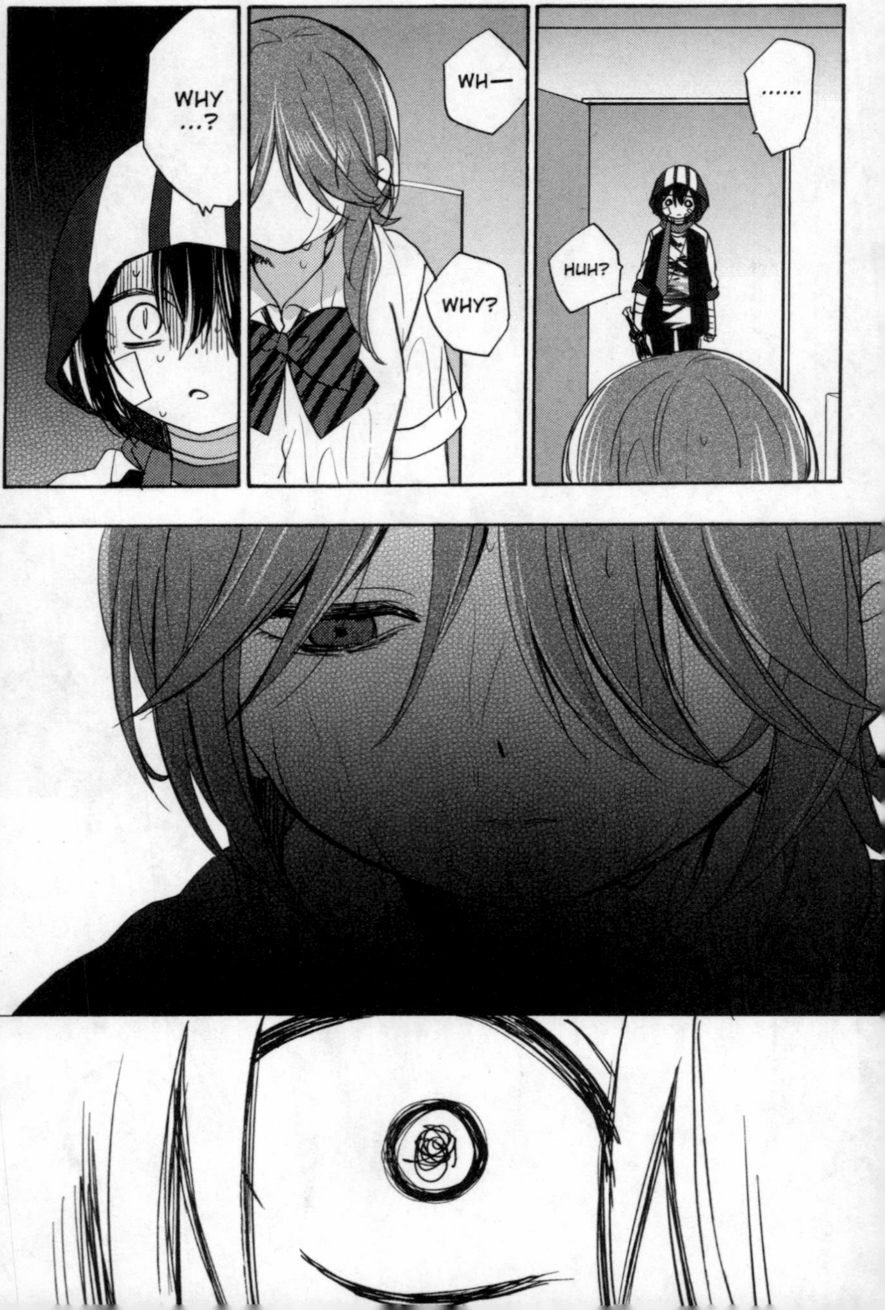
......
HUH?
WH—
WHY?
WHY ...?

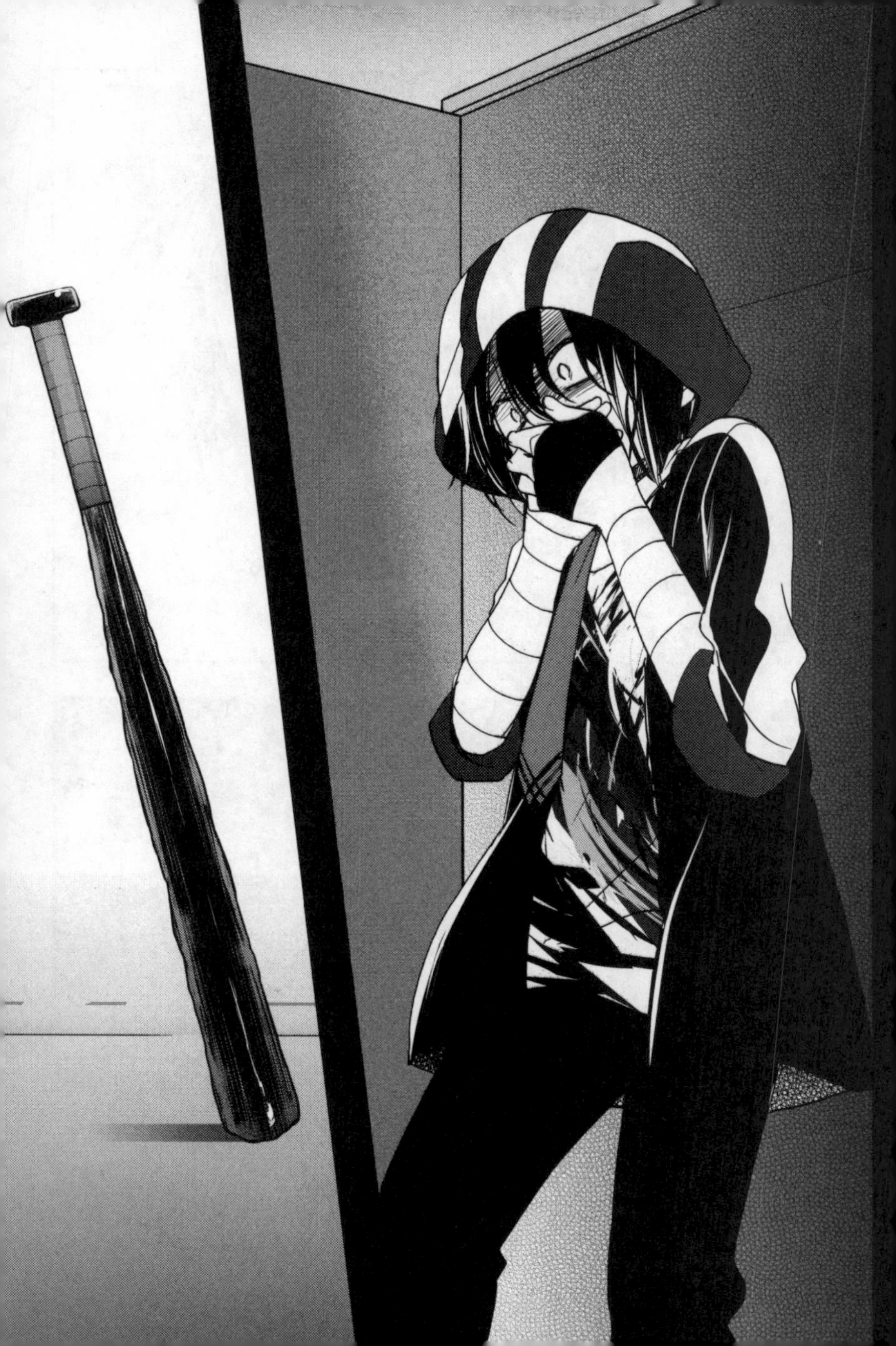

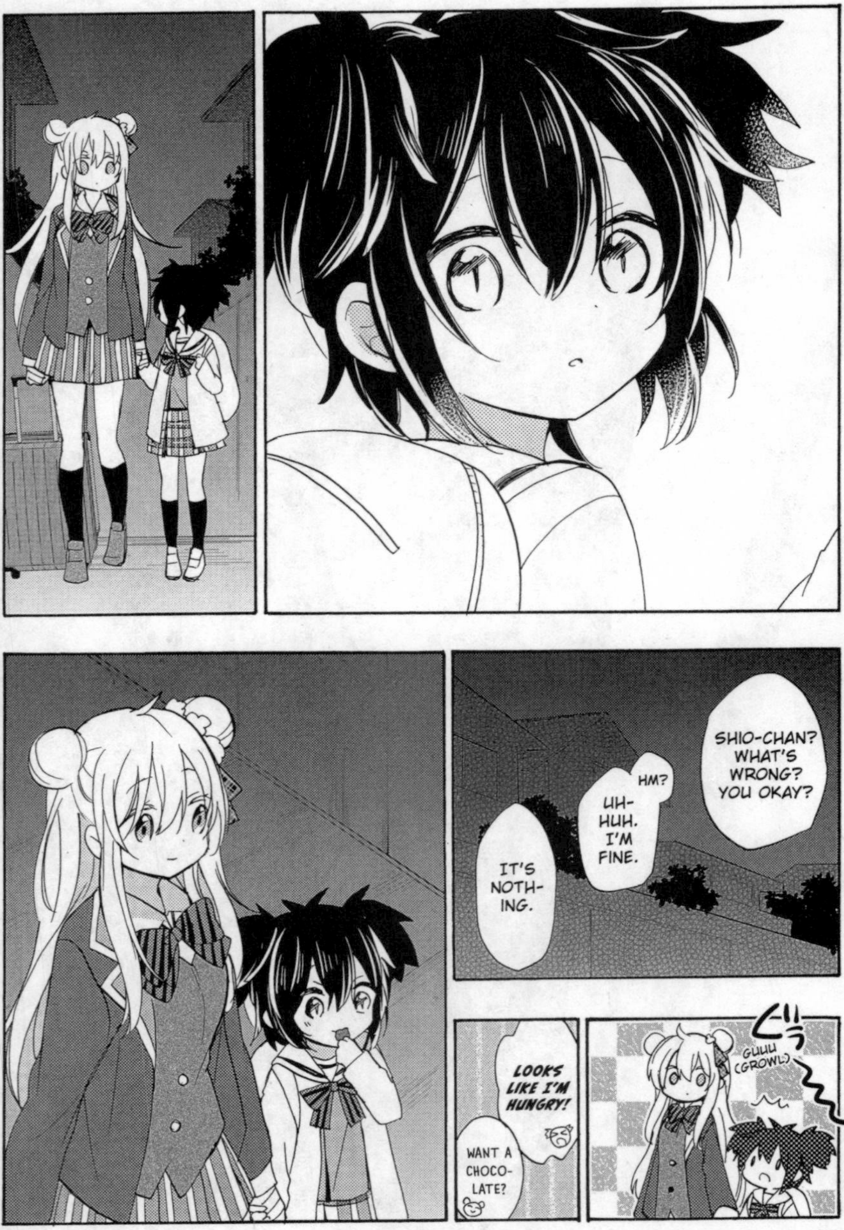
SHIO-CHAN? WHAT'S WRONG? YOU OKAY?
HM?
UH-HUH. I'M FINE.
IT'S NOTHING.
GUUU (GROWL)
LOOKS LIKE I'M HUNGRY!
WANT A CHOCOLATE?

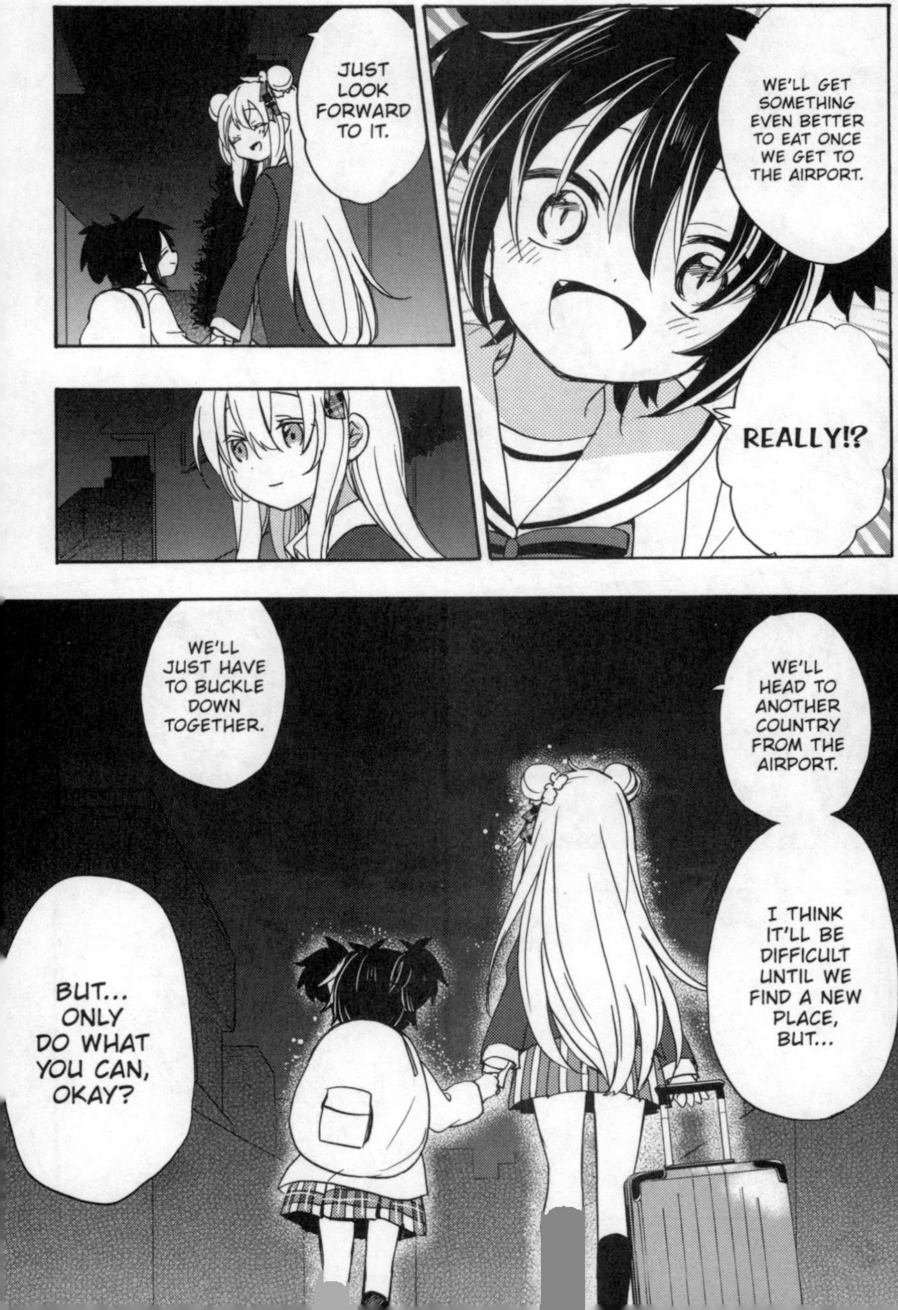
WE'LL GET SOMETHING EVEN BETTER TO EAT ONCE WE GET TO THE AIRPORT.
REALLY!?
JUST LOOK FORWARD TO IT.
WE'LL HEAD TO ANOTHER COUNTRY FROM THE AIRPORT.
I THINK IT'LL BE DIFFICULT UNTIL WE FIND A NEW PLACE, BUT...
WE'LL JUST HAVE TO BUCKLE DOWN TOGETHER.
BUT... ONLY DO WHAT YOU CAN, OKAY?

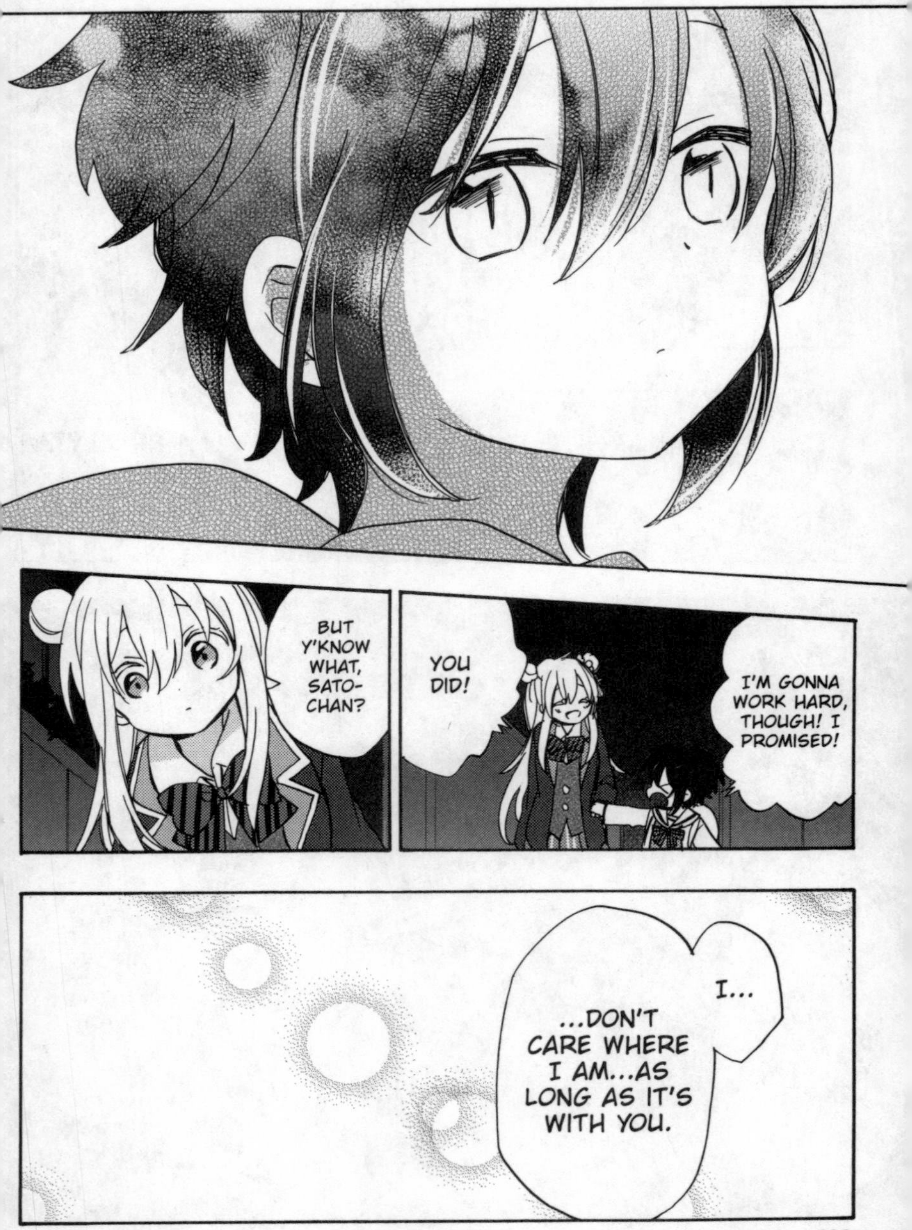
I'M GONNA WORK HARD, THOUGH! I PROMISED!
YOU DID!
BUT Y'KNOW WHAT, SATO-CHAN?
I...
...DON'T CARE WHERE I AM...AS LONG AS IT'S WITH YOU.

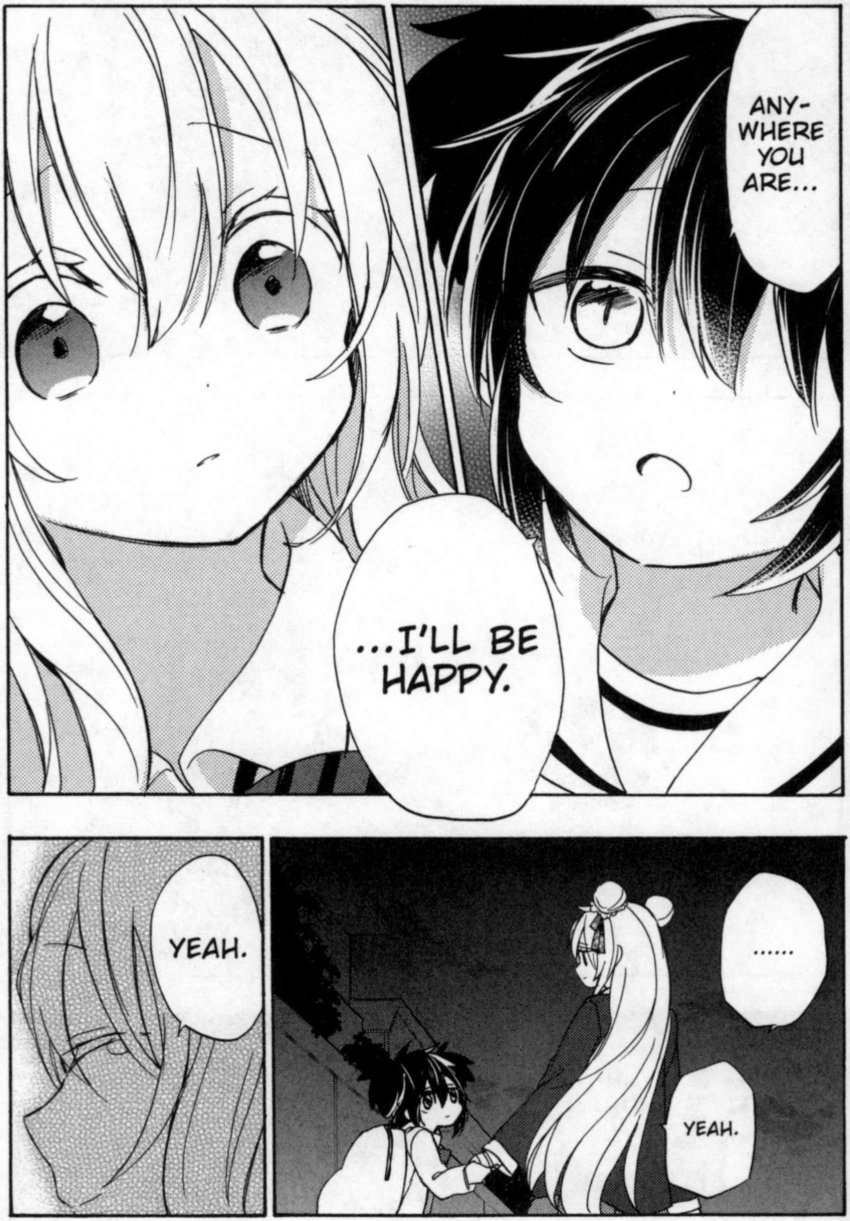
ANY-WHERE YOU ARE...
...I'LL BE HAPPY.
......
YEAH.
YEAH.

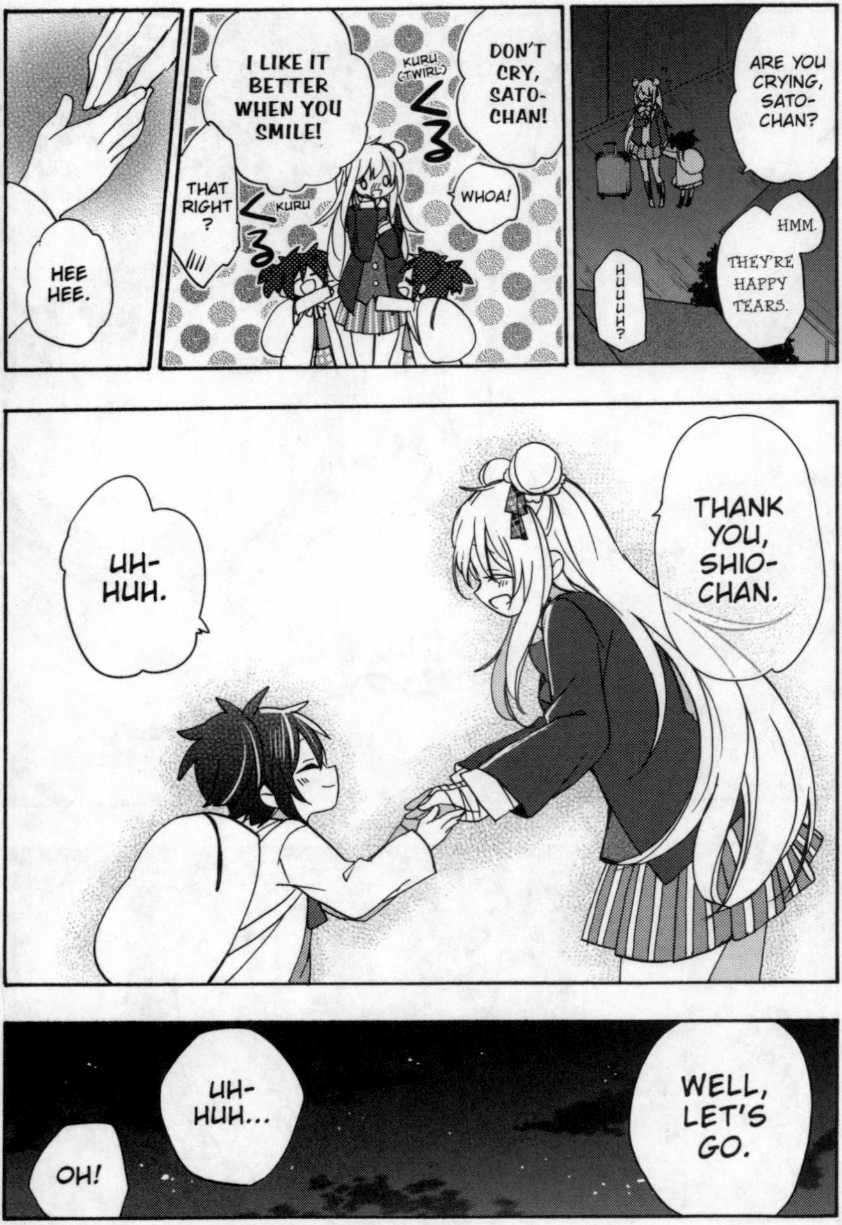
ARE YOU CRYING, SATO-CHAN?
HMM.
THEY'RE HAPPY TEARS.
HUUUH?
DON'T CRY, SATO-CHAN!
KURU (TWIRL)
くる
I LIKE IT BETTER WHEN YOU SMILE!
WHOA!
THAT RIGHT?
KURU
くる
HEE HEE.
THANK YOU, SHIO-CHAN.
UH-HUH.
WELL, LET'S GO.
UH-HUH...
OH!

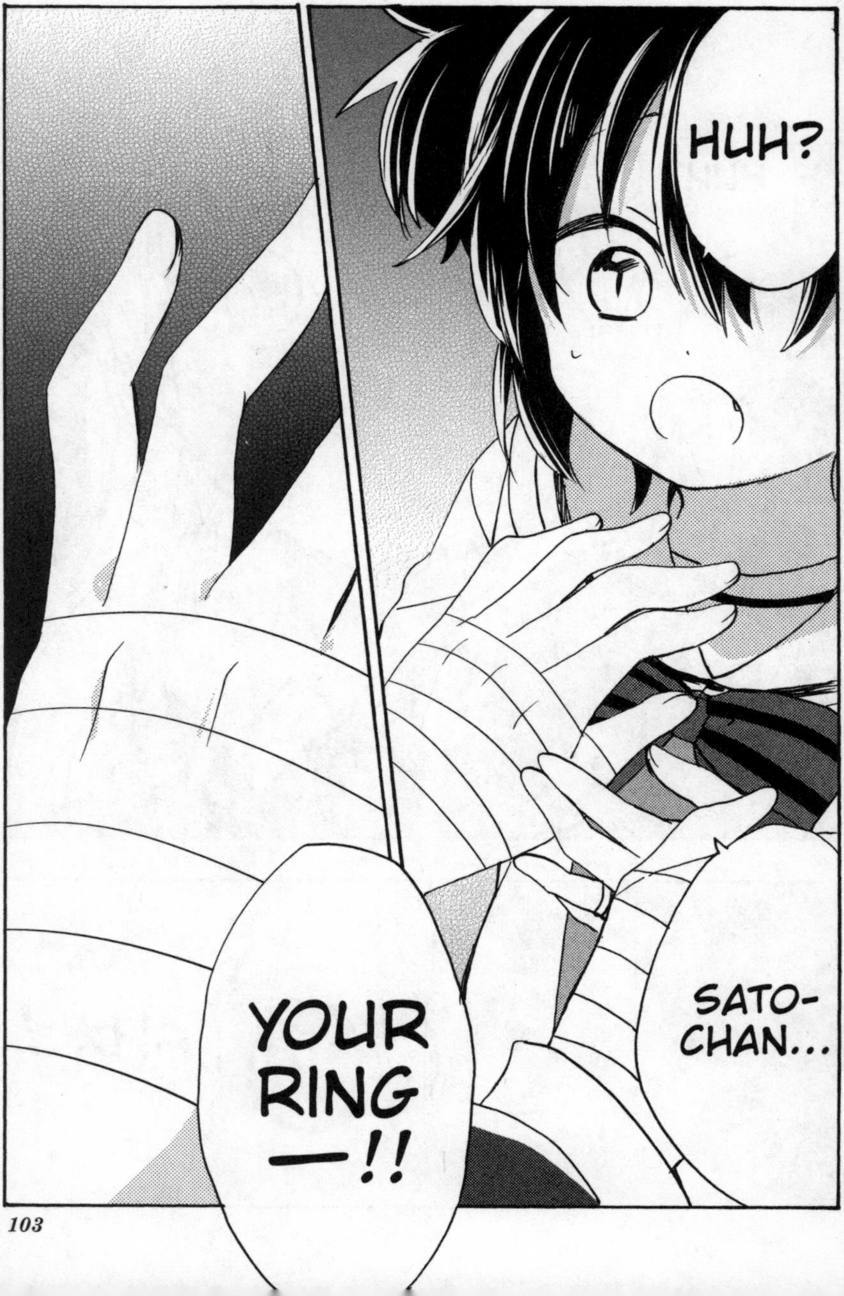
HUH?
SATO-CHAN...
YOUR RING—!!

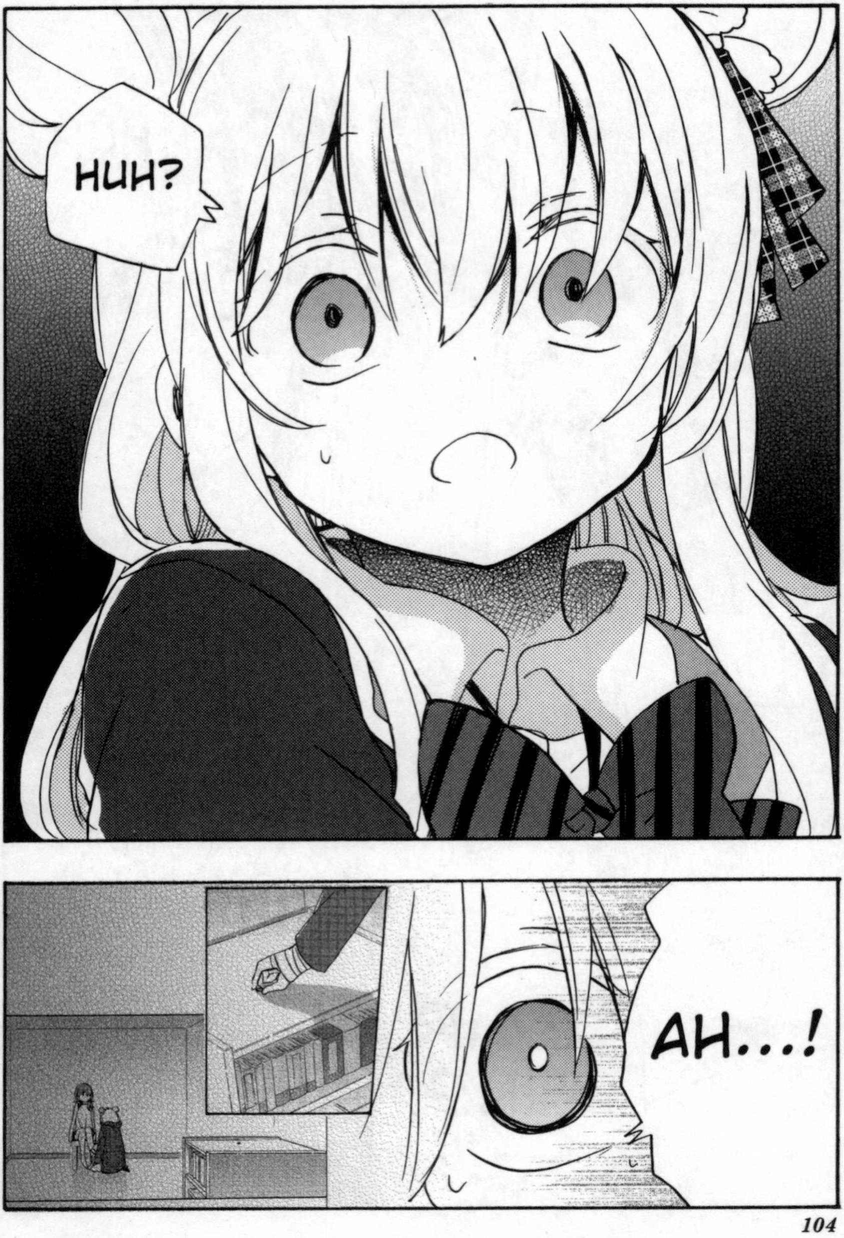
HUH?
AH...!

Happy
Sugar
Life

Happy
Sugar
Life

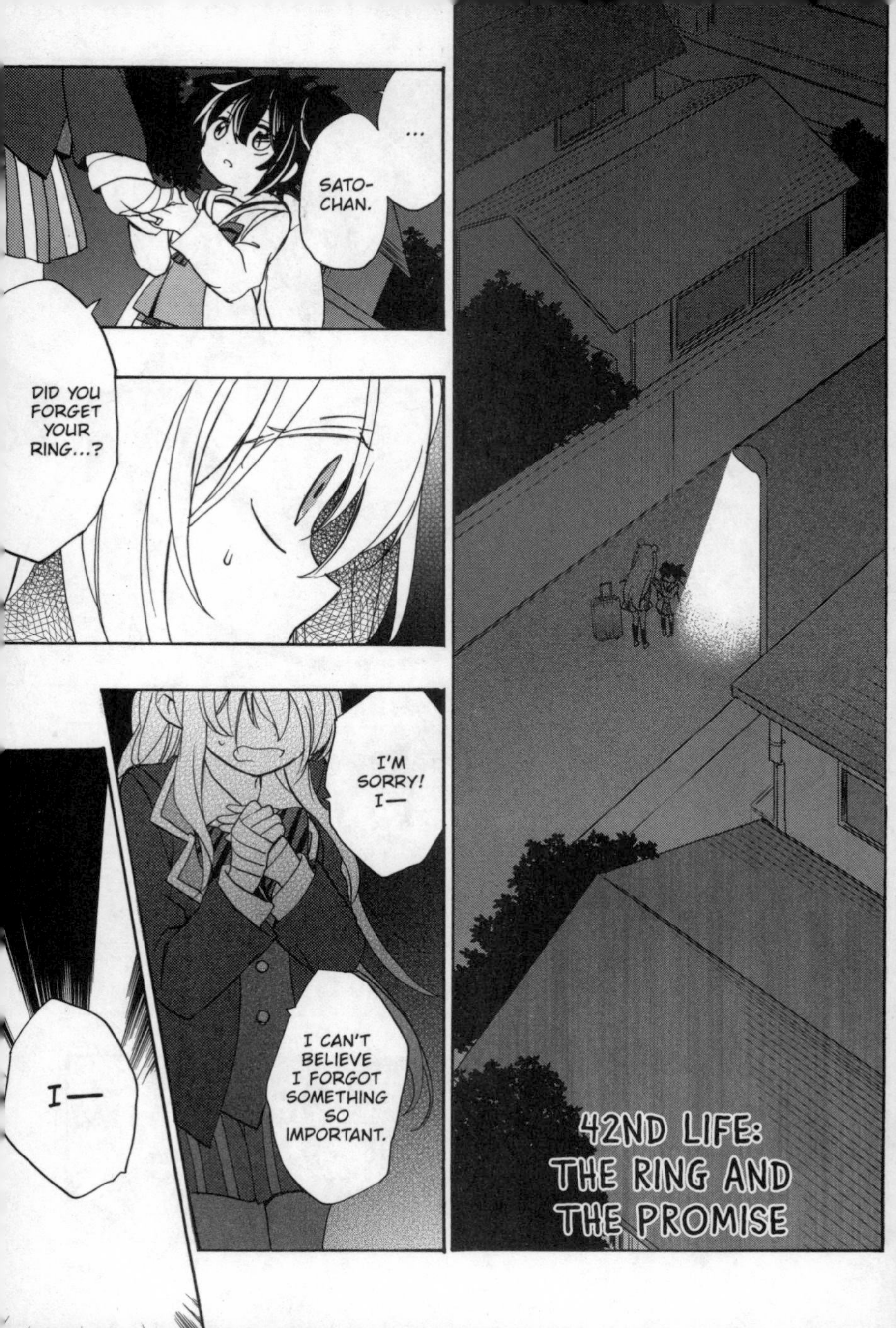
42ND LIFE:
THE RING AND THE PROMISE
...
SATO-CHAN.
DID YOU FORGET YOUR RING...?
I'M SORRY! I—
I CAN'T BELIEVE I FORGOT SOMETHING SO IMPORTANT.
I—

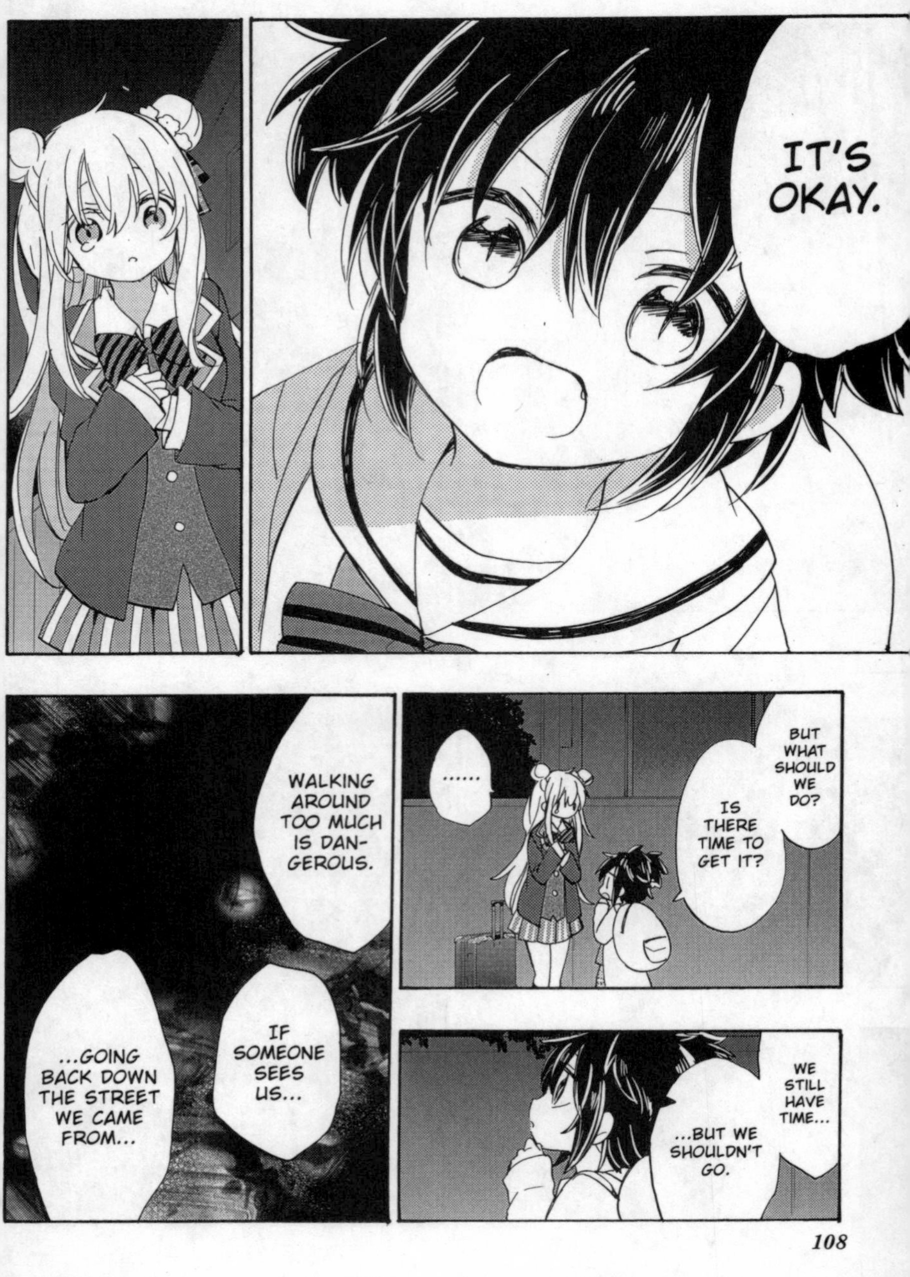
IT'S OKAY.
BUT WHAT SHOULD WE DO?
IS THERE TIME TO GET IT?
......
WE STILL HAVE TIME...
...BUT WE SHOULDN'T GO.
WALKING AROUND TOO MUCH IS DANGEROUS.
IF SOMEONE SEES US...
...GOING BACK DOWN THE STREET WE CAME FROM...

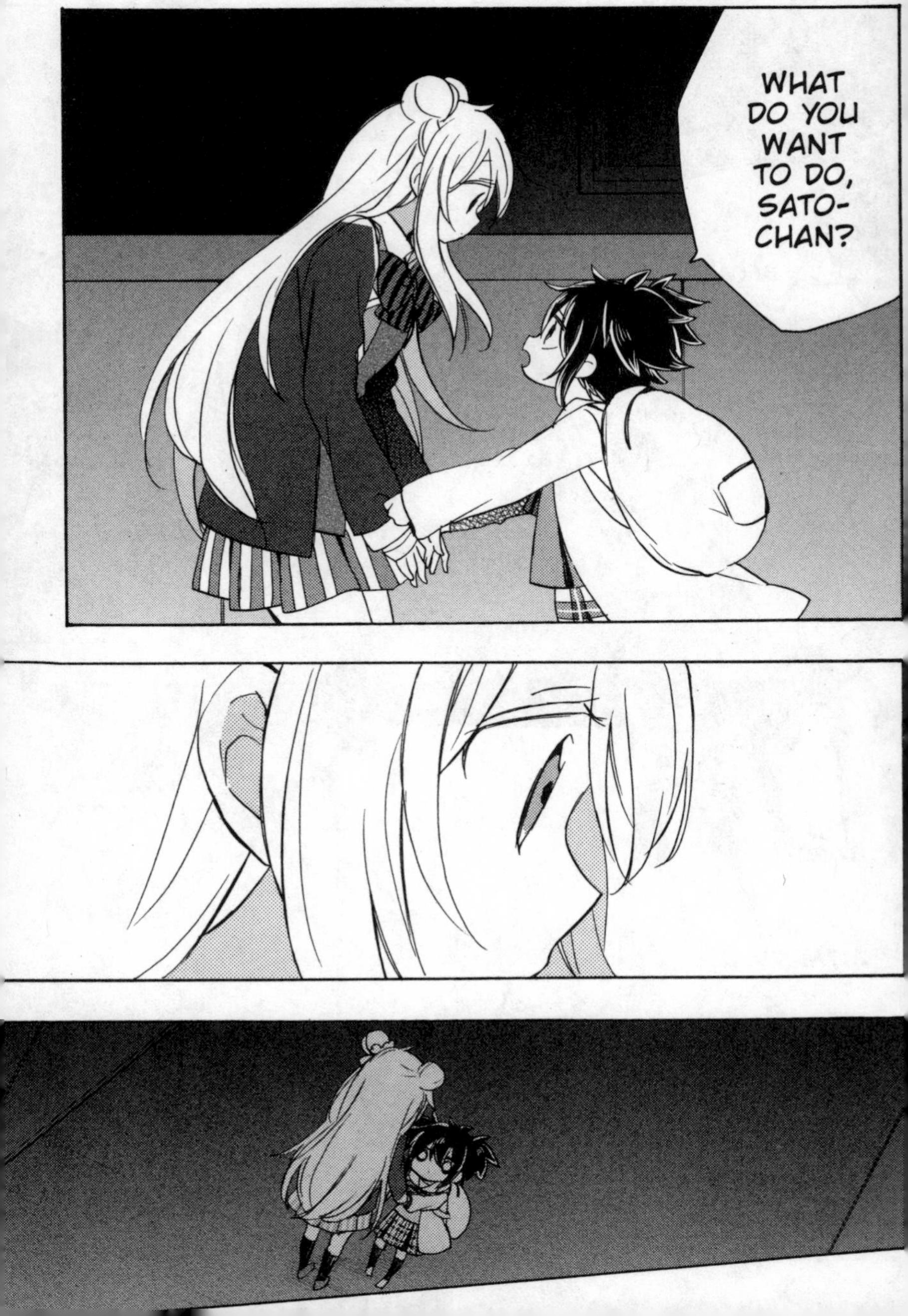
WHAT DO YOU WANT TO DO, SATO-CHAN?

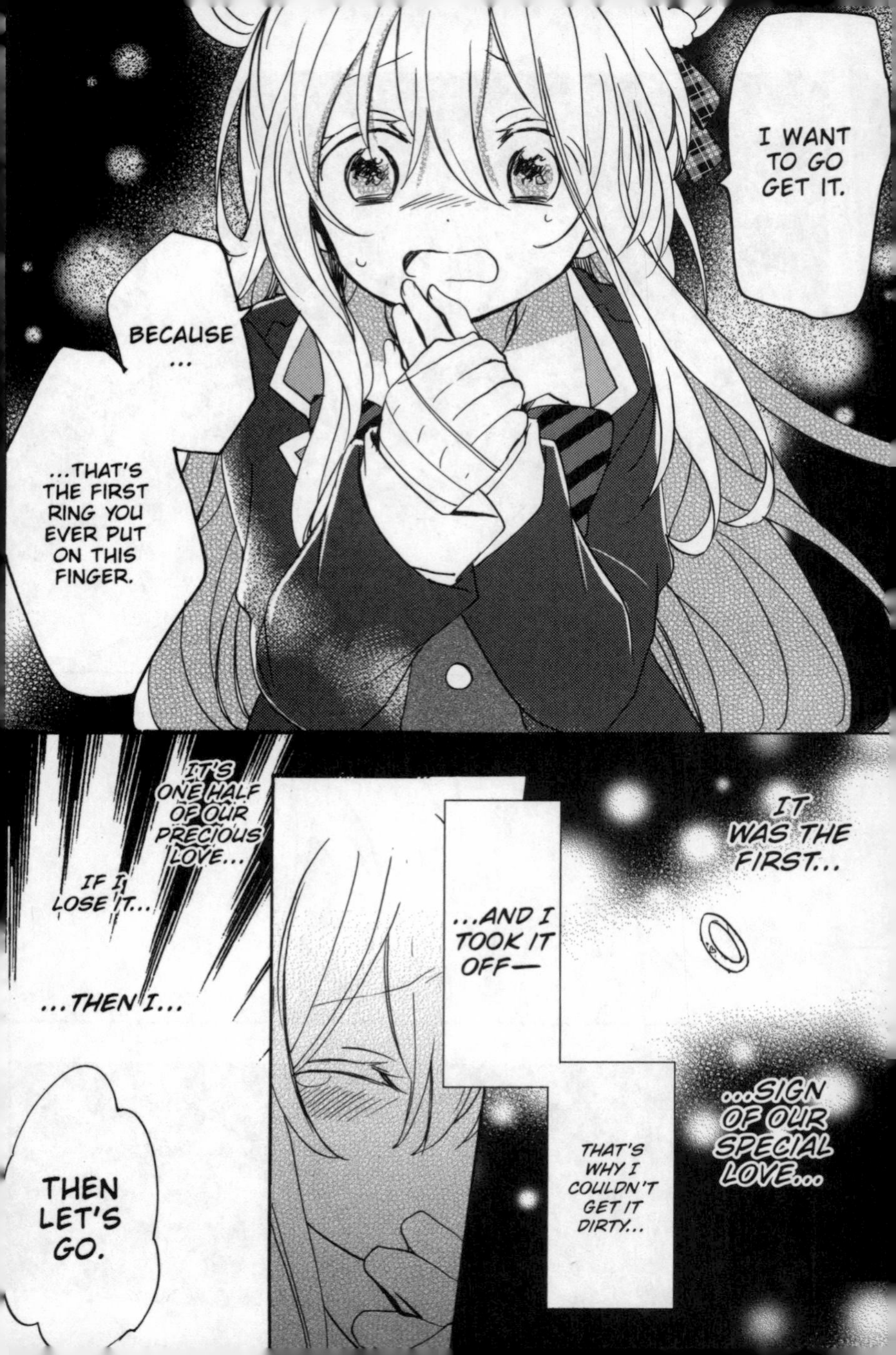
I WANT TO GO GET IT.
BECAUSE ...
...THAT'S THE FIRST RING YOU EVER PUT ON THIS FINGER.
IT WAS THE FIRST...
...SIGN OF OUR SPECIAL LOVE...
...AND I TOOK IT OFF—
THAT'S WHY I COULDN'T GET IT DIRTY...
IT'S ONE HALF OF OUR PRECIOUS LOVE...
IF I LOSE IT...
...THEN I...
THEN LET'S GO.

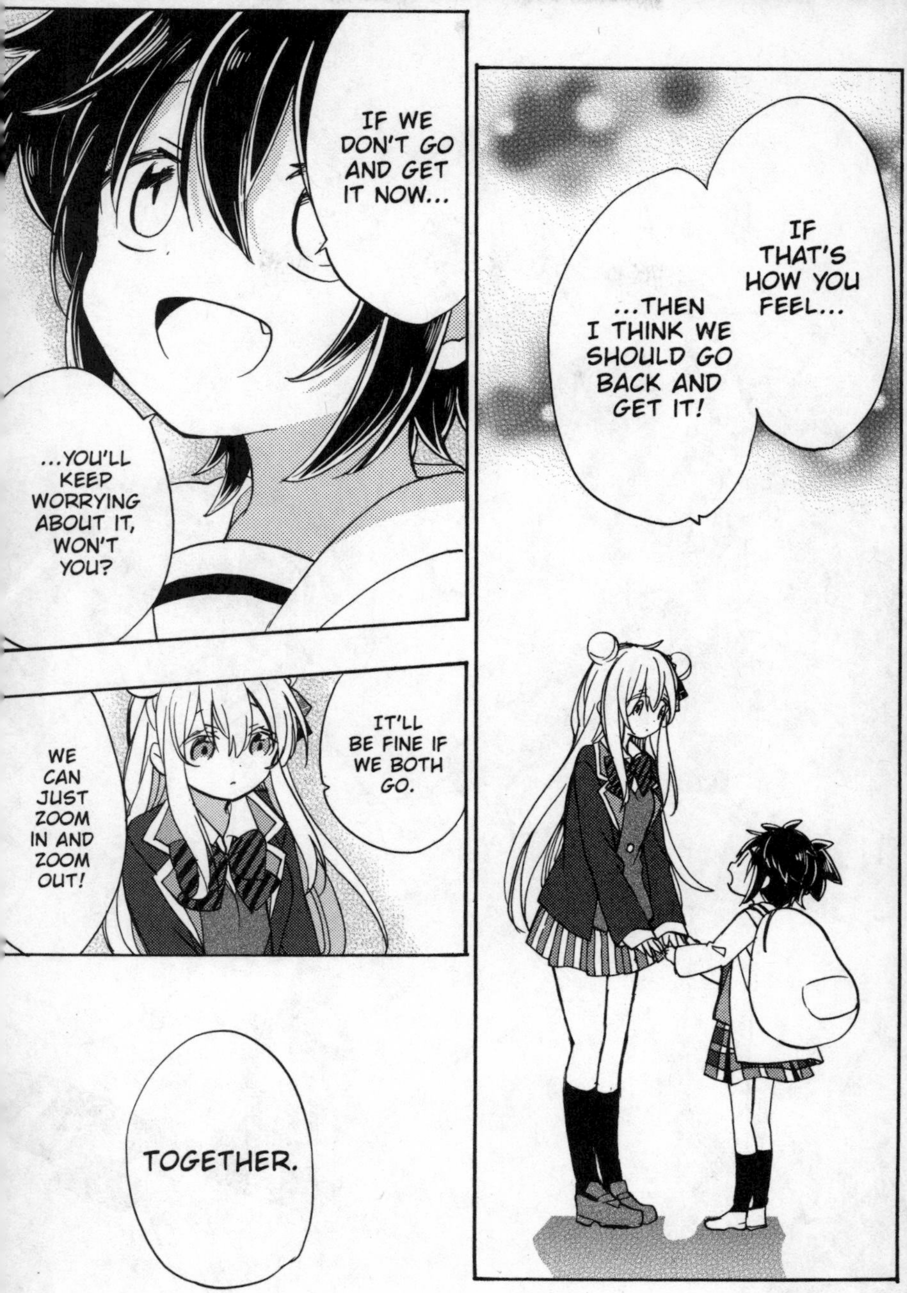
IF THAT'S HOW YOU FEEL...
...THEN I THINK WE SHOULD GO BACK AND GET IT!
IF WE DON'T GO AND GET IT NOW...
...YOU'LL KEEP WORRYING ABOUT IT, WON'T YOU?
IT'LL BE FINE IF WE BOTH GO.
WE CAN JUST ZOOM IN AND ZOOM OUT!
TOGETHER.

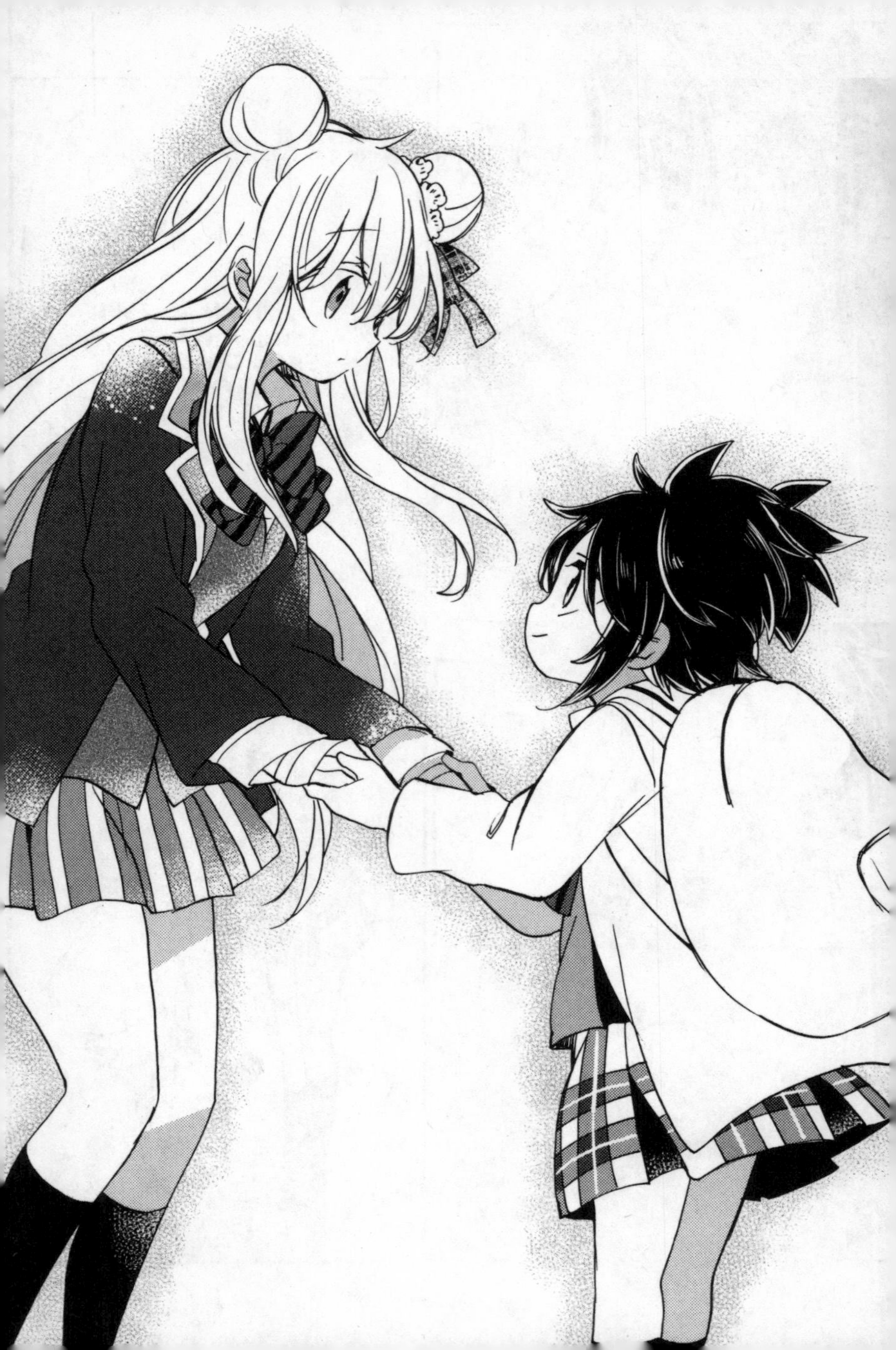

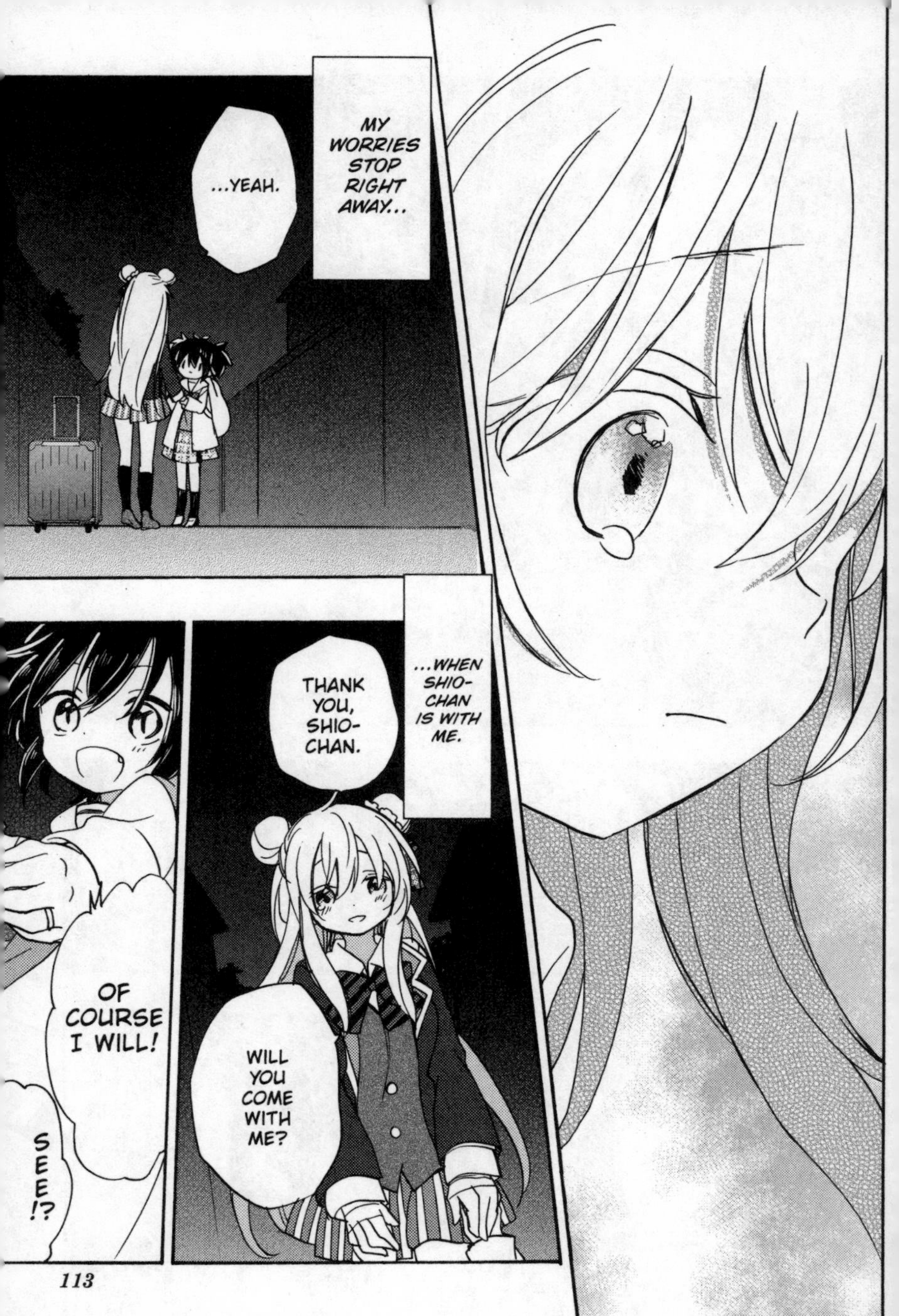
MY WORRIES STOP RIGHT AWAY...
...WHEN SHIO-CHAN IS WITH ME.
...YEAH.
THANK YOU, SHIO-CHAN.
WILL YOU COME WITH ME?
OF COURSE I WILL!
SEE!?

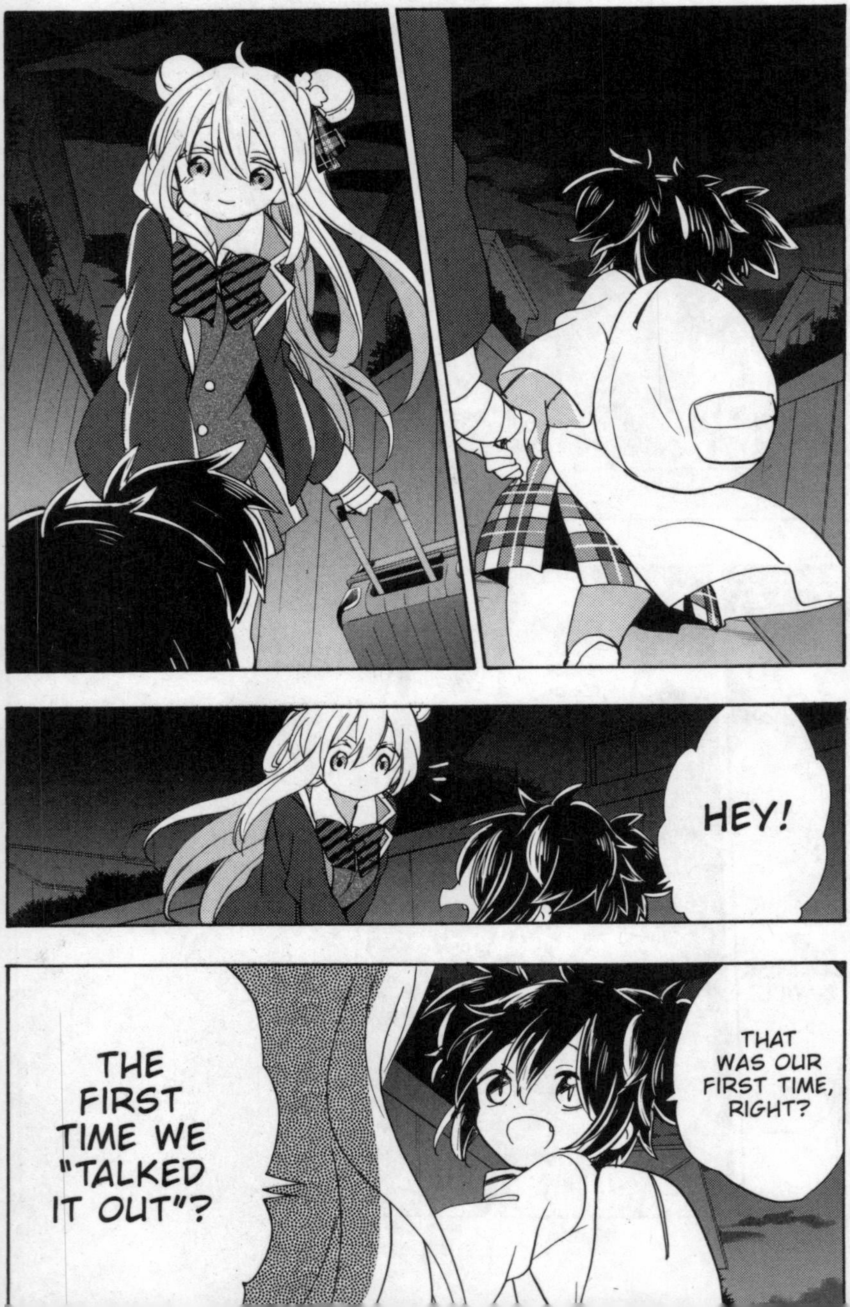
HEY!
THAT WAS OUR FIRST TIME, RIGHT?
THE FIRST TIME WE "TALKED IT OUT"?

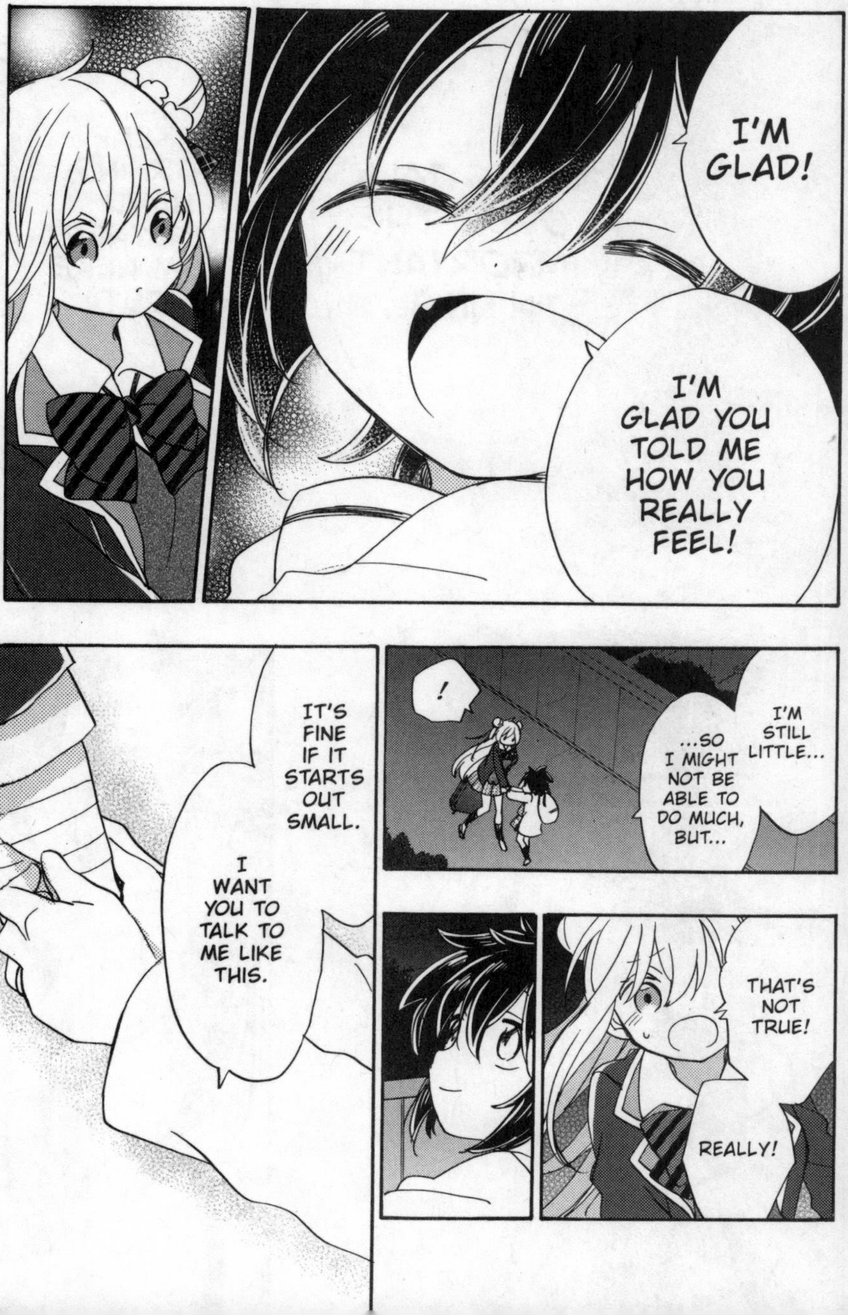
I'M GLAD!
I'M GLAD YOU TOLD ME HOW YOU REALLY FEEL!
I'M STILL LITTLE...
...SO I MIGHT NOT BE ABLE TO DO MUCH, BUT...
!
THAT'S NOT TRUE!
REALLY!
IT'S FINE IF IT STARTS OUT SMALL.
I WANT YOU TO TALK TO ME LIKE THIS.

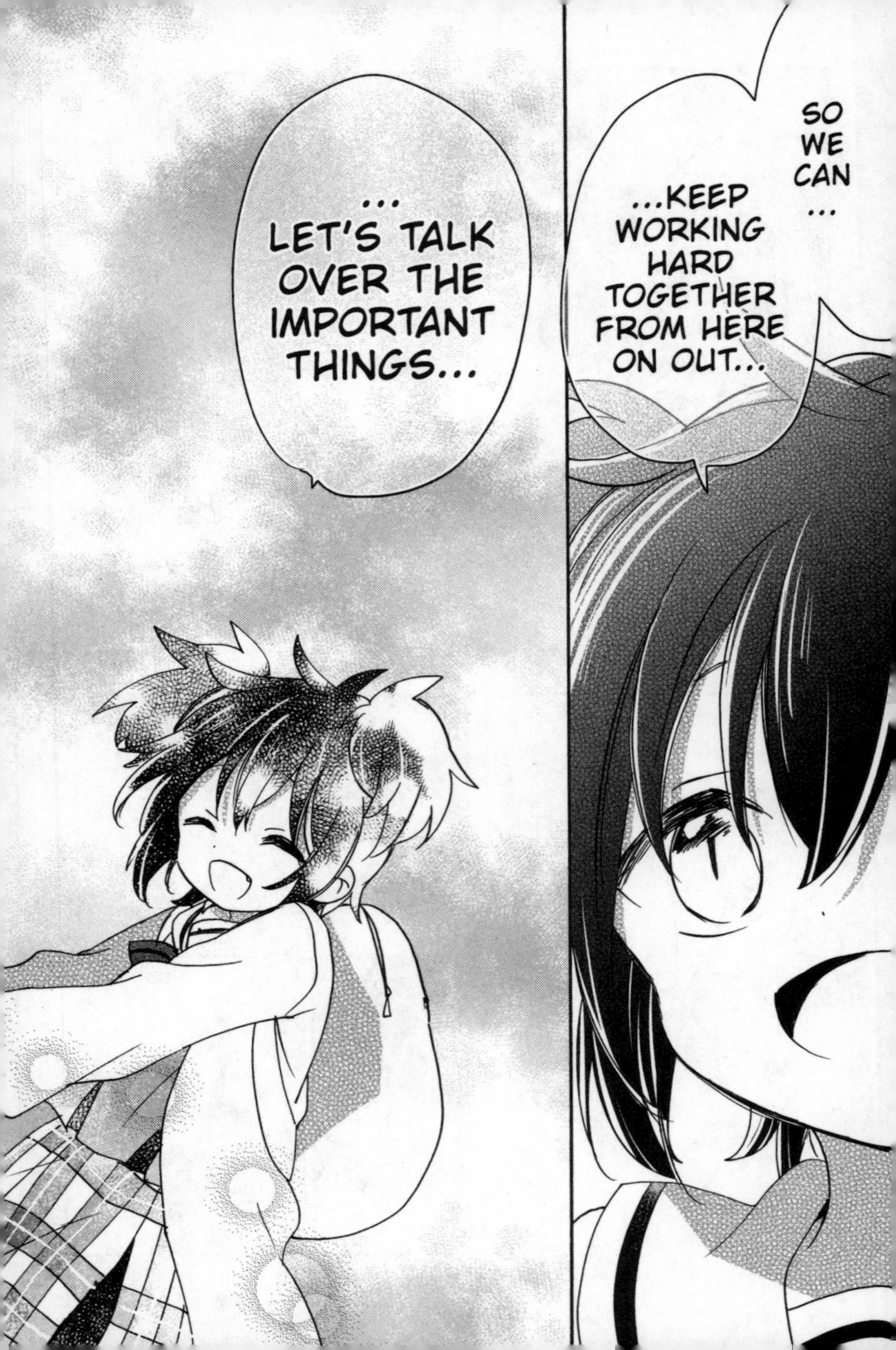
SO WE CAN ...
...KEEP WORKING HARD TOGETHER FROM HERE ON OUT...
... LET'S TALK OVER THE IMPORTANT THINGS...

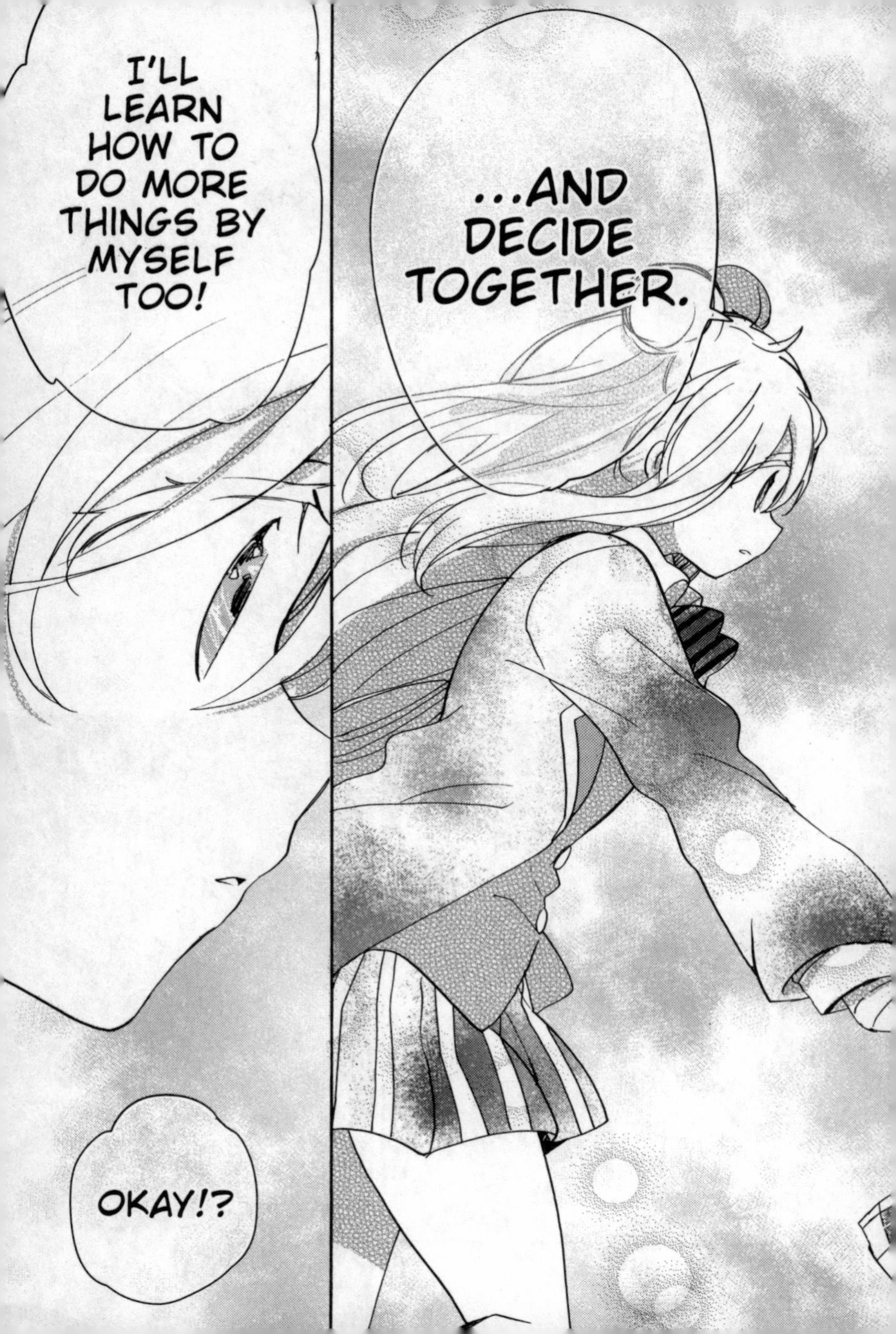
...AND DECIDE TOGETHER.
I'LL LEARN HOW TO DO MORE THINGS BY MYSELF TOO!
OKAY!?

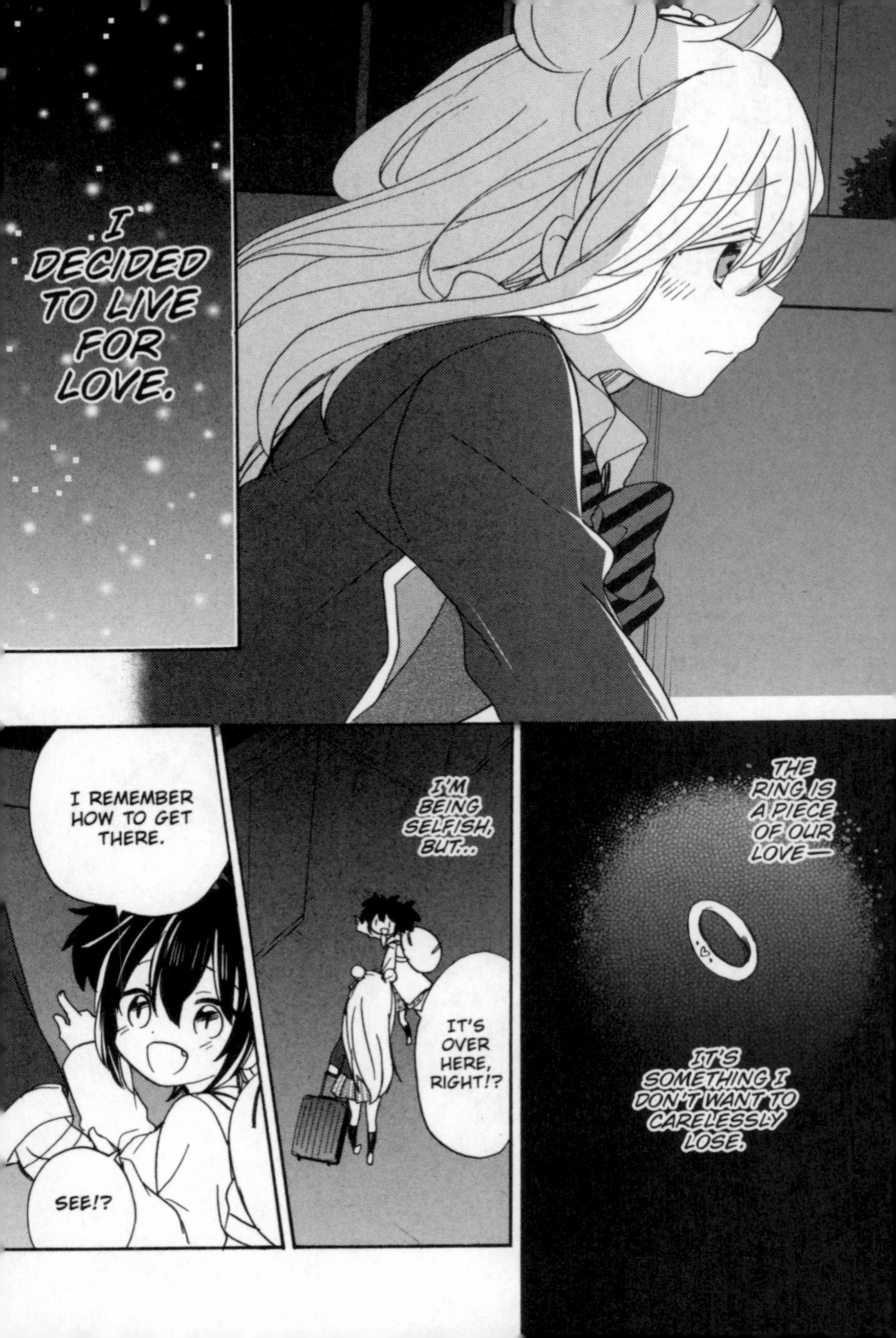
I DECIDED TO LIVE FOR LOVE.
THE RING IS A PIECE OF OUR LOVE—
IT'S SOMETHING I DON'T WANT TO CARELESSLY LOSE.
I'M BEING SELFISH, BUT...
IT'S OVER HERE, RIGHT!?
I REMEMBER HOW TO GET THERE.
SEE!?

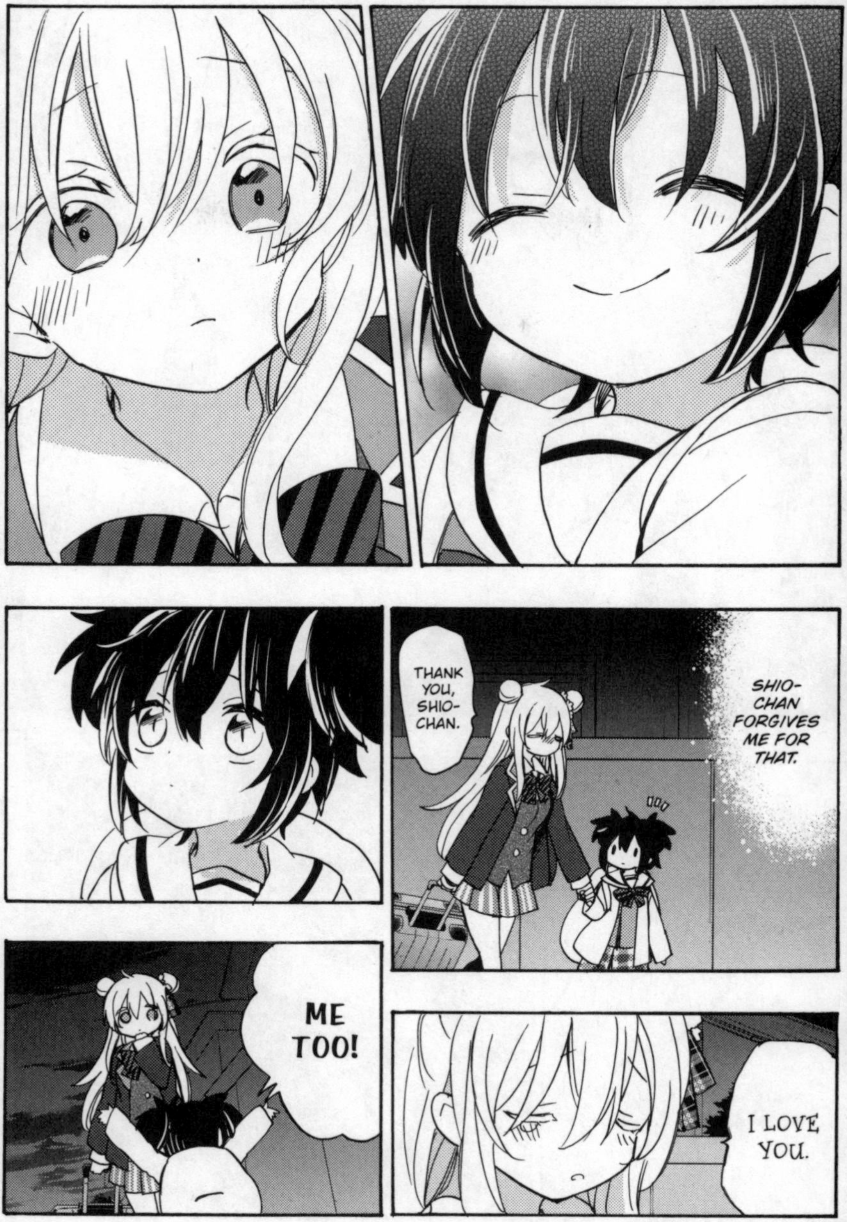
SHIO-CHAN FORGIVES ME FOR THAT.
THANK YOU, SHIO-CHAN.
I LOVE YOU.
ME TOO!

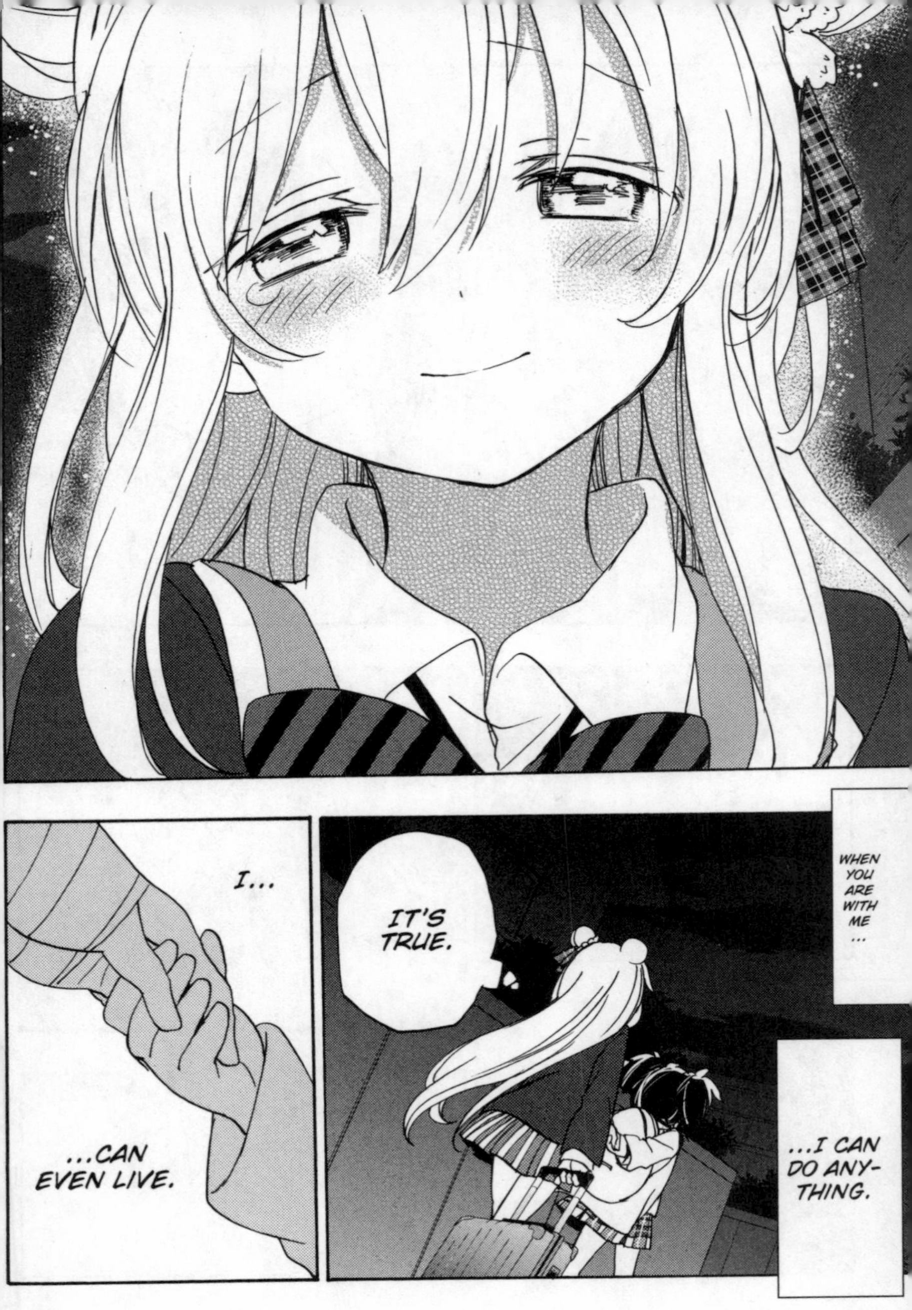
WHEN YOU ARE WITH ME ...
...I CAN DO ANY-THING.
IT'S TRUE.
I...
...CAN EVEN LIVE.

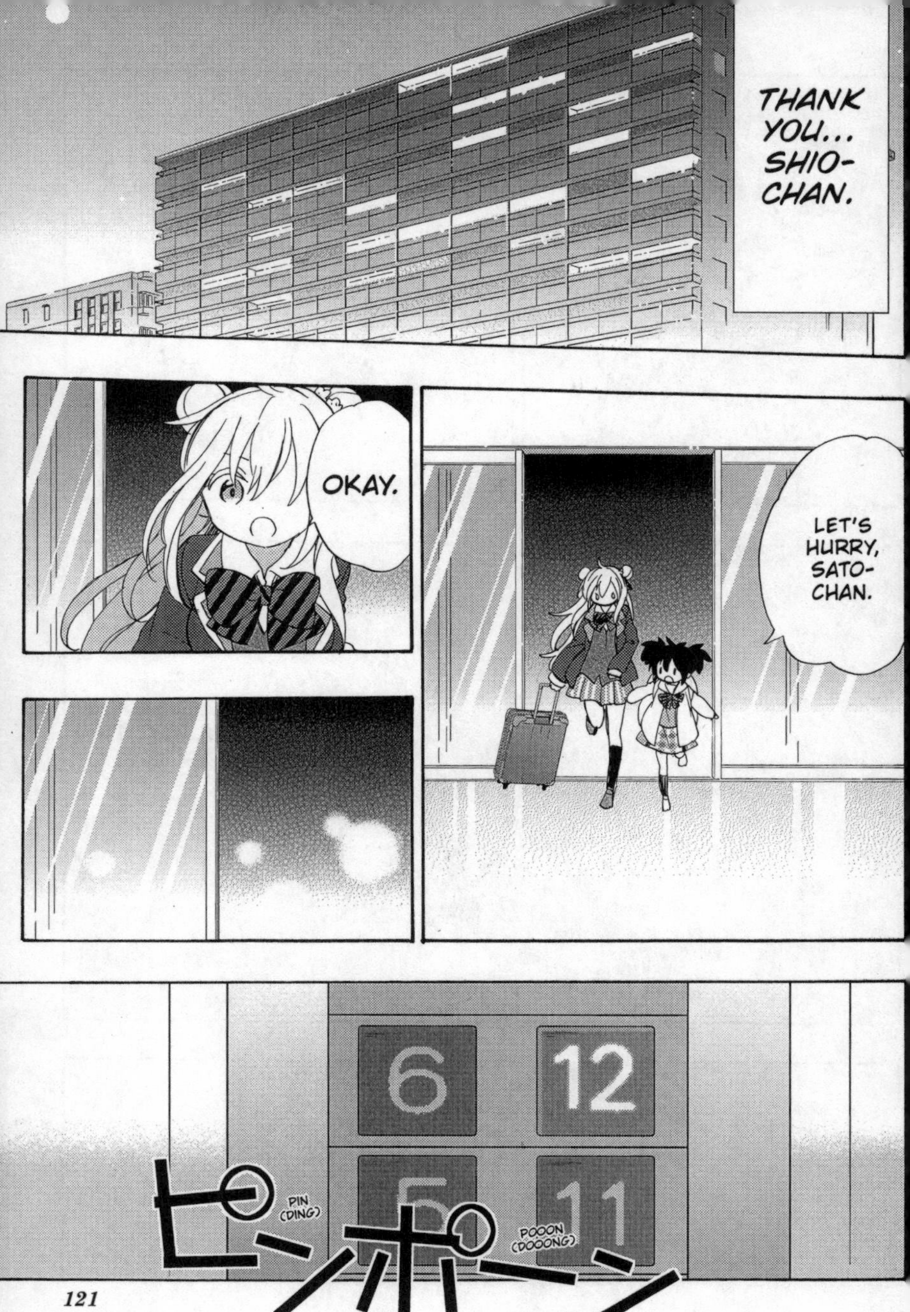
THANK YOU... SHIO-CHAN.
LET'S HURRY, SATO-CHAN.
OKAY.
6
12
11
ピーンポーン
PIN (DING)
POOON (DOOONG)

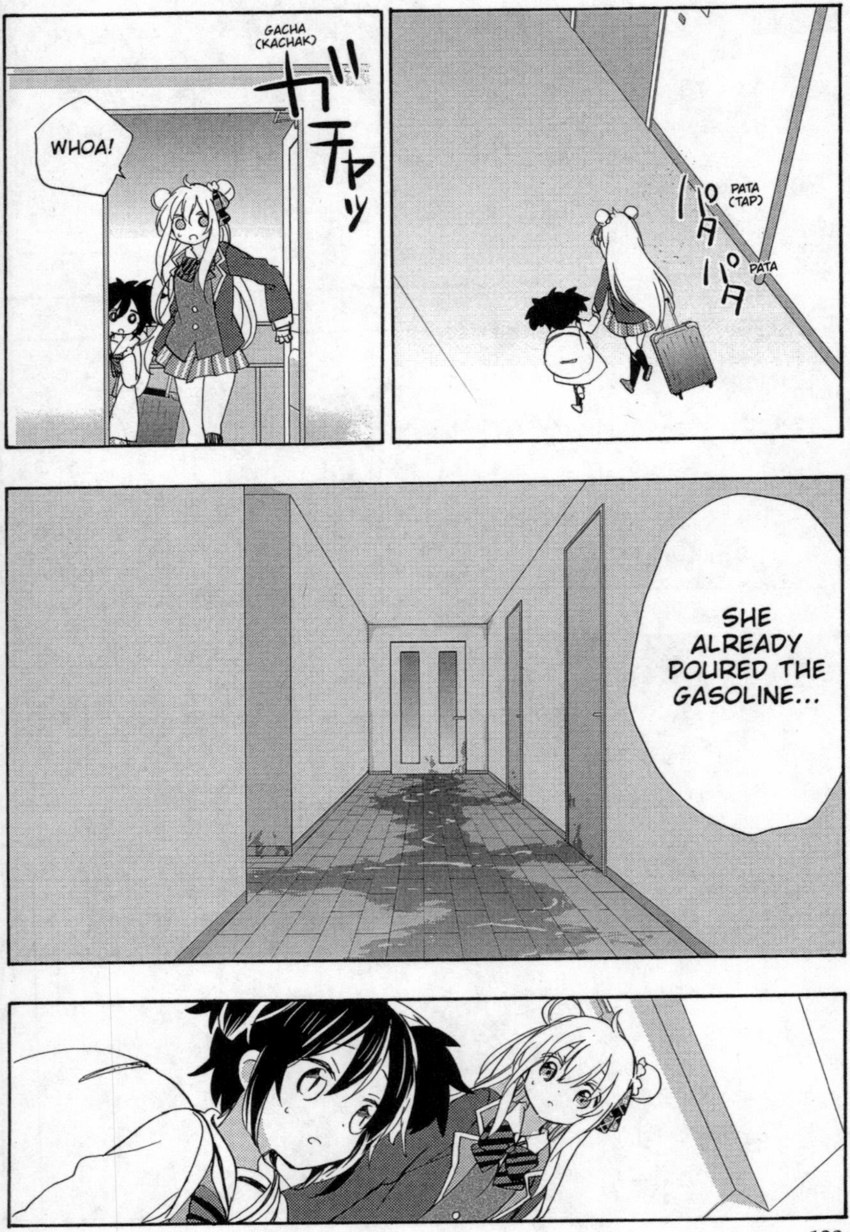
パタ
PATA (TAP)
パタ
PATA
ガチャッ
GACHA (KACHAK)
WHOA!
SHE ALREADY POURED THE GASOLINE...

OKAY.

YOU WAIT HERE, SHIO-CHAN!

I DON'T WANT YOU TO GET DIRTY.

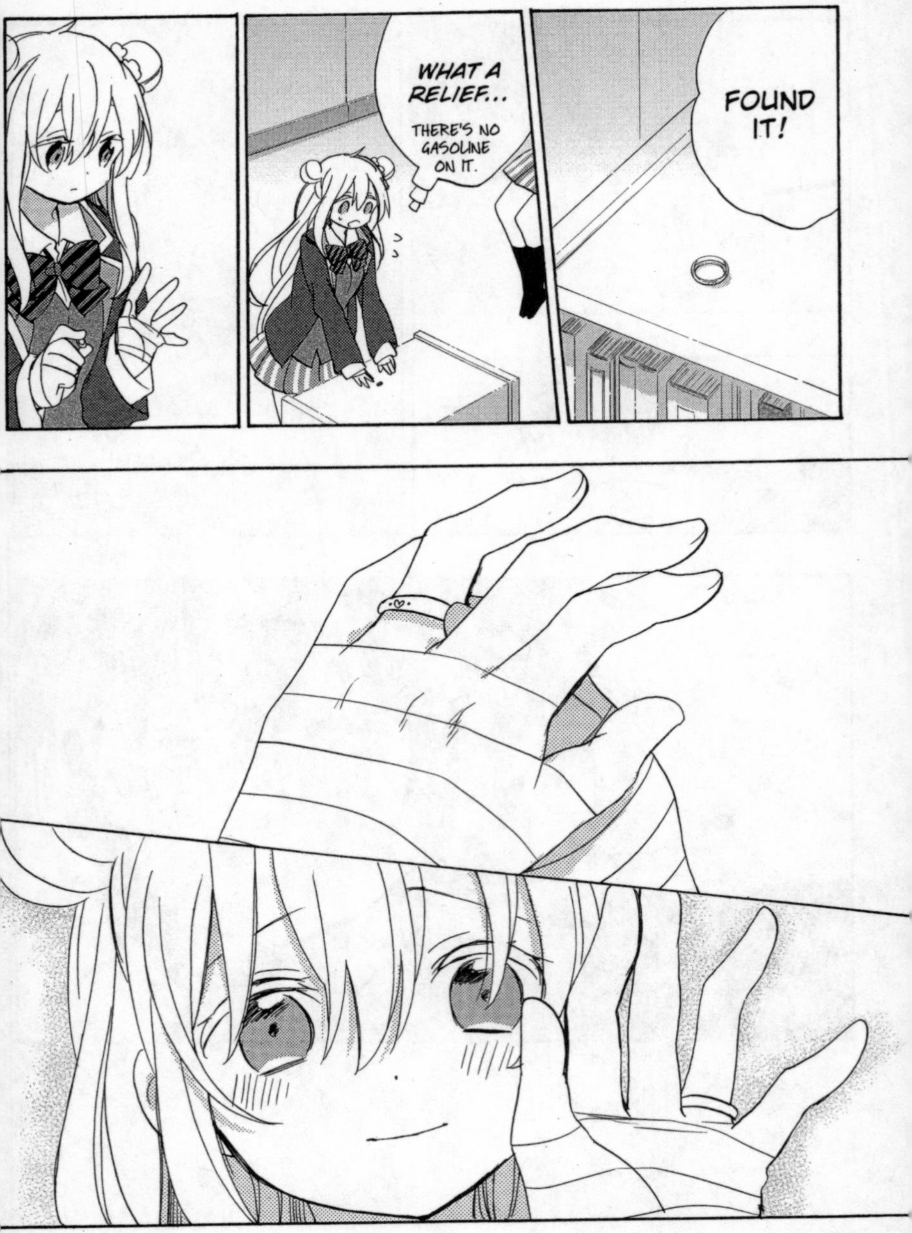
FOUND IT!
WHAT A RELIEF...
THERE'S NO GASOLINE ON IT.

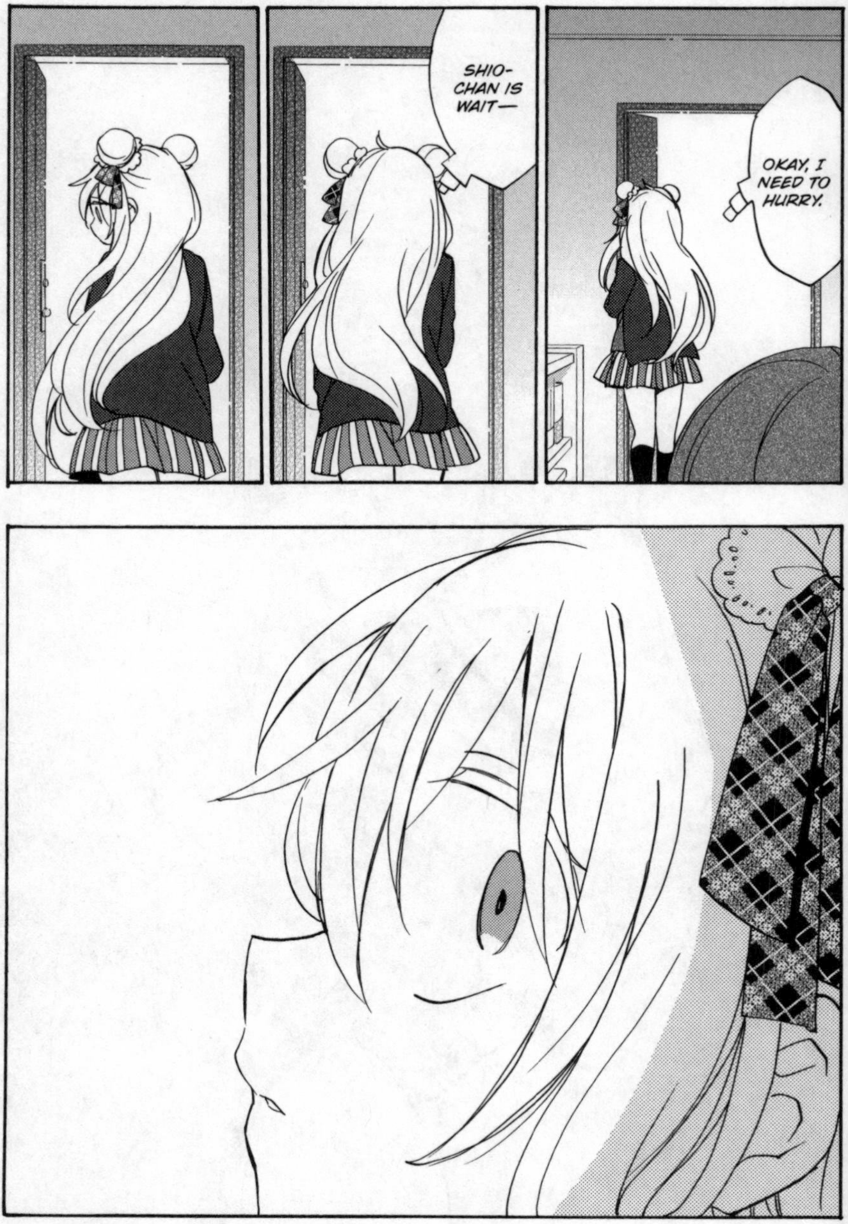
OKAY, I NEED TO HURRY.
SHIO-CHAN IS WAIT—

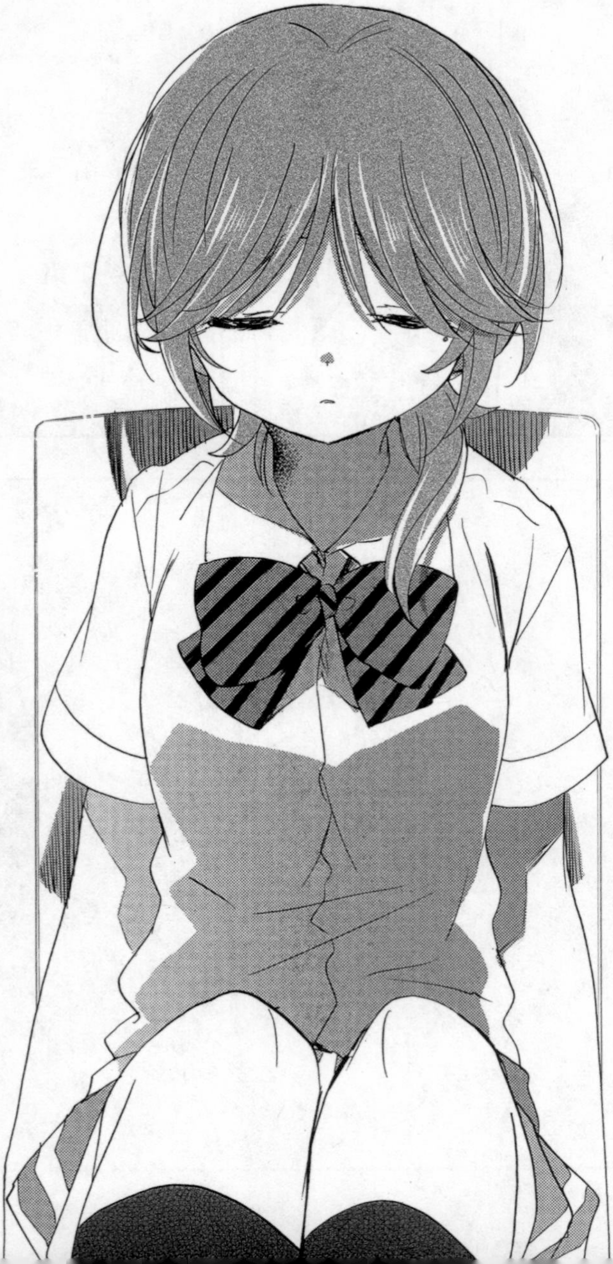

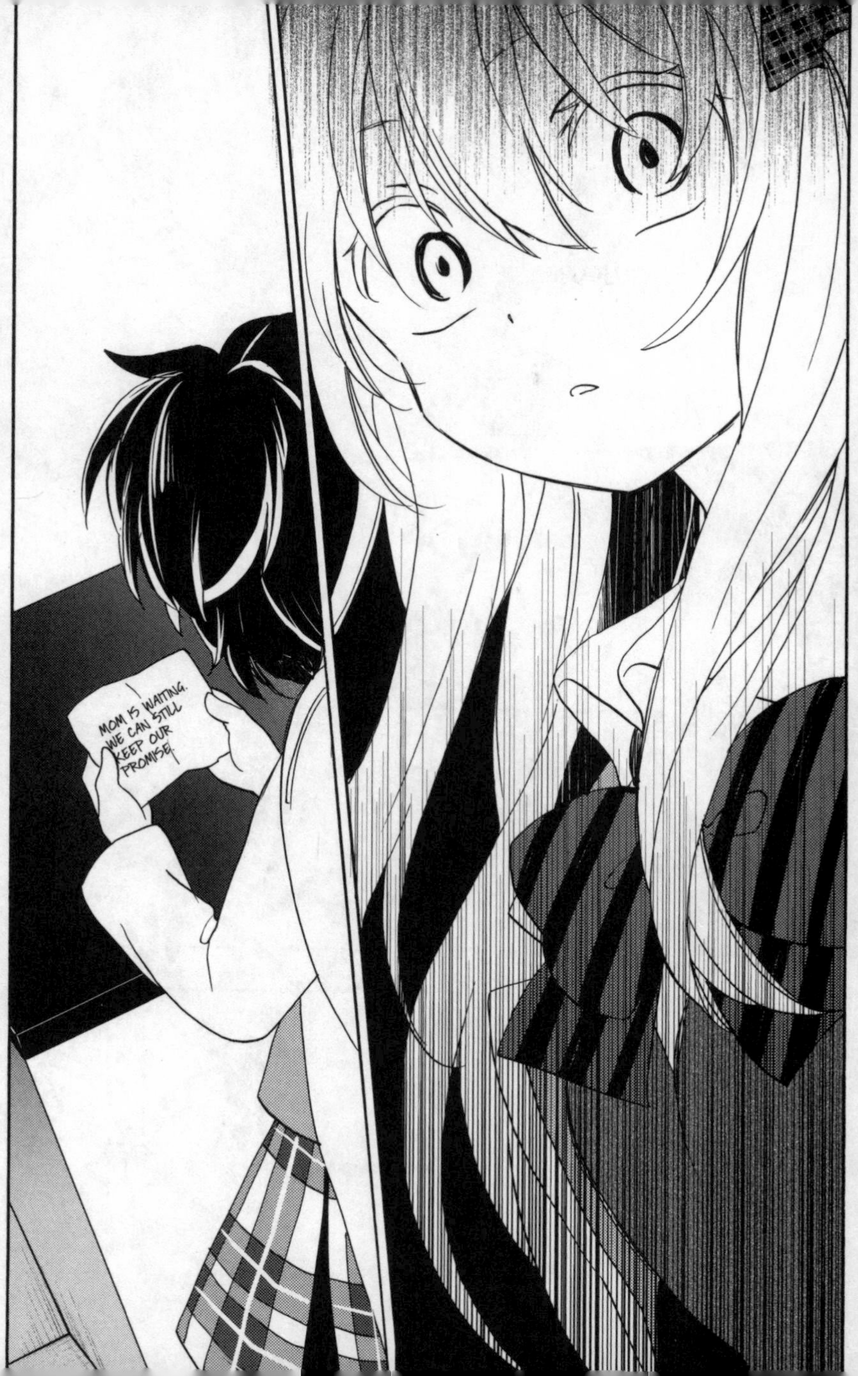
MOM IS WAITING. WE CAN STILL KEEP OUR PROMISE.

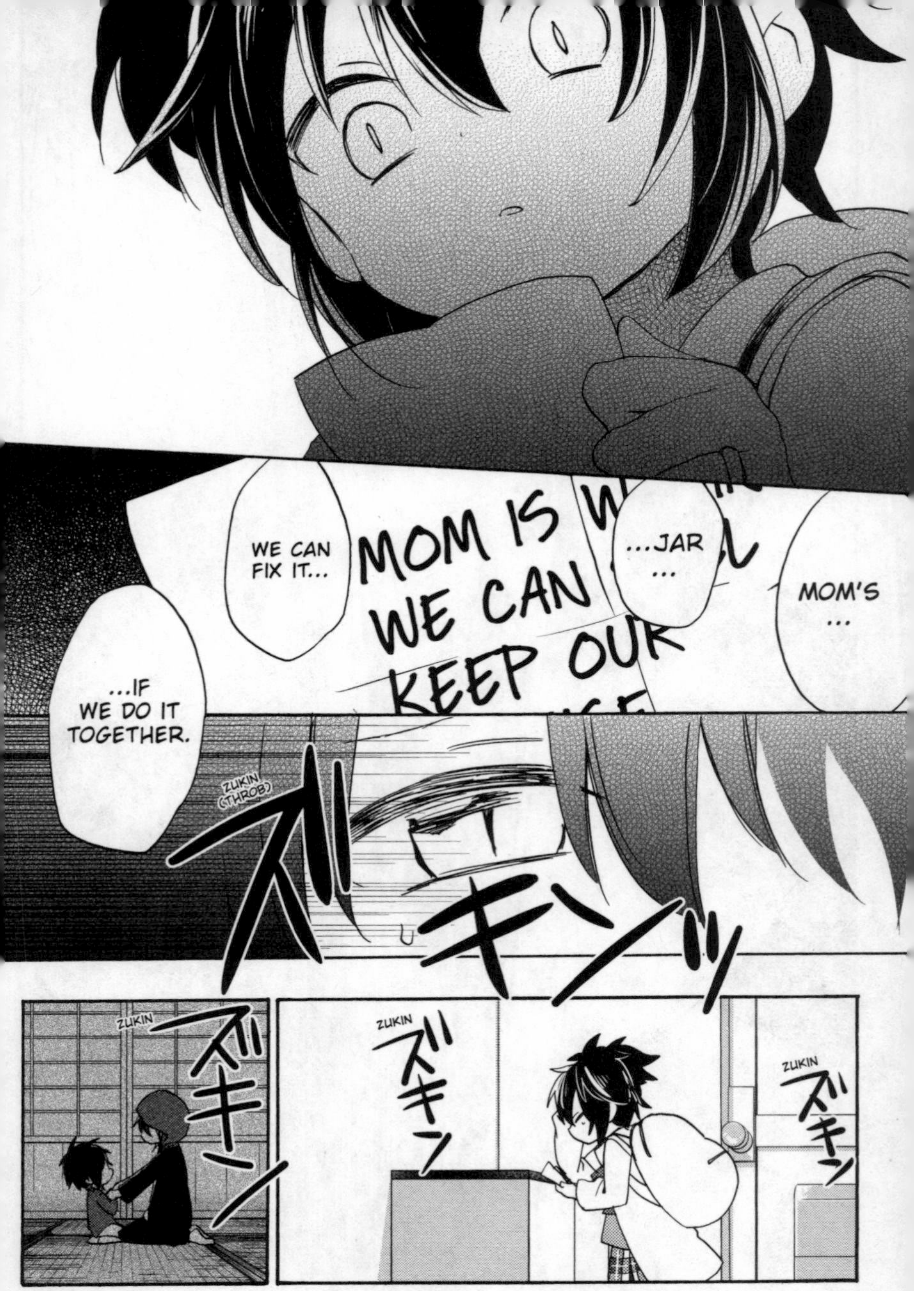
MOM'S ...
...JAR ...
MOM IS
WE CAN
KEEP OUR
WE CAN FIX IT...
...IF WE DO IT TOGETHER.
ZUKIN (THROB)
ZUKIN
ZUKIN
ZUKIN

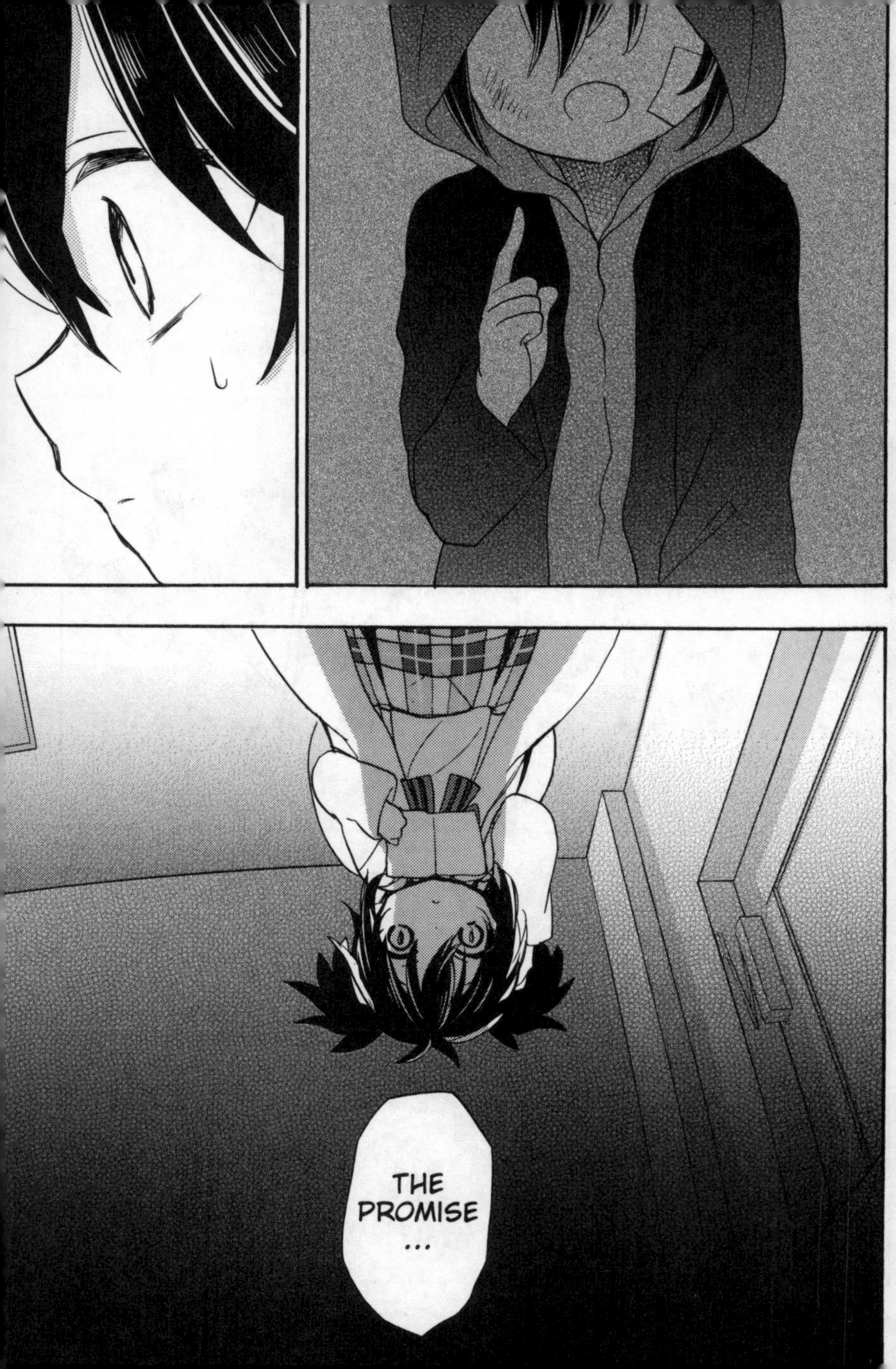
THE PROMISE ...

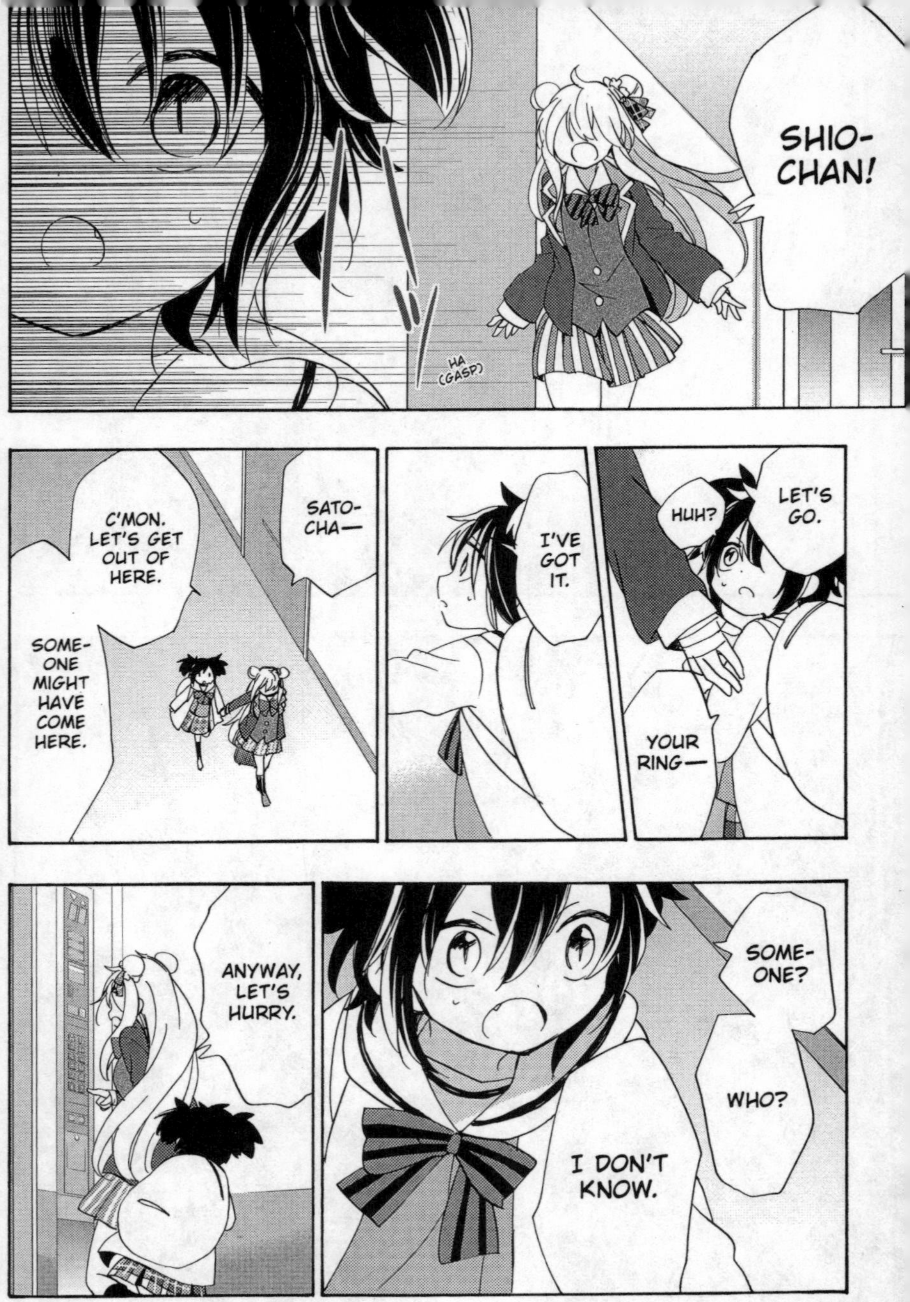
SHIO-CHAN!
HA (GASP)
LET'S GO.
HUH?
YOUR RING—
I'VE GOT IT.
SATO-CHA—
C'MON. LET'S GET OUT OF HERE.
SOME-ONE MIGHT HAVE COME HERE.
SOME-ONE?
WHO?
I DON'T KNOW.
ANYWAY, LET'S HURRY.

SATO-CHAN...

THIS...

UIIIN (VREEN)

ZUKIN (THROB)

ZUKIN

ZUKIN

......

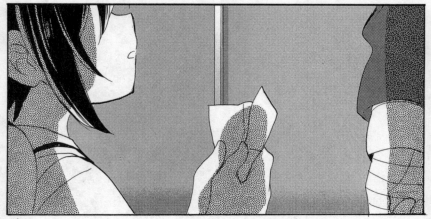

DING 1 DOOONG

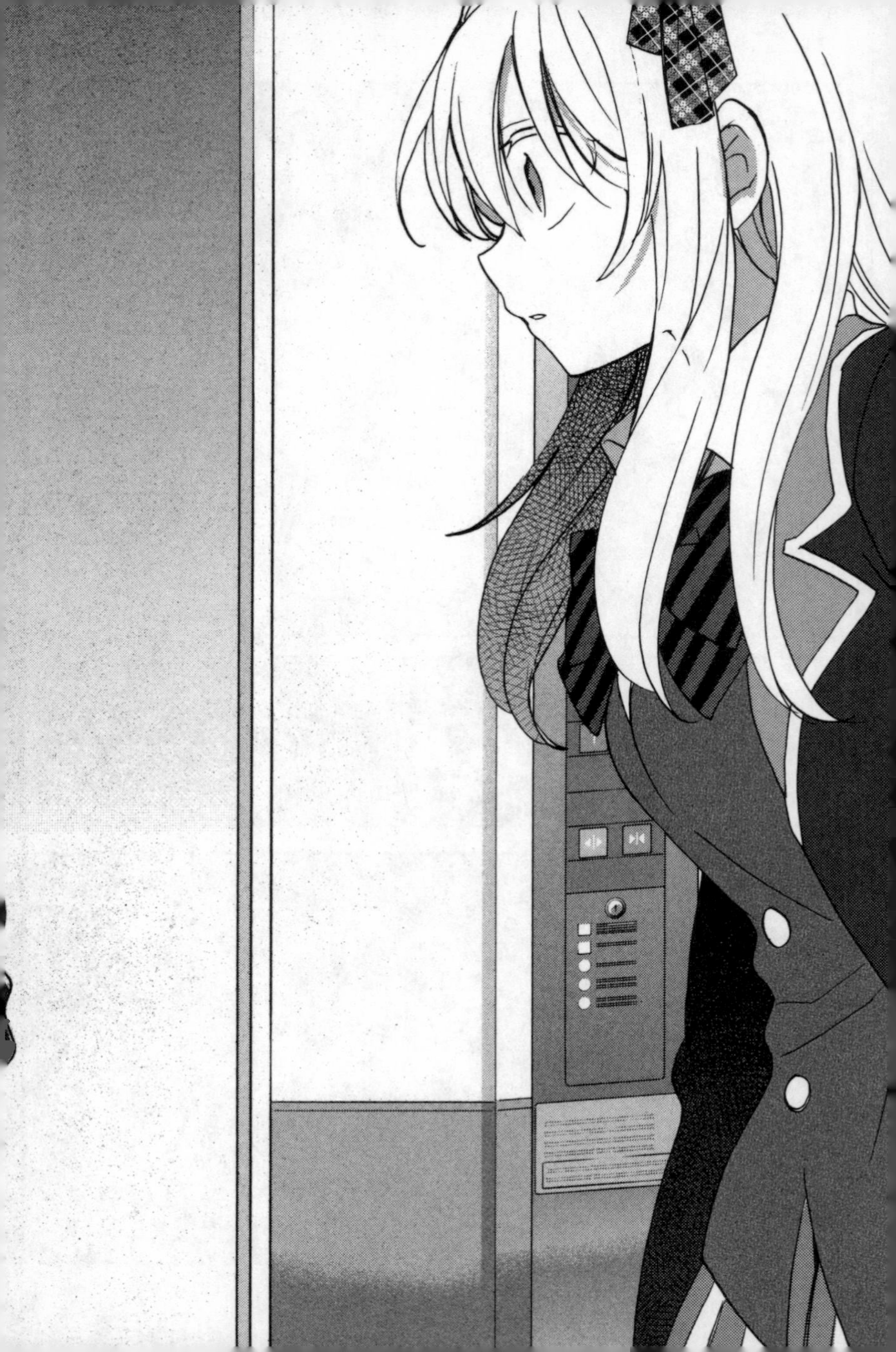

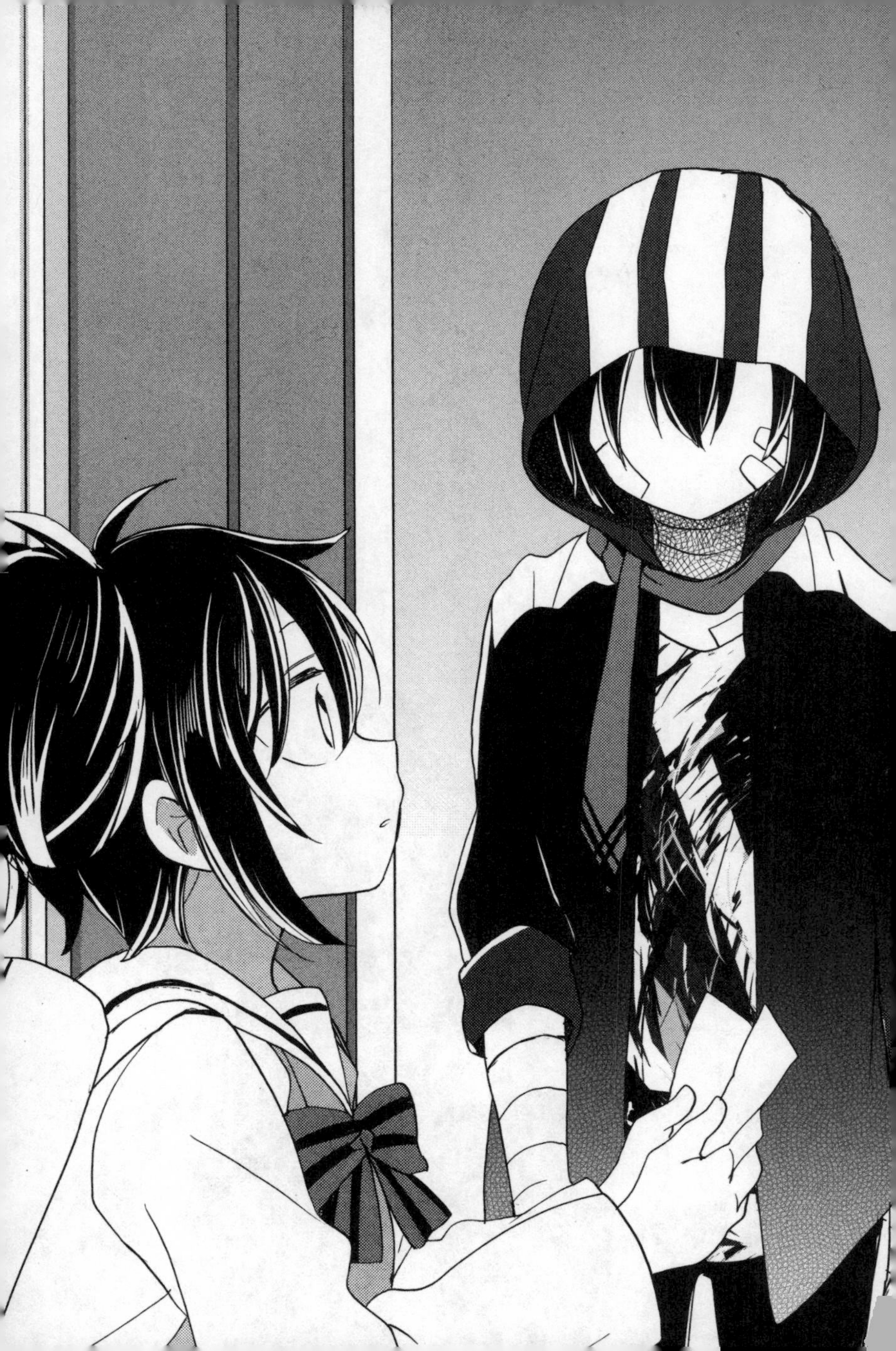

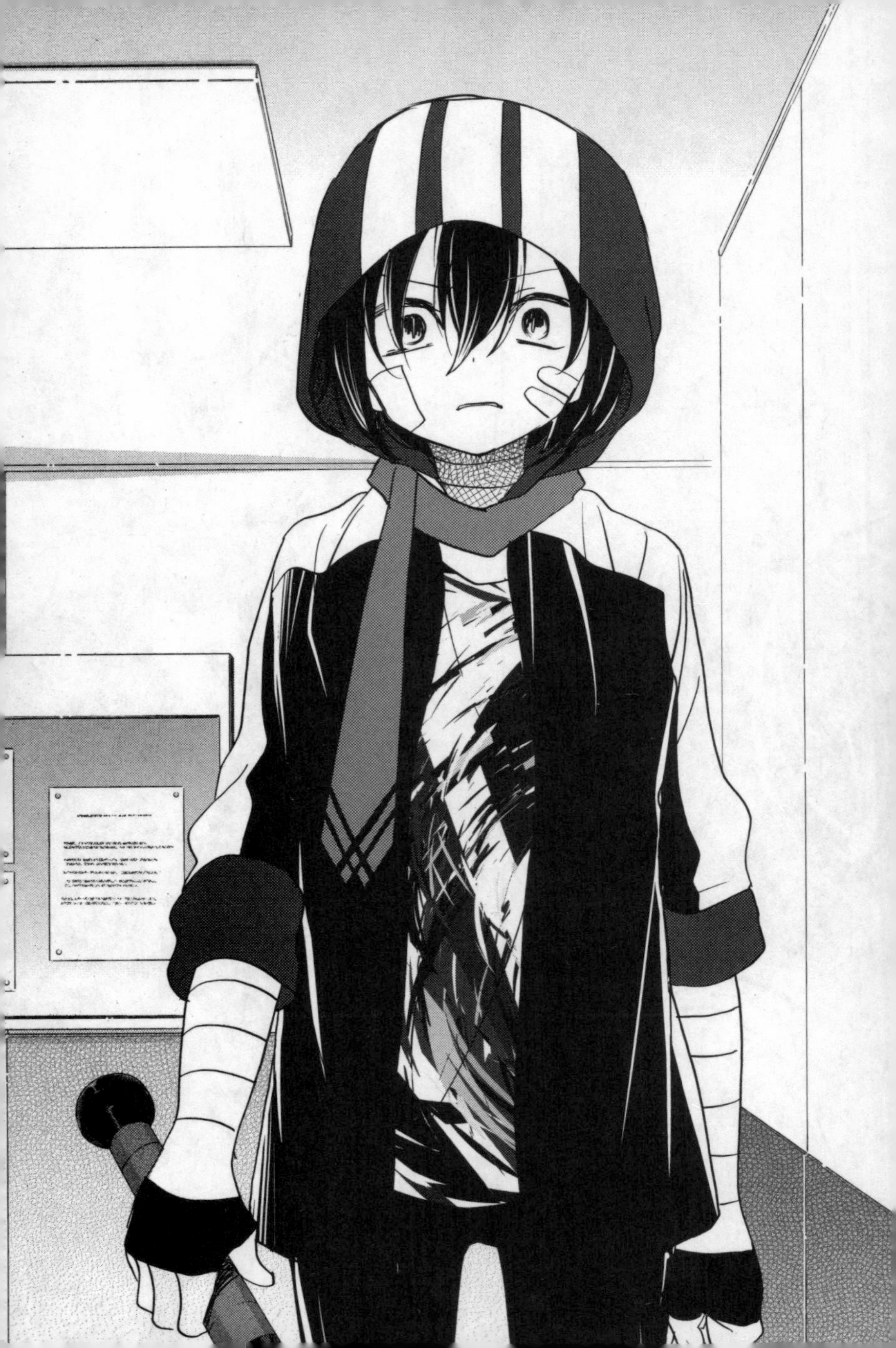

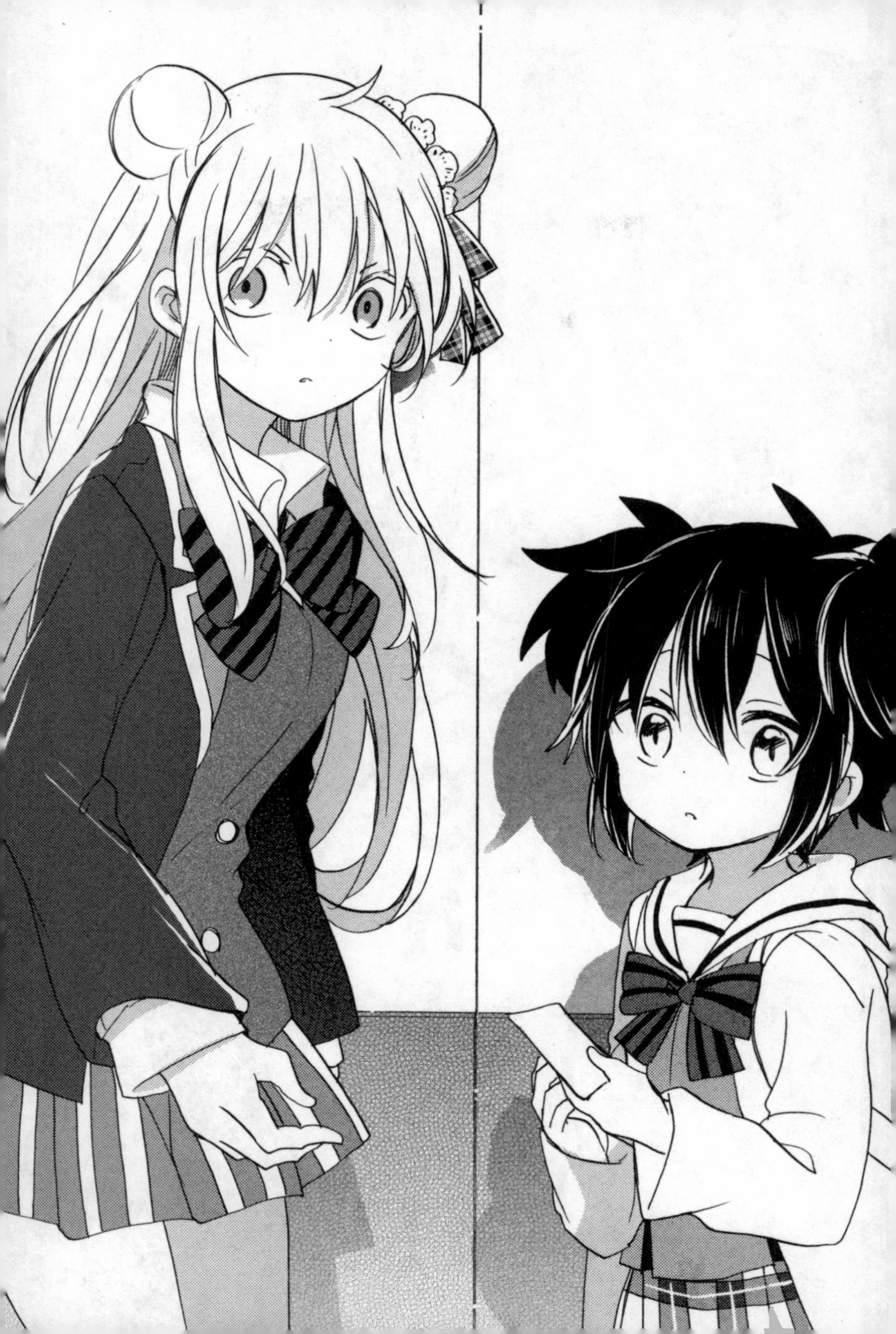

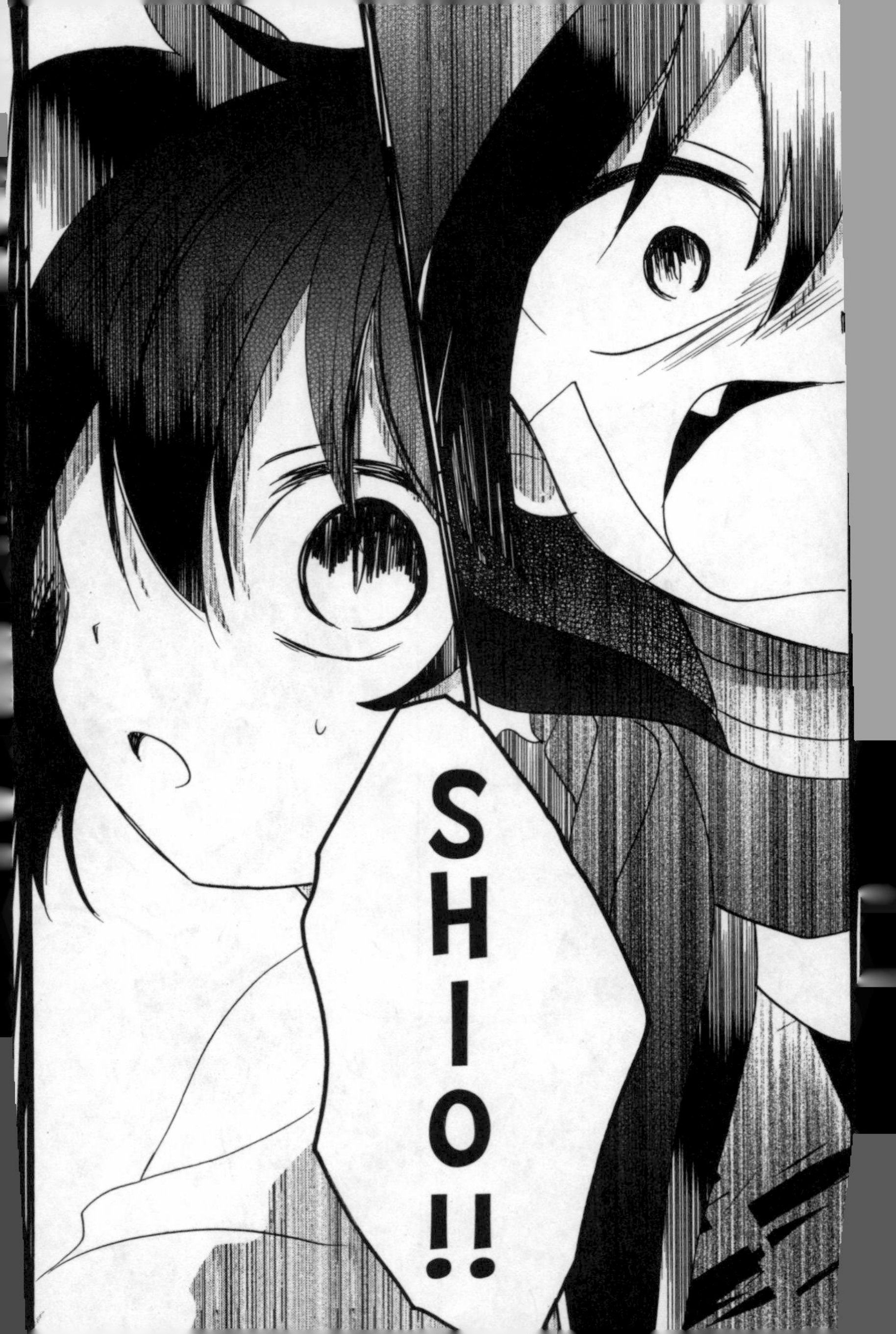
SHIO!!

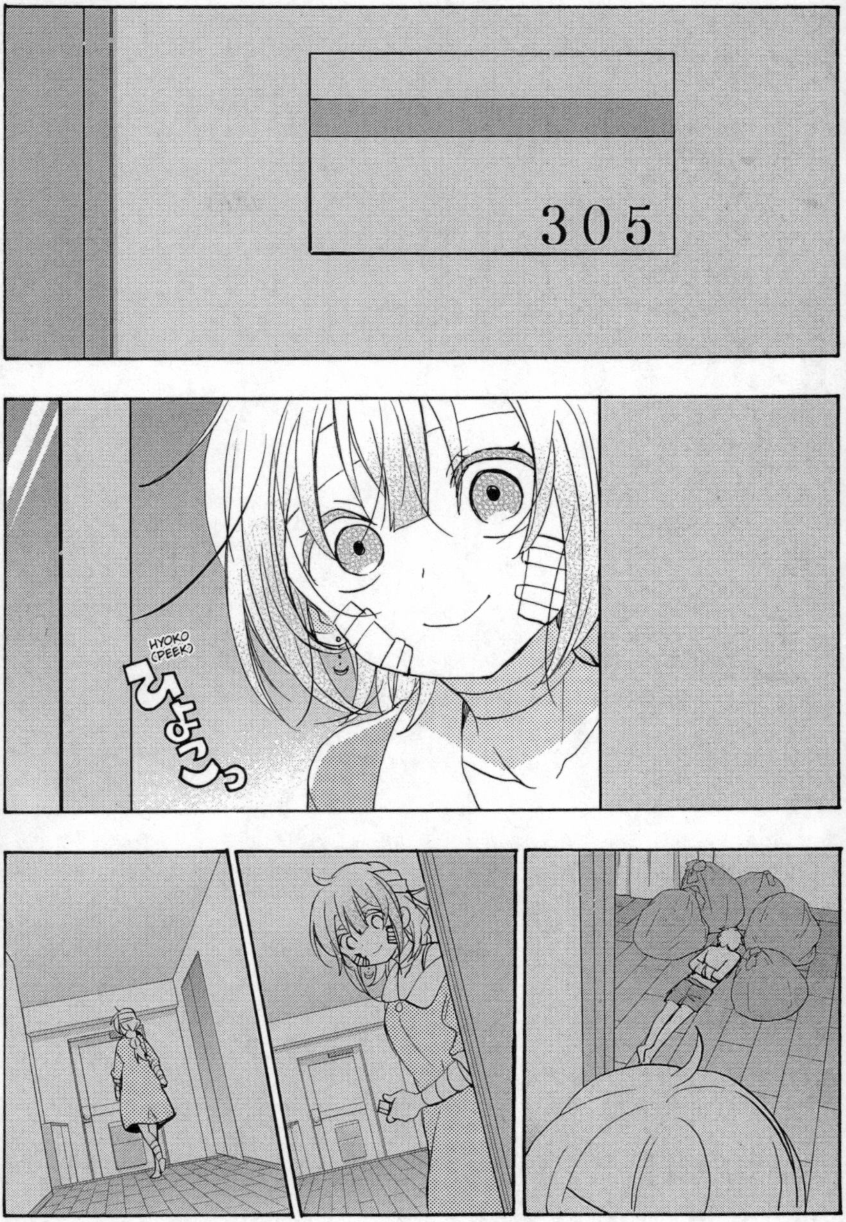
305
HYOKO (PEEK)
ひょこっ

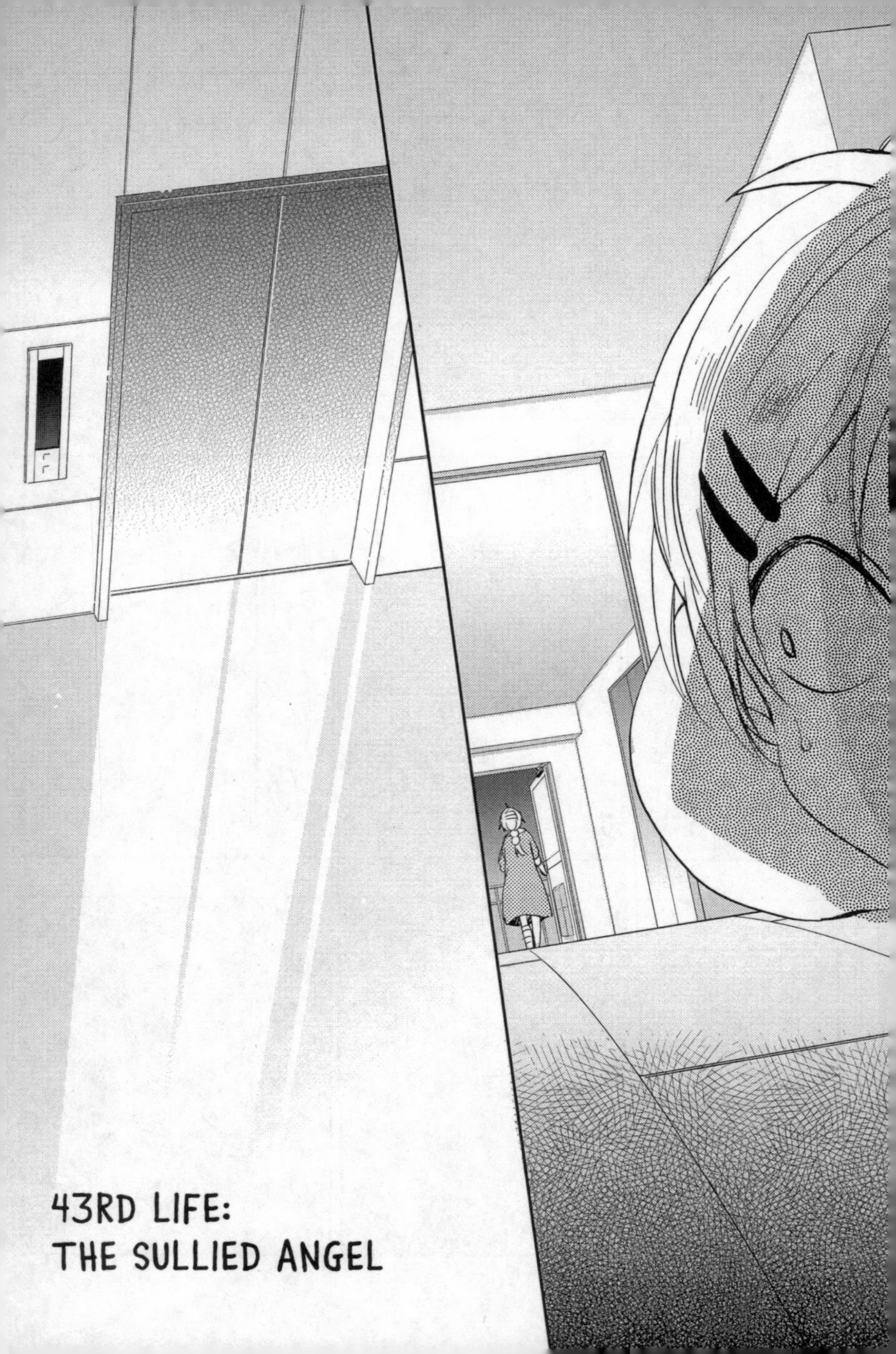
43RD LIFE:
THE SULLIED ANGEL

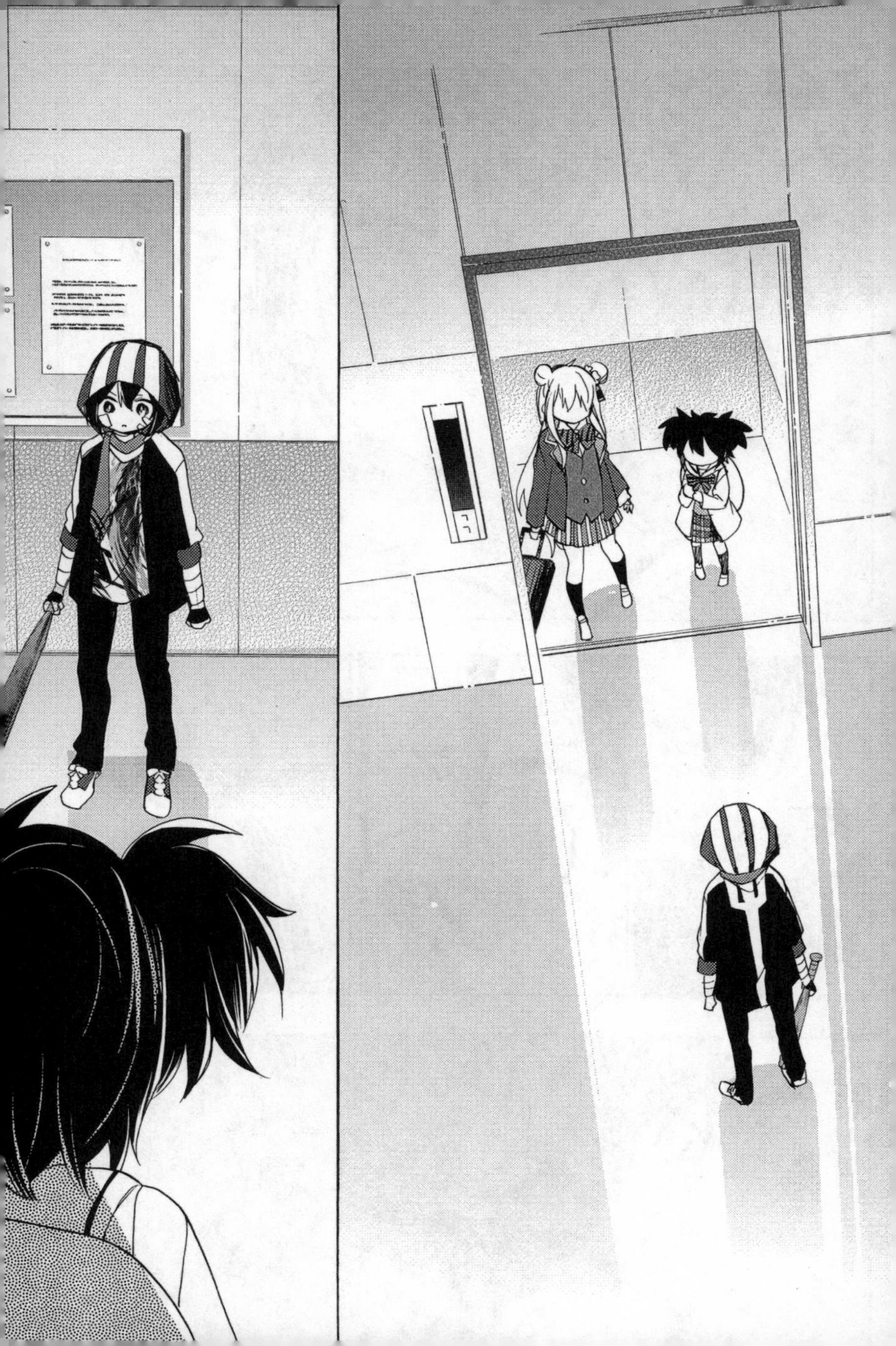

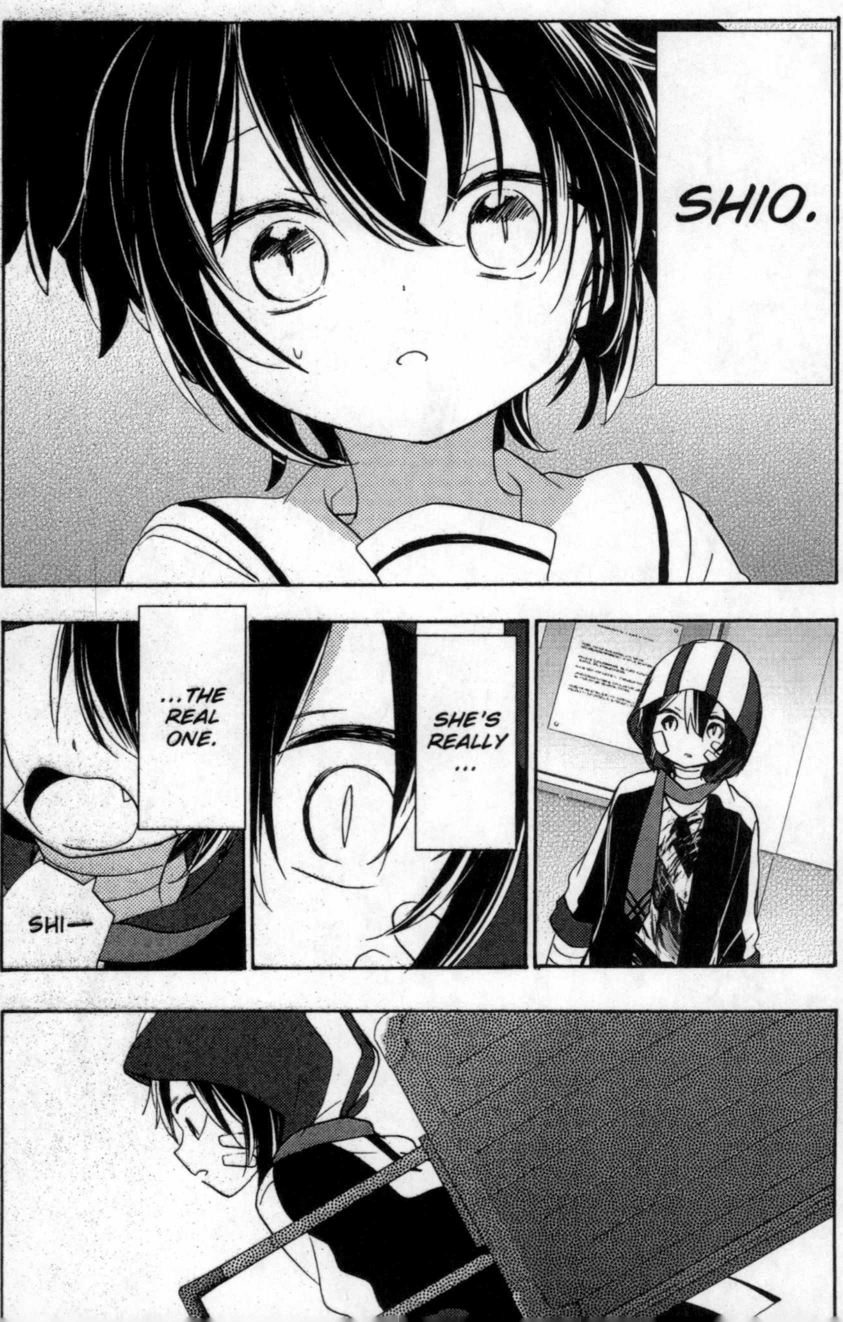
SHIO.
SHE'S REALLY ...
...THE REAL ONE.
SHI—

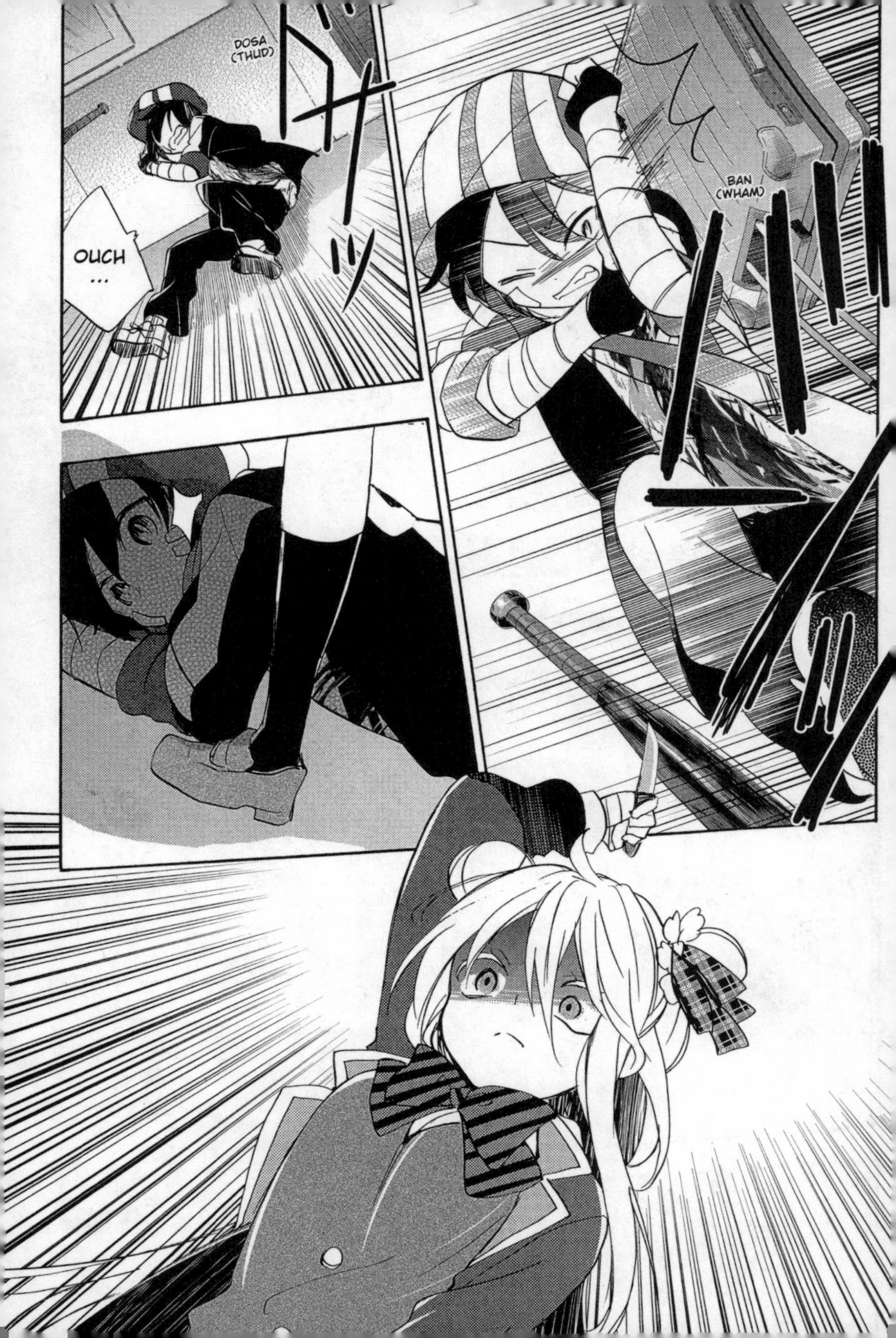
BAN
(WHAM)
DOSA
(THUD)
OUCH
...

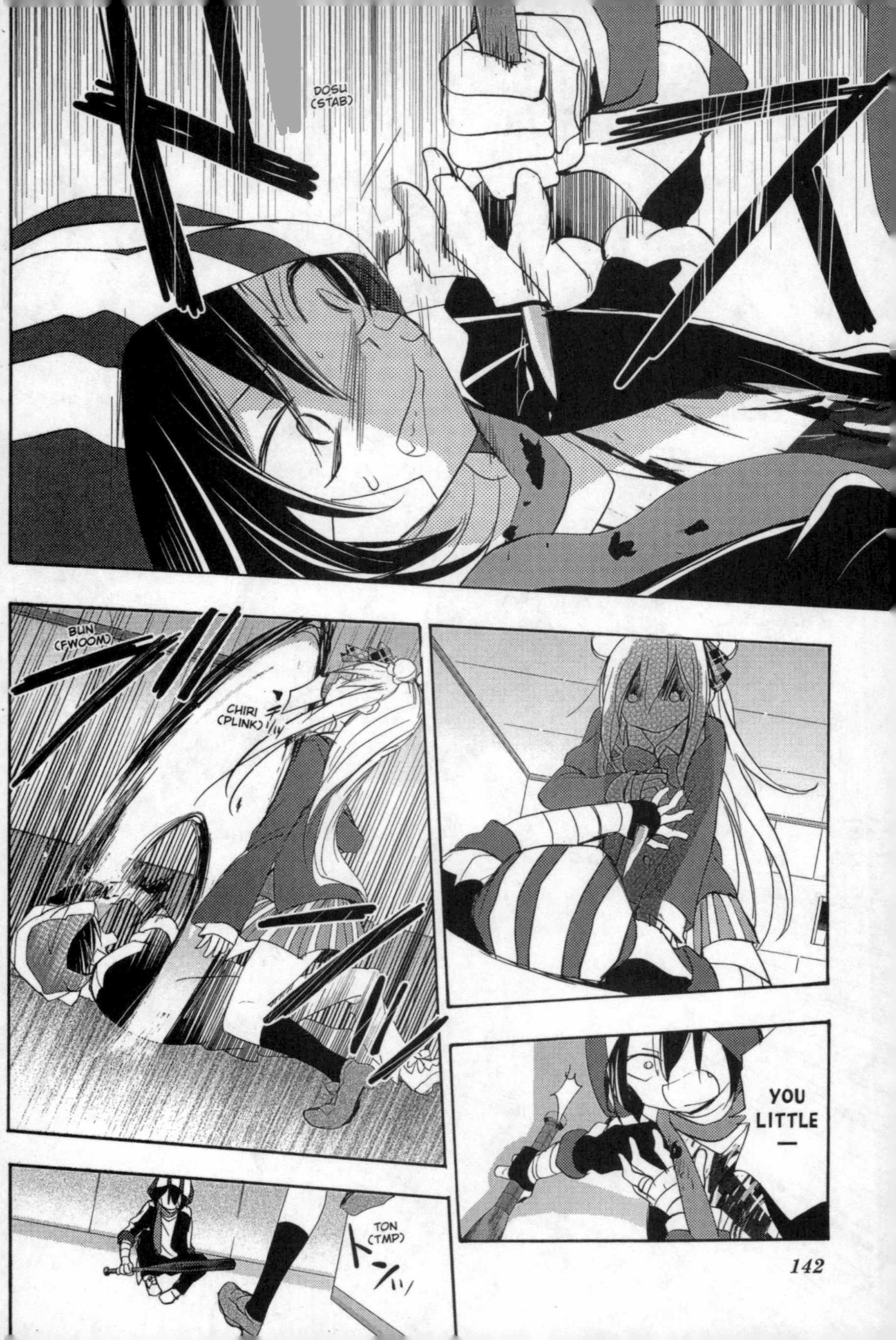
DOSU
(STAB)
BUN
(FWOOM)
CHIRI
(PLINK)
YOU LITTLE—
TON
(TMP)

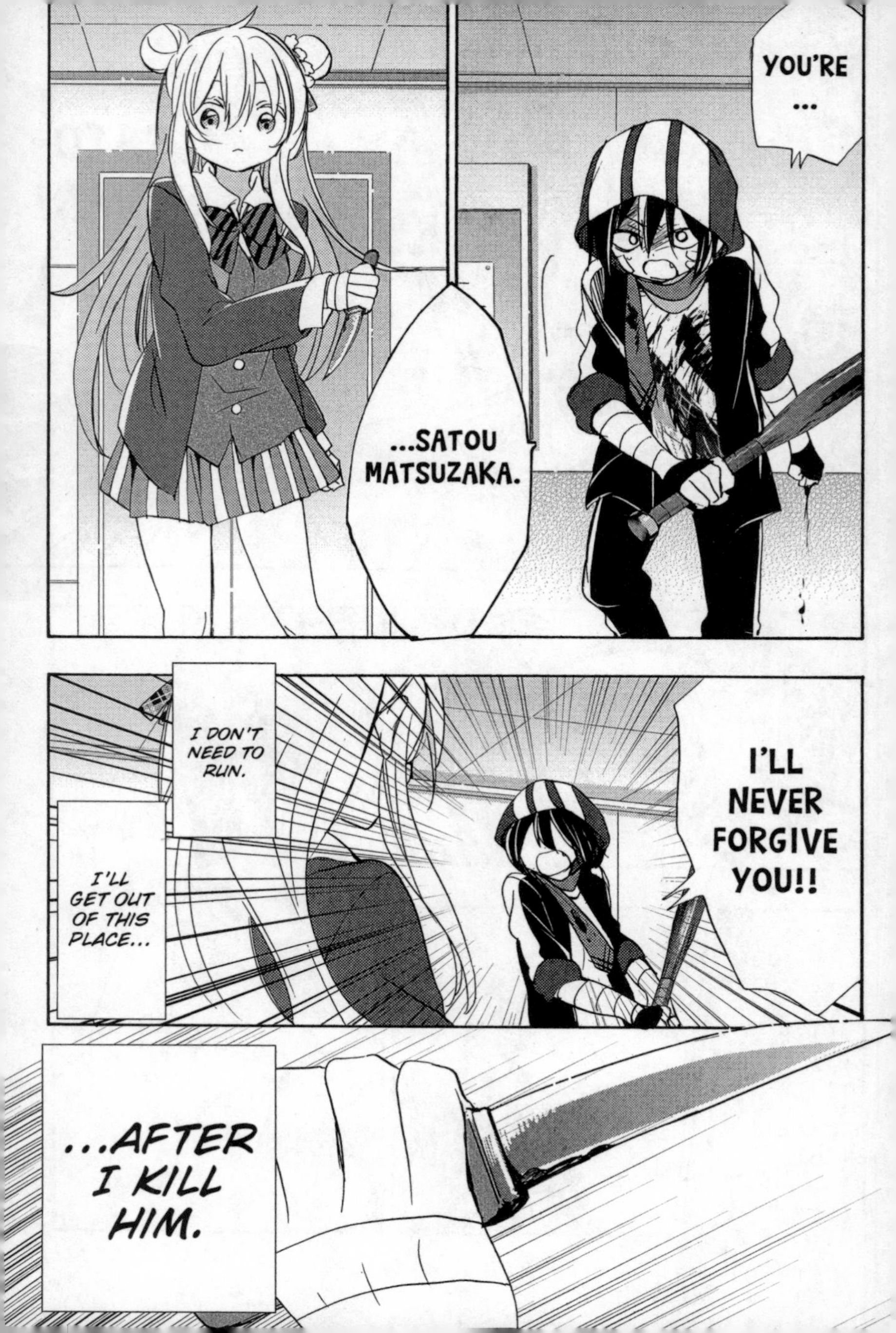
YOU'RE ...
...SATOU MATSUZAKA.
I'LL NEVER FORGIVE YOU!!
I DON'T NEED TO RUN.
I'LL GET OUT OF THIS PLACE...
...AFTER I KILL HIM.

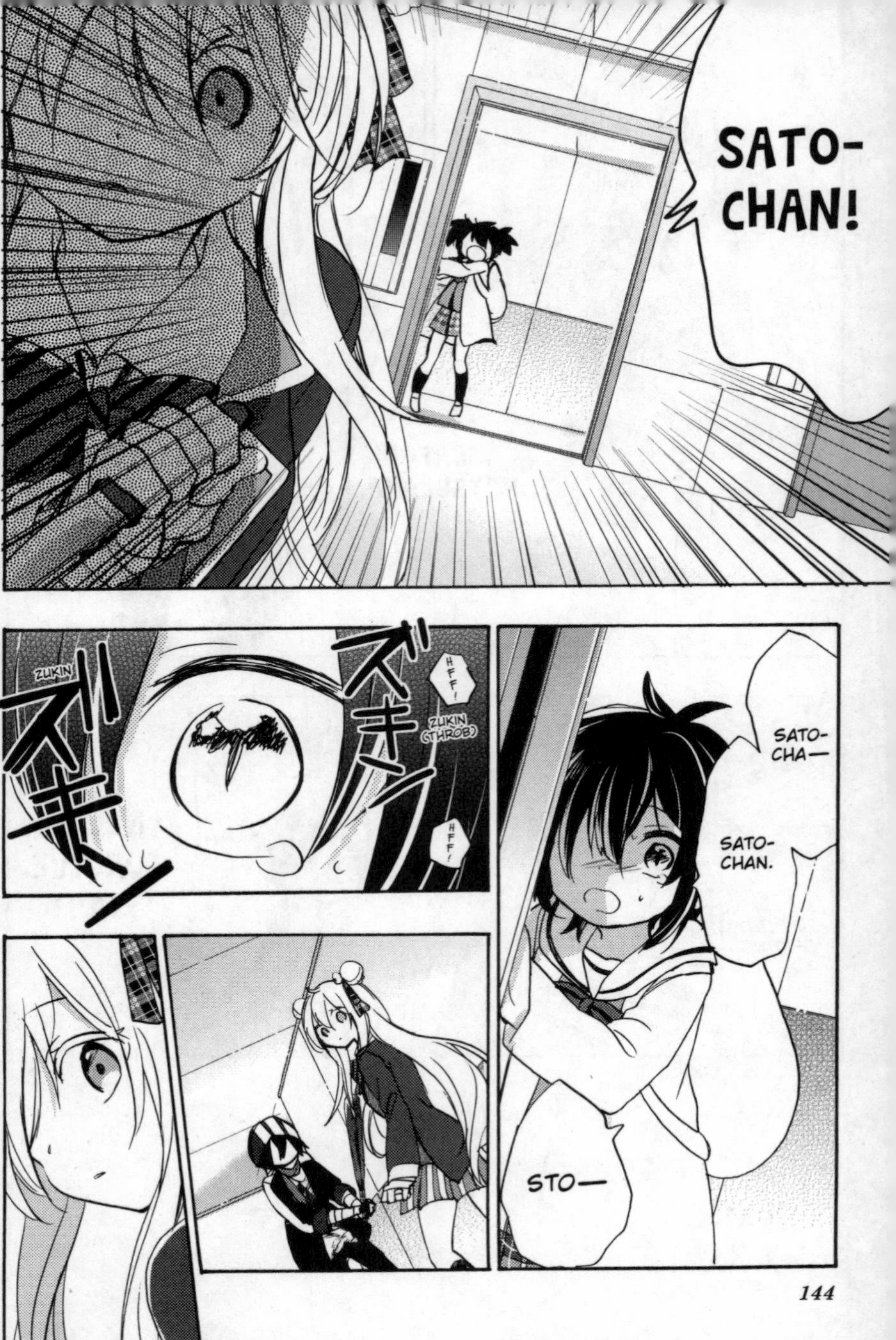
SATO-CHAN!
SATO-CHA—
SATO-CHAN.
STO—
HFF!
ZUKIN (THROB)
ズキン
HFF!
ZUKIN
ズキン

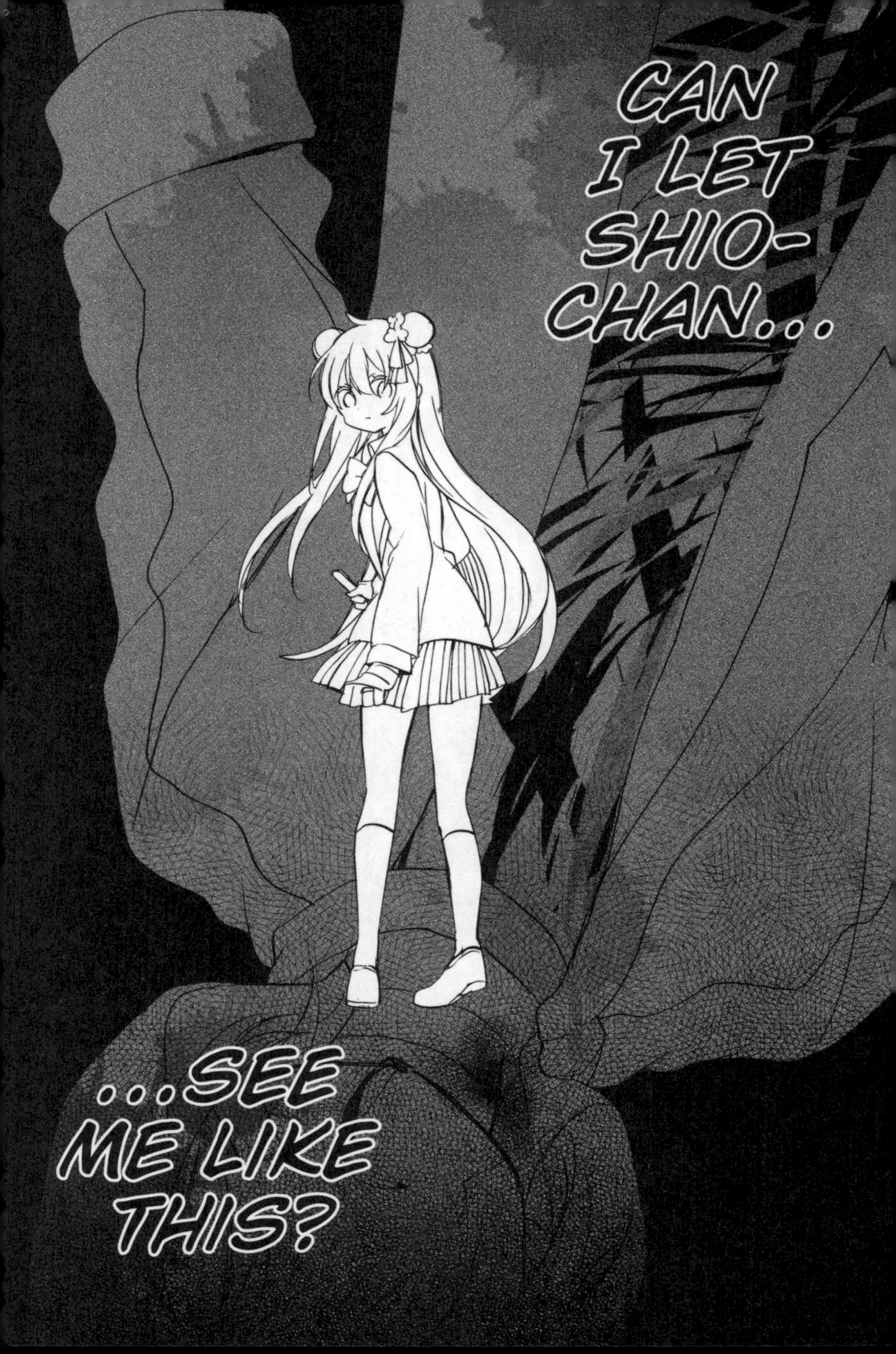
CAN I LET SHIO-CHAN...
...SEE ME LIKE THIS?

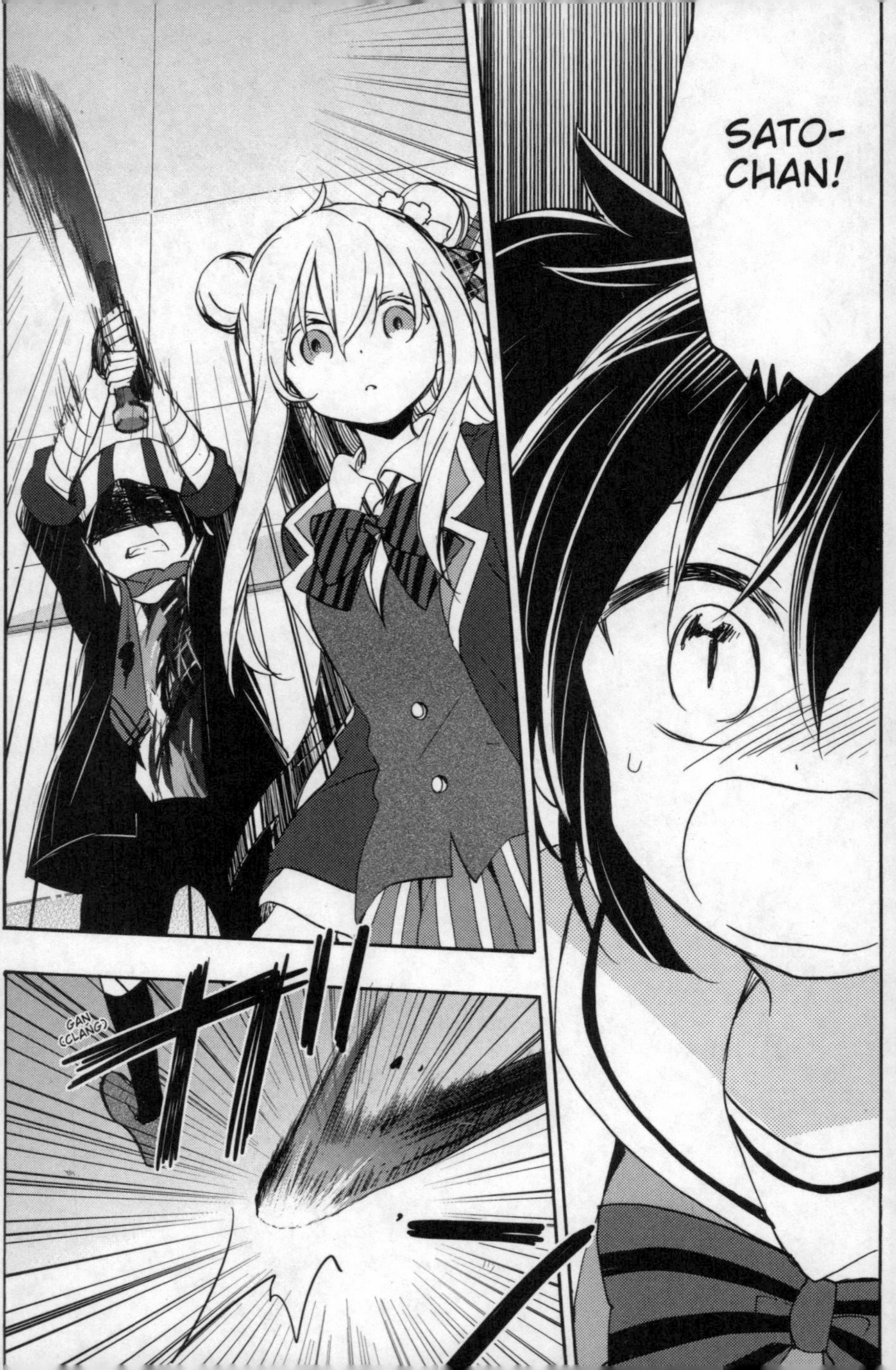
SATO-CHAN!
GAN (CLANG)

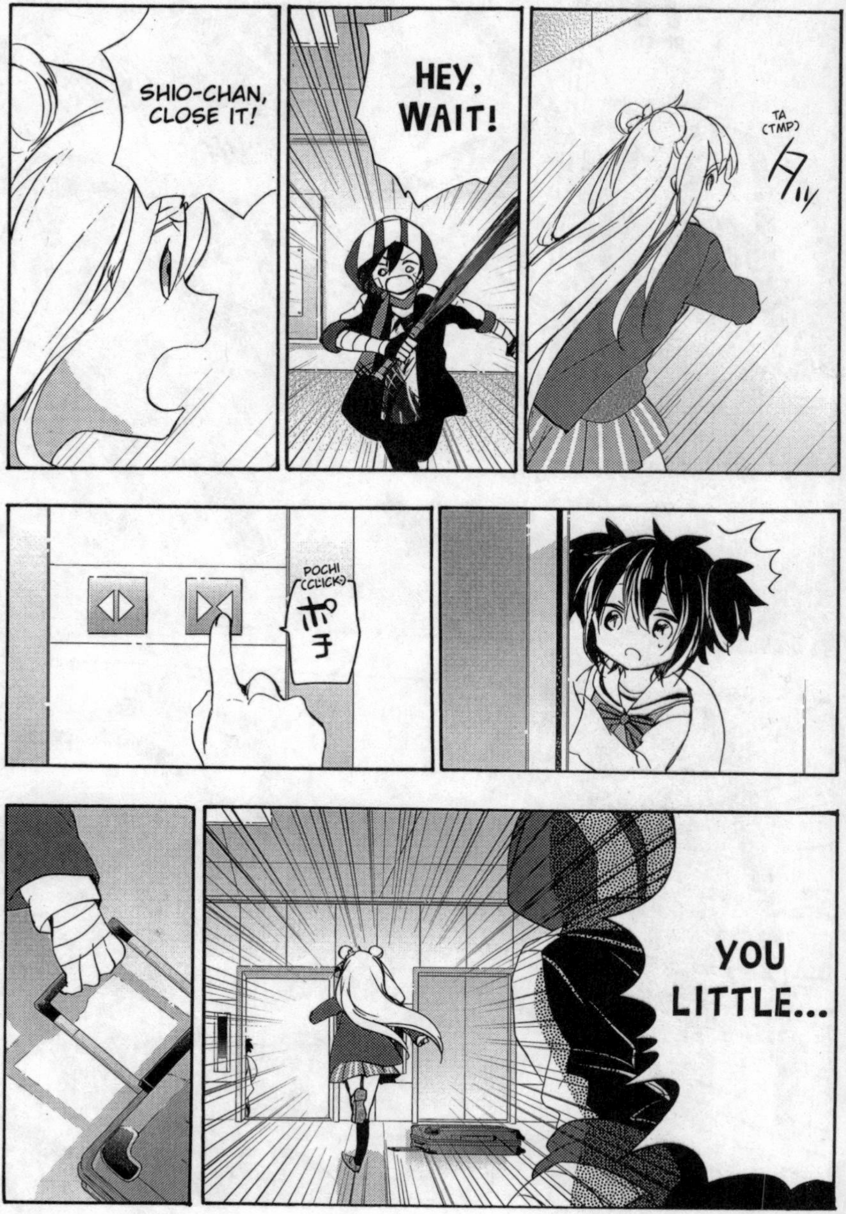
TA (TMP)
タッ
HEY, WAIT!
SHIO-CHAN, CLOSE IT!
POCHI (CLICK)
ポチ
YOU LITTLE...

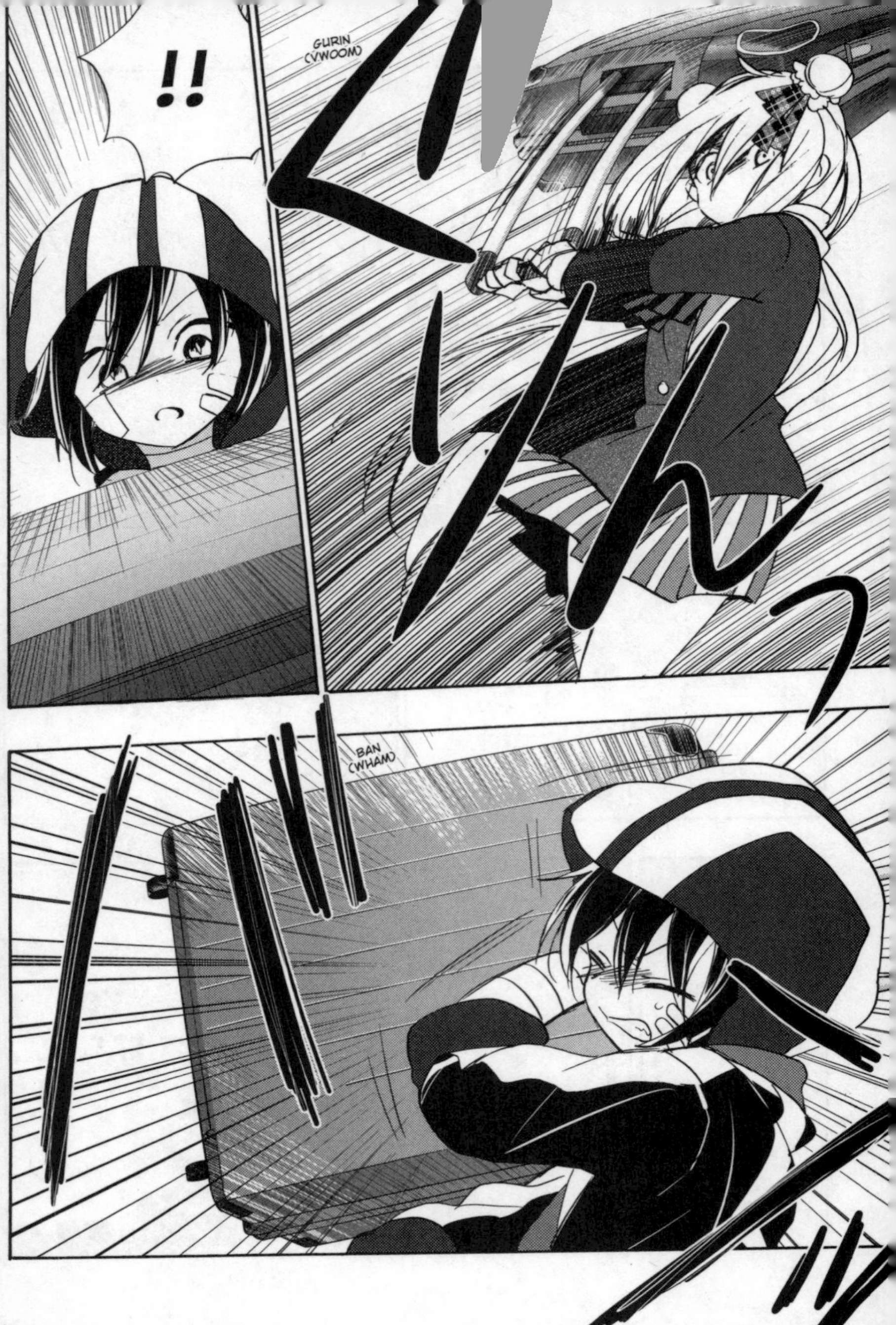
GURIN (V'WOOM)
!!
BAN (WHAM)

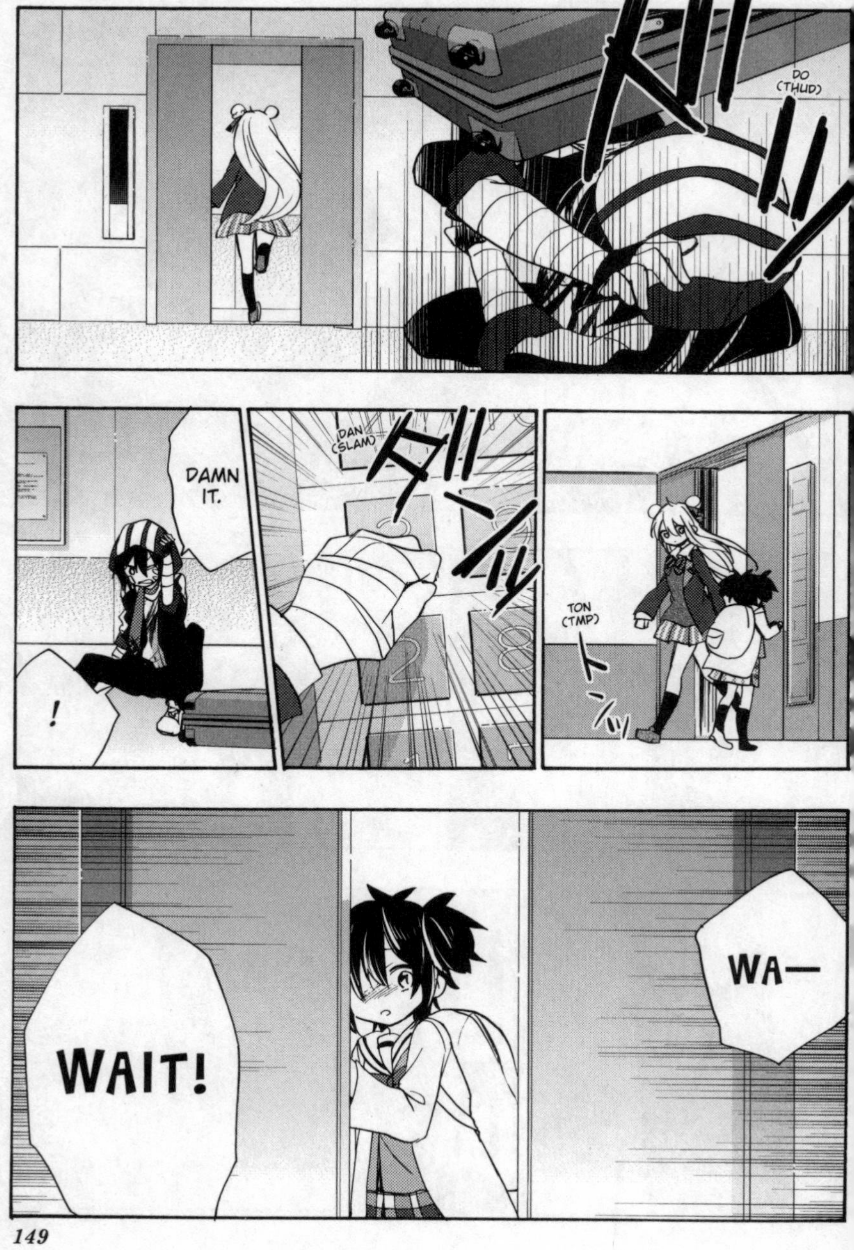
DO
(THUD)
TON
(TMP)
DAN
(SLAM)
DAMN IT.
!
WA—
WAIT!

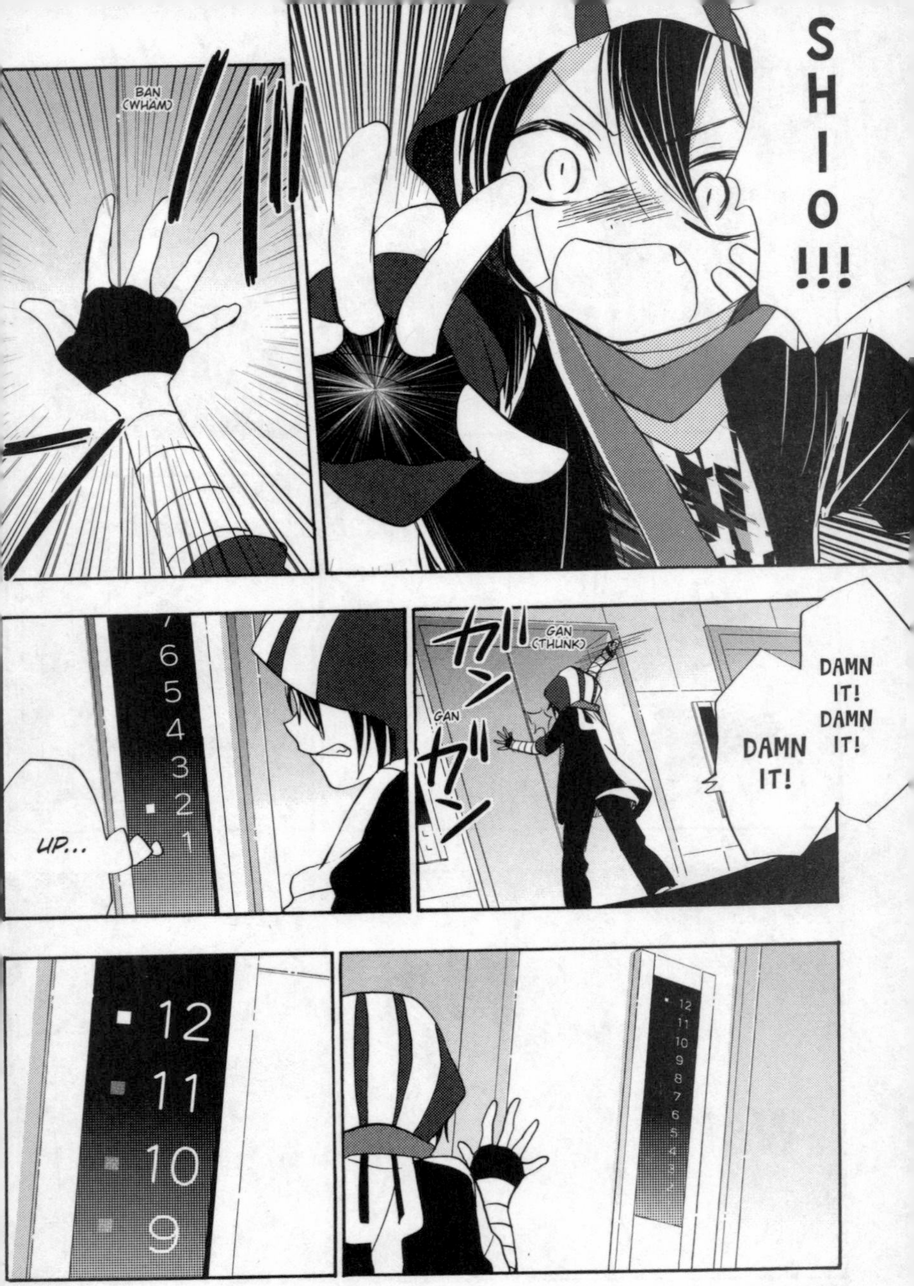
SHIO!!!
BAN (WHAM)
GAN (THUNK)
GAN
DAMN IT!
DAMN IT!
DAMN IT!
UP...

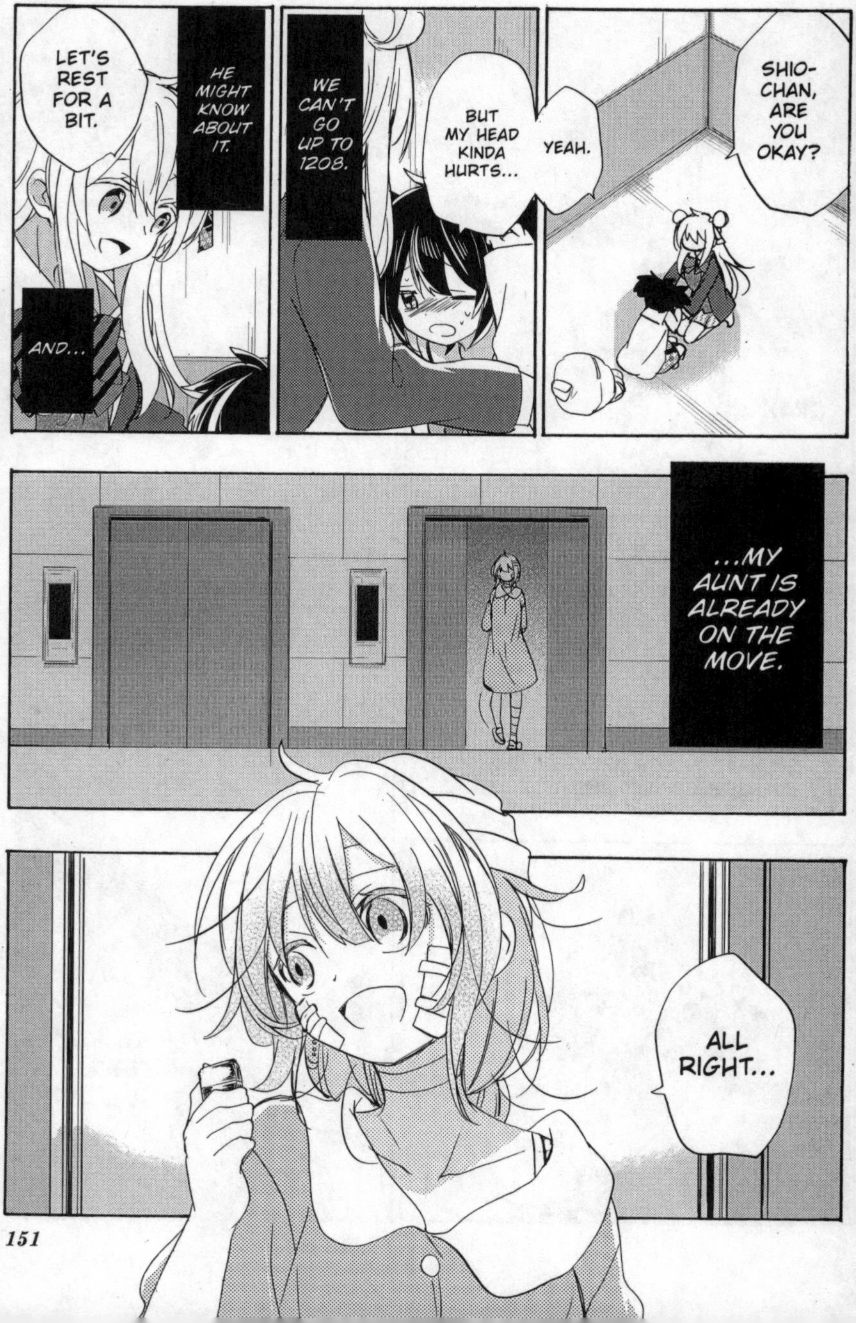
SHIO-CHAN, ARE YOU OKAY?
YEAH.
BUT MY HEAD KINDA HURTS...
WE CAN'T GO UP TO 1208.
HE MIGHT KNOW ABOUT IT.
LET'S REST FOR A BIT.
AND...
...MY AUNT IS ALREADY ON THE MOVE.
ALL RIGHT...

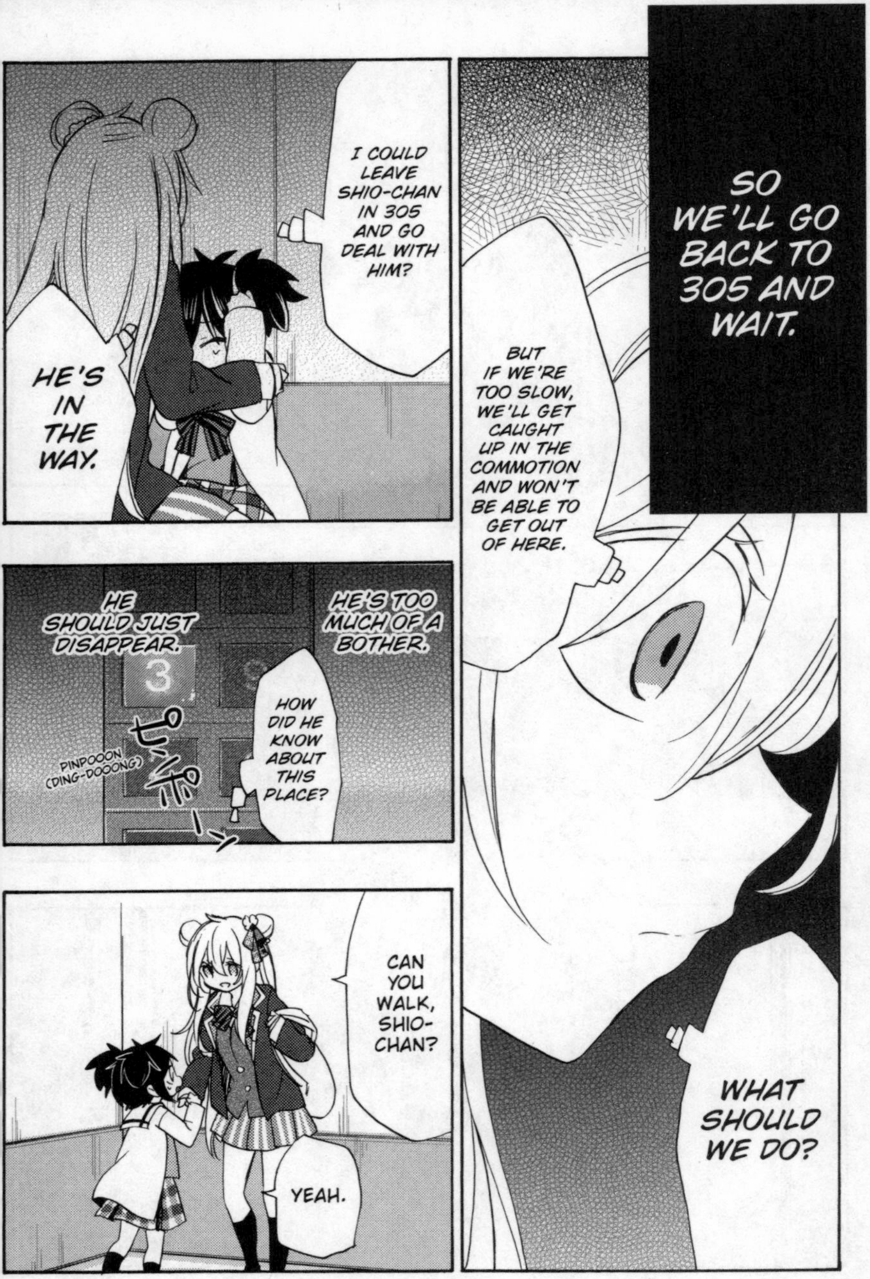
SO WE'LL GO BACK TO 305 AND WAIT.
BUT IF WE'RE TOO SLOW, WE'LL GET CAUGHT UP IN THE COMMOTION AND WON'T BE ABLE TO GET OUT OF HERE.
WHAT SHOULD WE DO?
I COULD LEAVE SHIO-CHAN IN 305 AND GO DEAL WITH HIM?
HE'S IN THE WAY.
HE'S TOO MUCH OF A BOTHER.
HE SHOULD JUST DISAPPEAR.
HOW DID HE KNOW ABOUT THIS PLACE?
ピンポーン
PINPOOON (DING-DOOONG)
CAN YOU WALK, SHIO-CHAN?
YEAH.

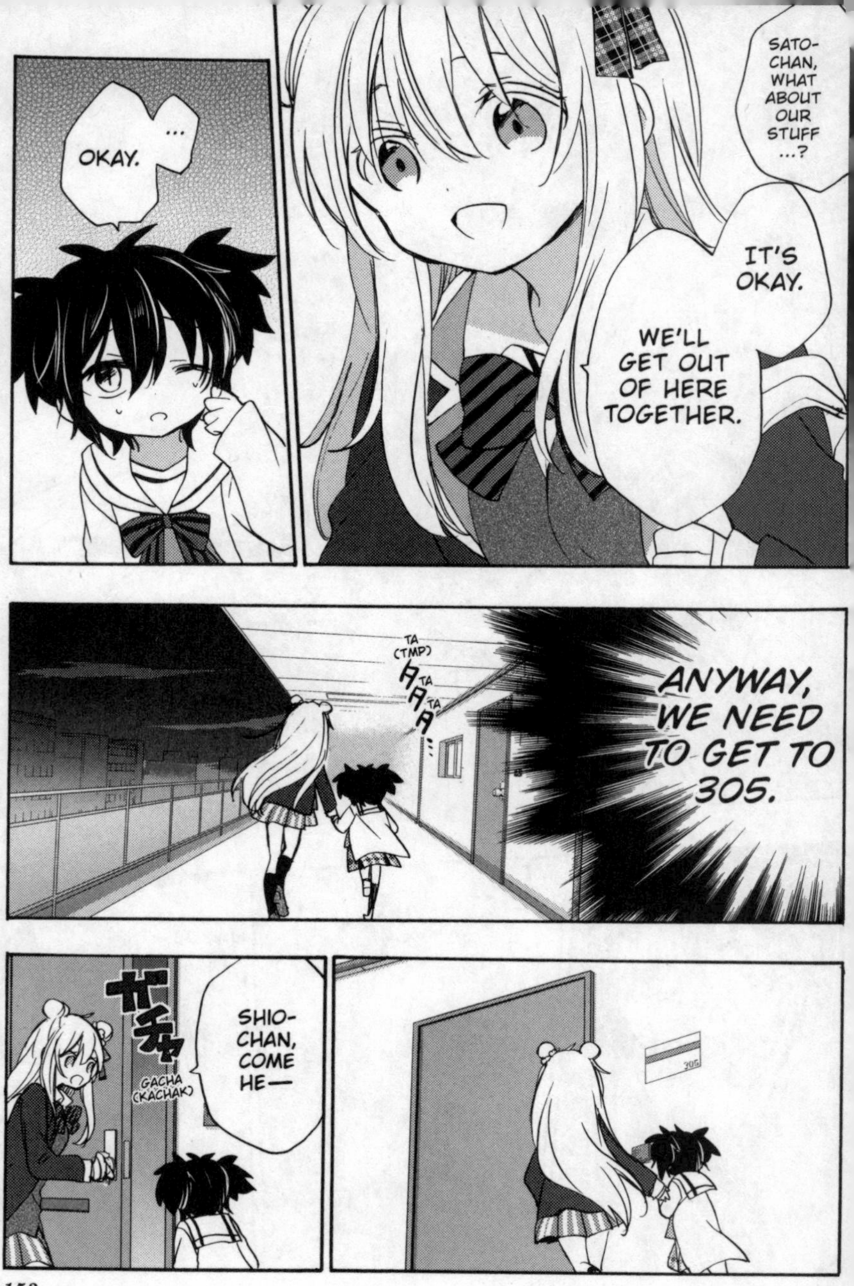
SATO-CHAN, WHAT ABOUT OUR STUFF ...?
IT'S OKAY.
WE'LL GET OUT OF HERE TOGETHER.
... OKAY.
ANYWAY, WE NEED TO GET TO 305.
TA (TMP) TA TA TA
305
SHIO-CHAN, COME HE—
ガチャ
GACHA (KACHAK)

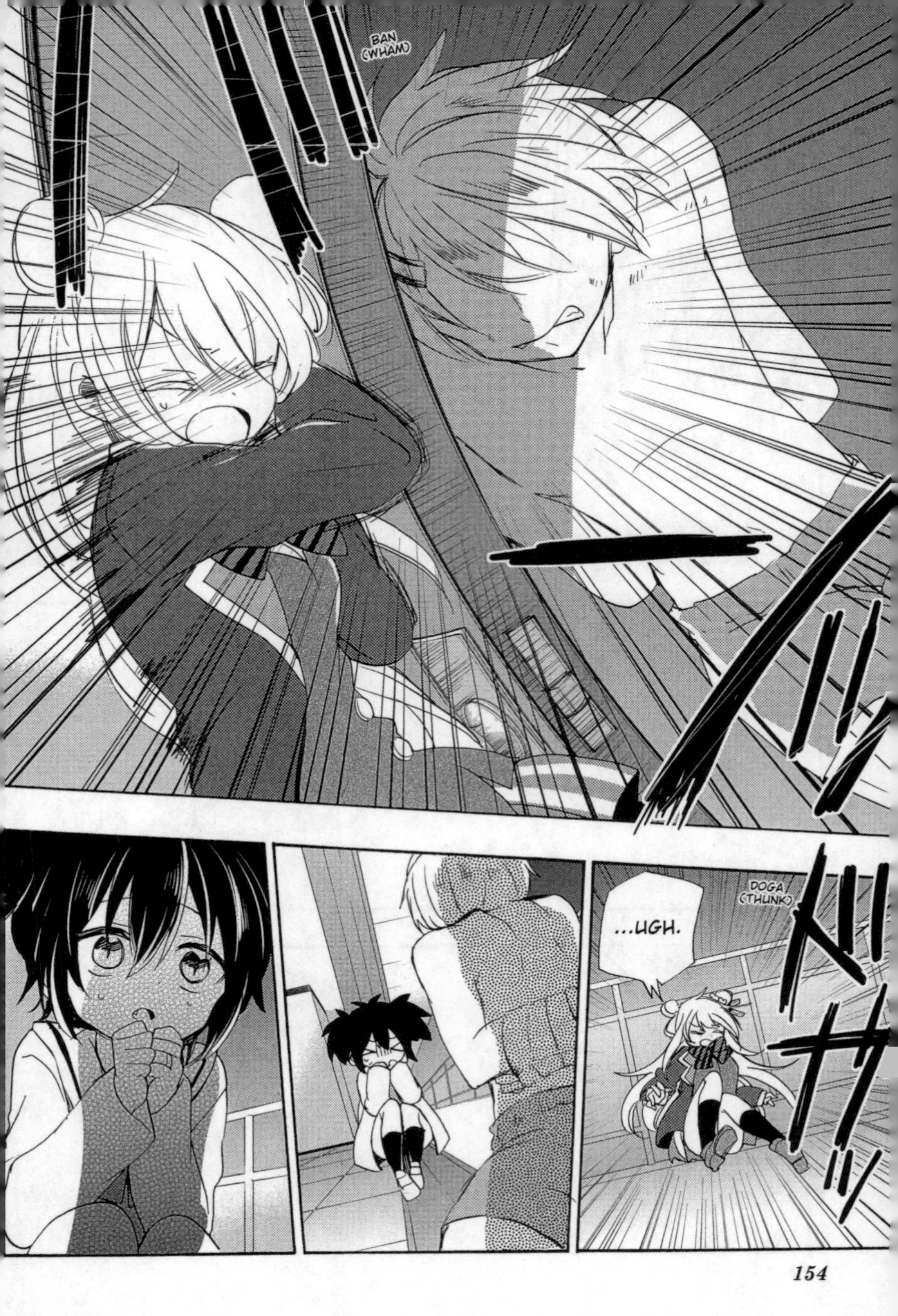
BAN
(WHAM)
DOGA
(THUNK)
...UGH.

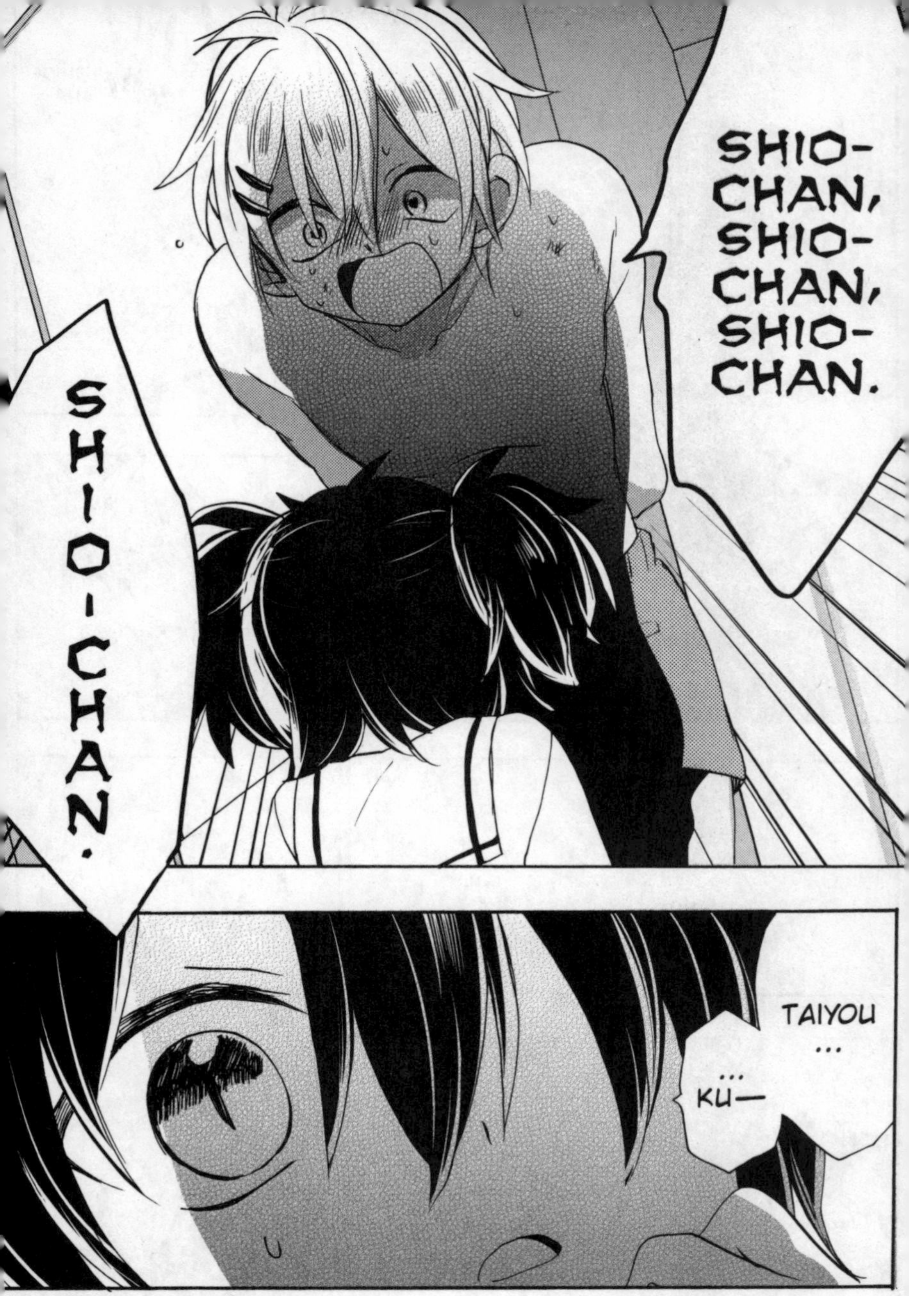
SHIO-CHAN, SHIO-CHAN, SHIO-CHAN.
SHIO-CHAN.
TAIYOU ... ...KU—

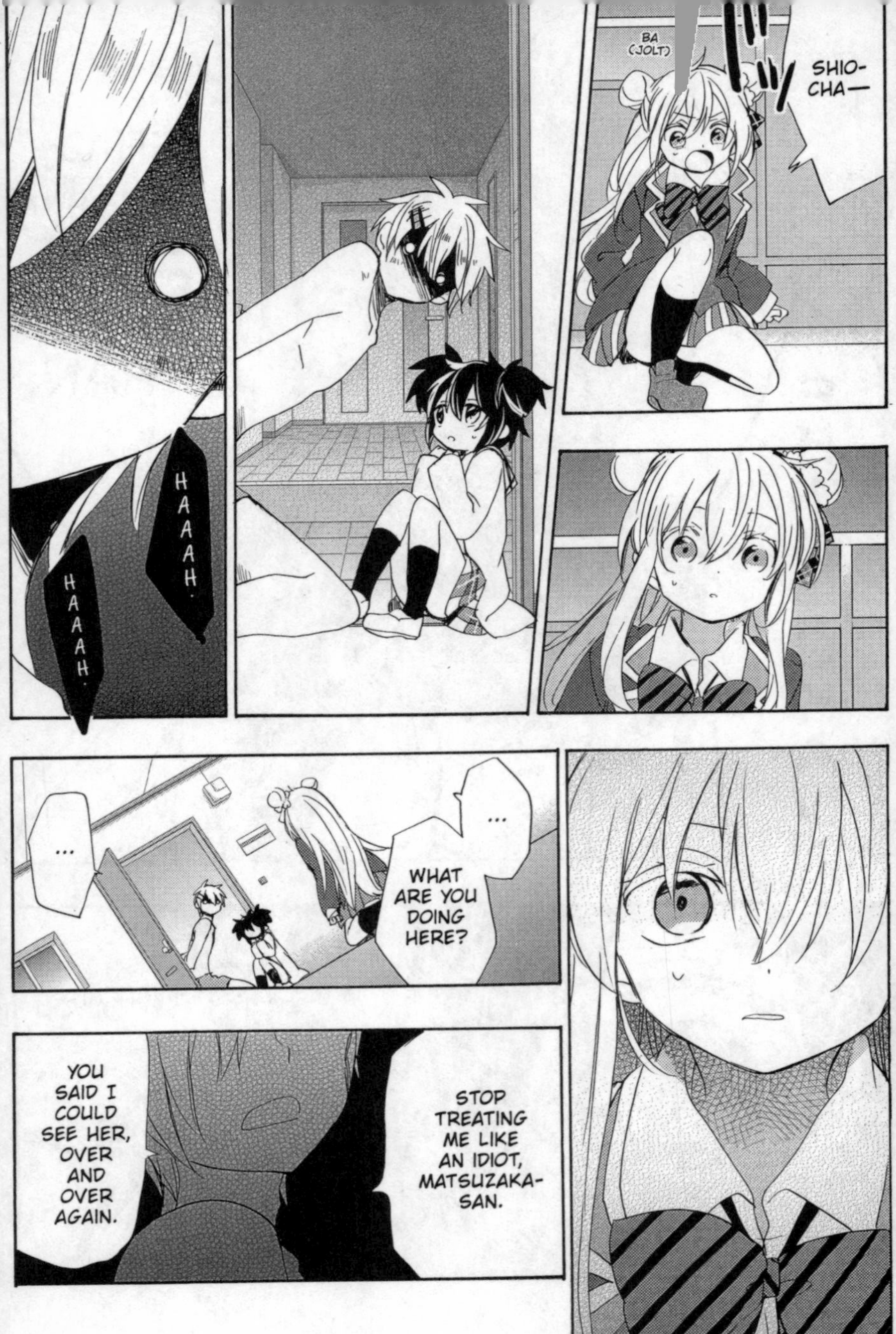

BA (JOLT)
SHIO-CHA—
HAAAAH.
HAAAAH.
...
WHAT ARE YOU DOING HERE?
...
STOP TREATING ME LIKE AN IDIOT, MATSUZAKA-SAN.
YOU SAID I COULD SEE HER, OVER AND OVER AGAIN.

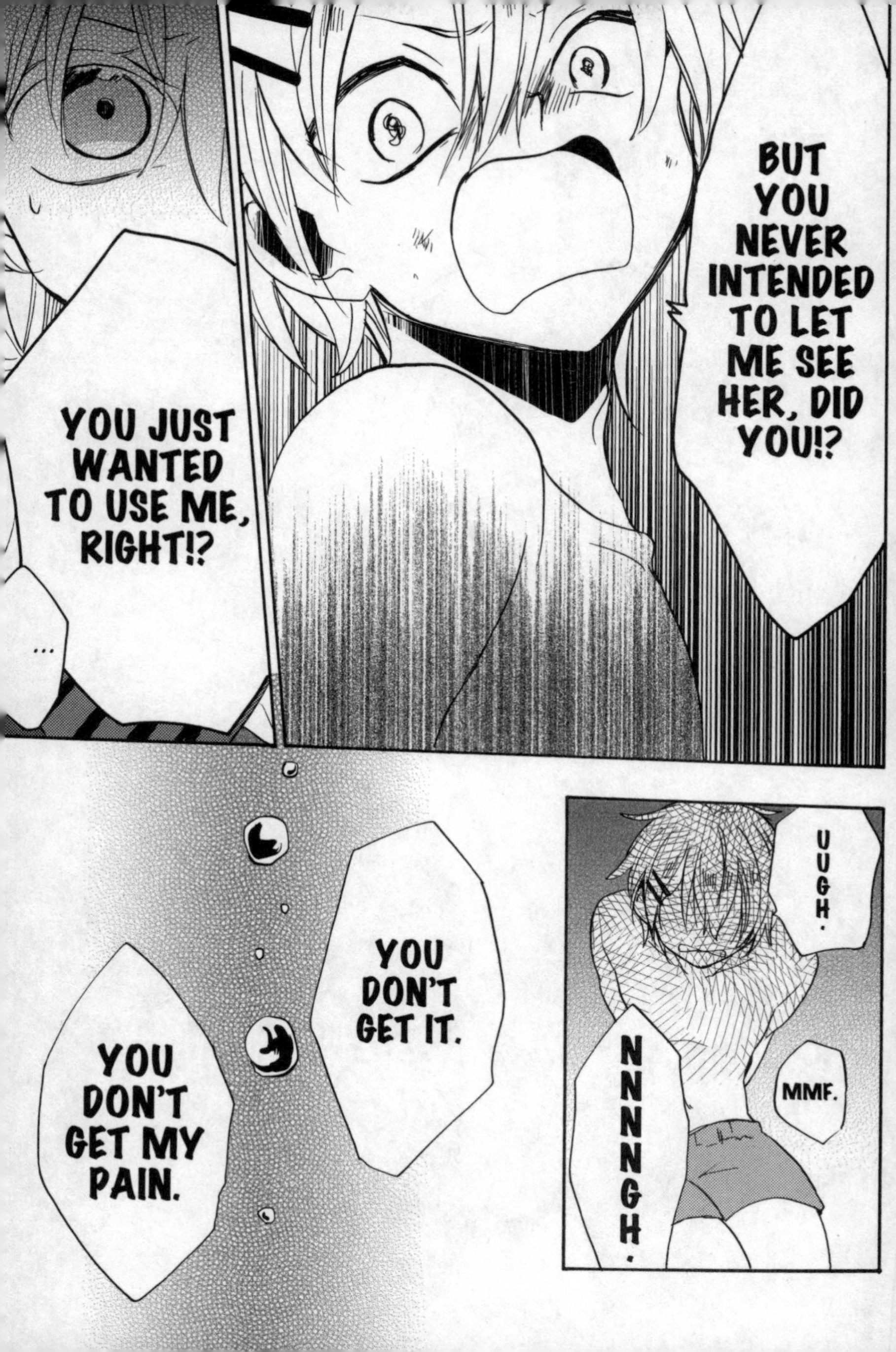
BUT YOU NEVER INTENDED TO LET ME SEE HER, DID YOU!?
YOU JUST WANTED TO USE ME, RIGHT!?
...
UUGH.
NNNNGH.
MMF.
YOU DON'T GET IT.
YOU DON'T GET MY PAIN.

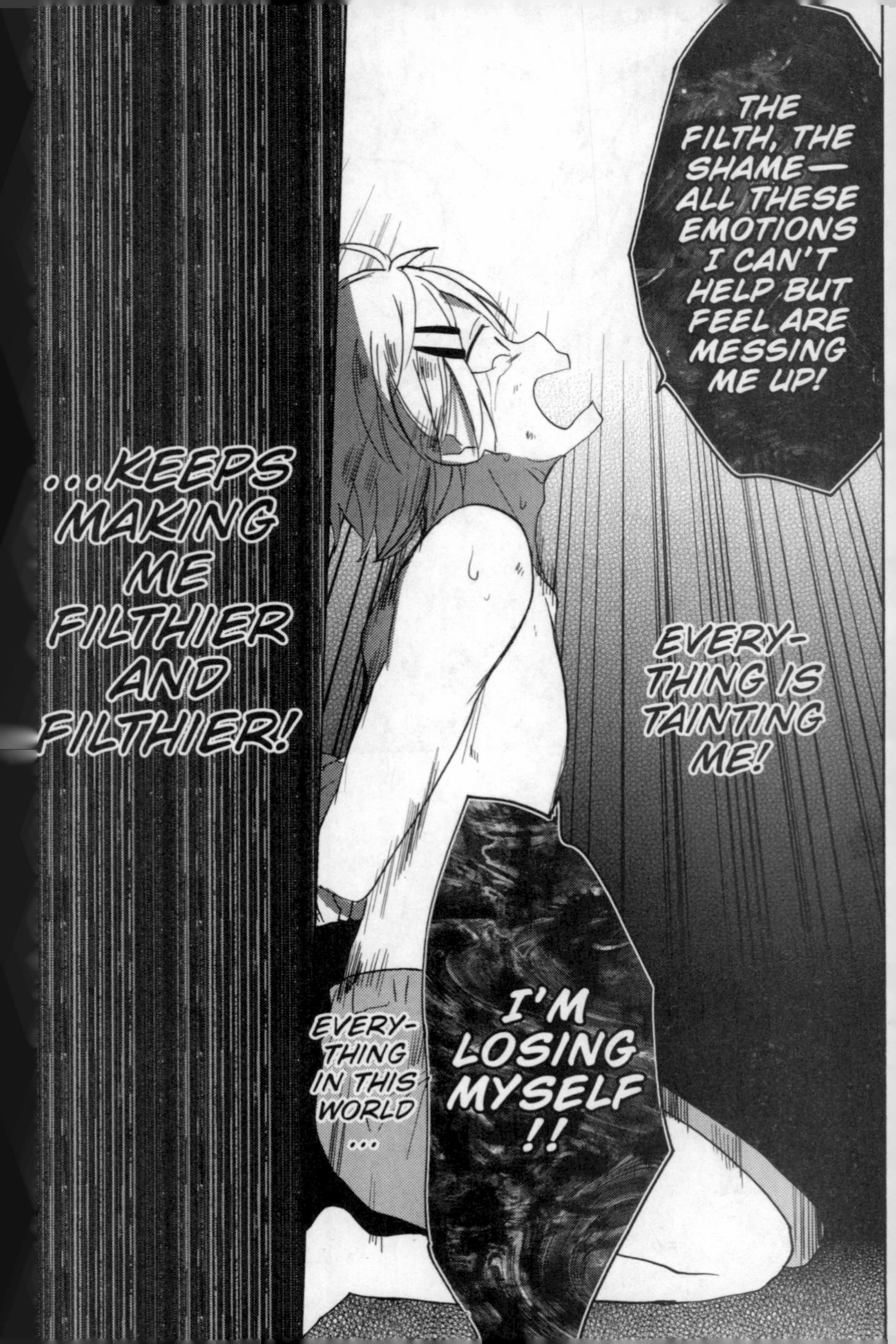
THE FILTH, THE SHAME—ALL THESE EMOTIONS I CAN'T HELP BUT FEEL ARE MESSING ME UP!
EVERY-THING IS TAINTING ME!
I'M LOSING MYSELF!!
EVERY-THING IN THIS WORLD...
...KEEPS MAKING ME FILTHIER AND FILTHIER!

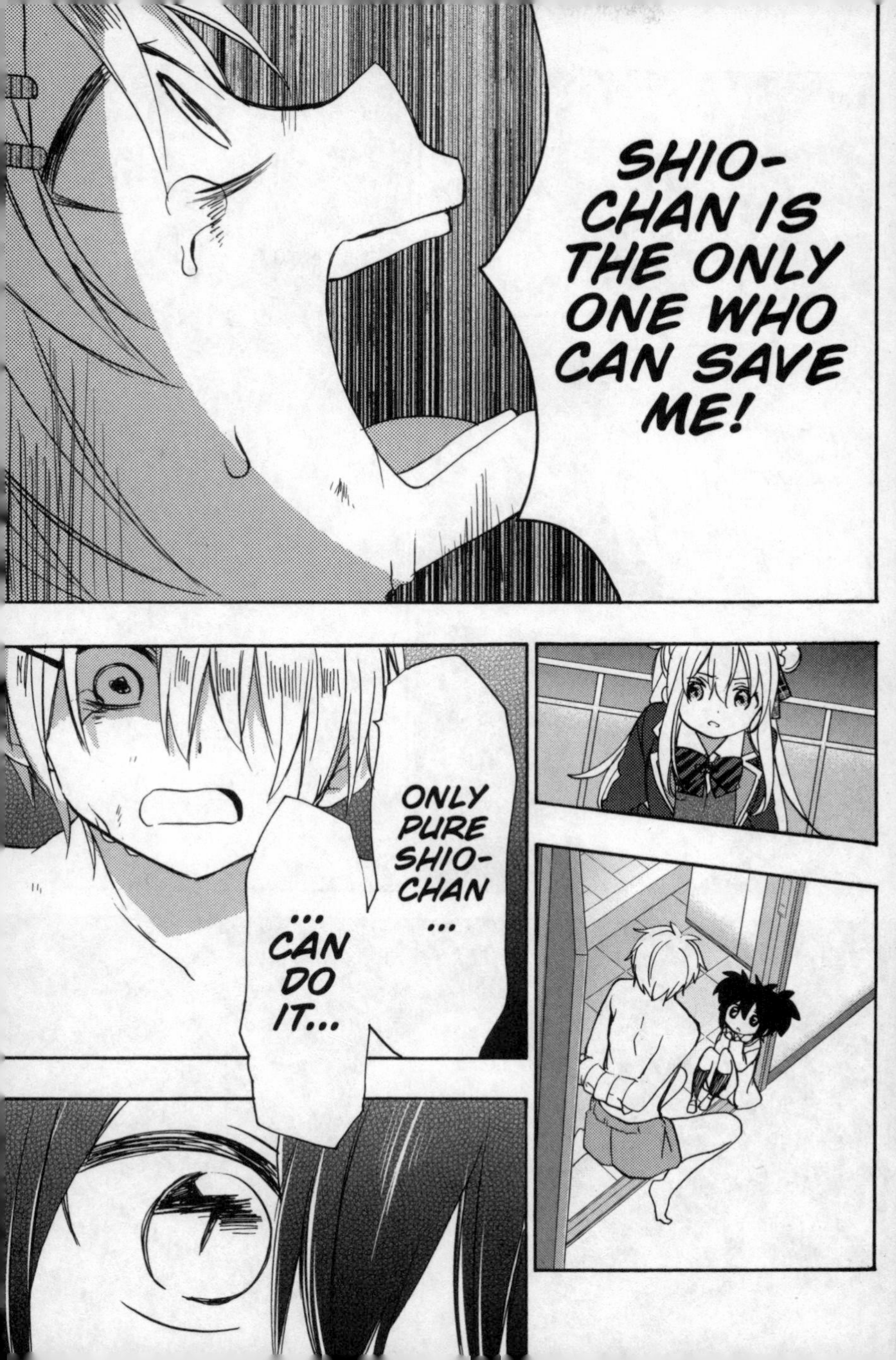
SHIO-CHAN IS THE ONLY ONE WHO CAN SAVE ME!
ONLY PURE SHIO-CHAN...
...CAN DO IT...

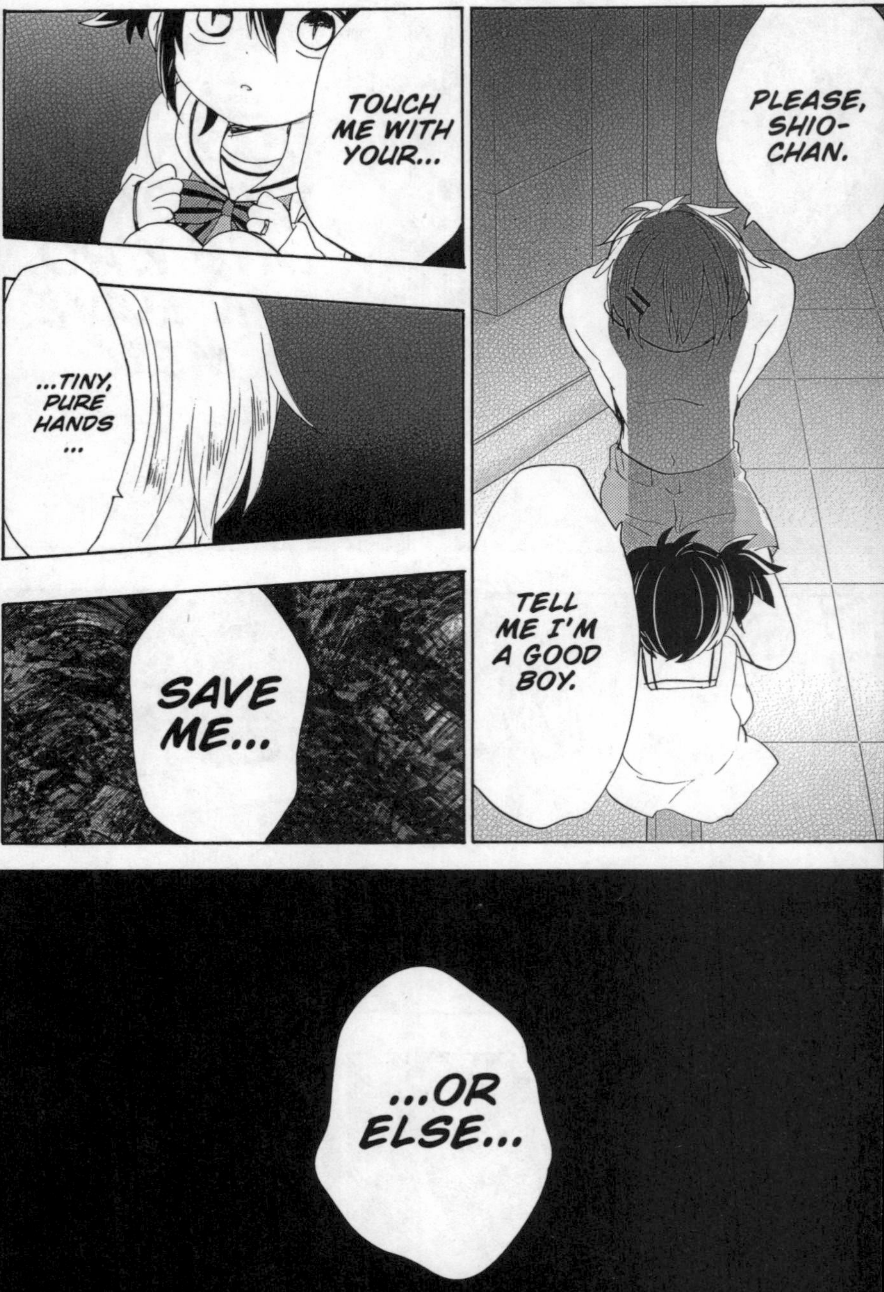
PLEASE, SHIO-CHAN.
TELL ME I'M A GOOD BOY.
TOUCH ME WITH YOUR...
...TINY, PURE HANDS...
SAVE ME...
...OR ELSE...

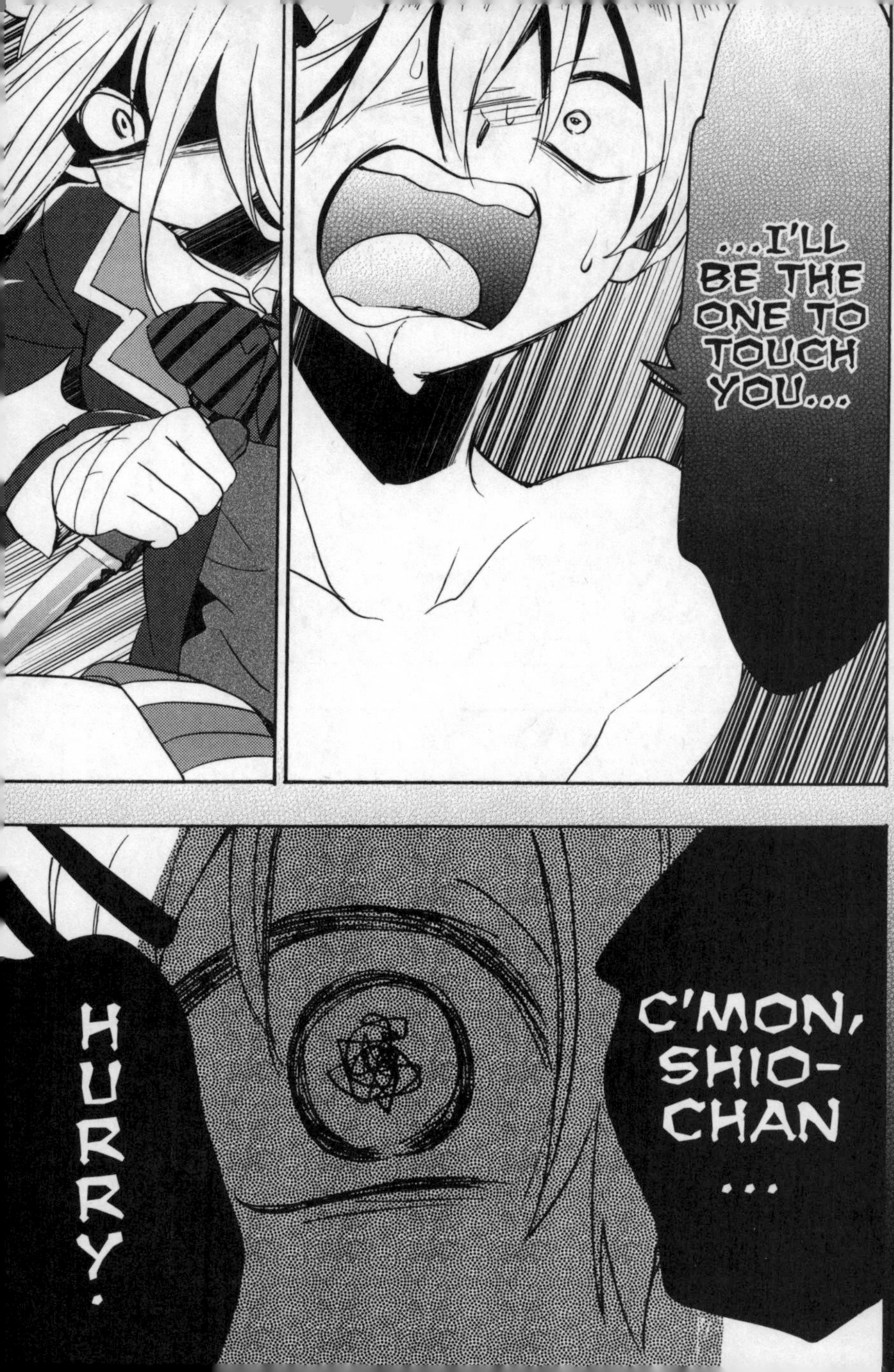
...I'LL BE THE ONE TO TOUCH YOU...
C'MON, SHIO-CHAN...
HURRY.

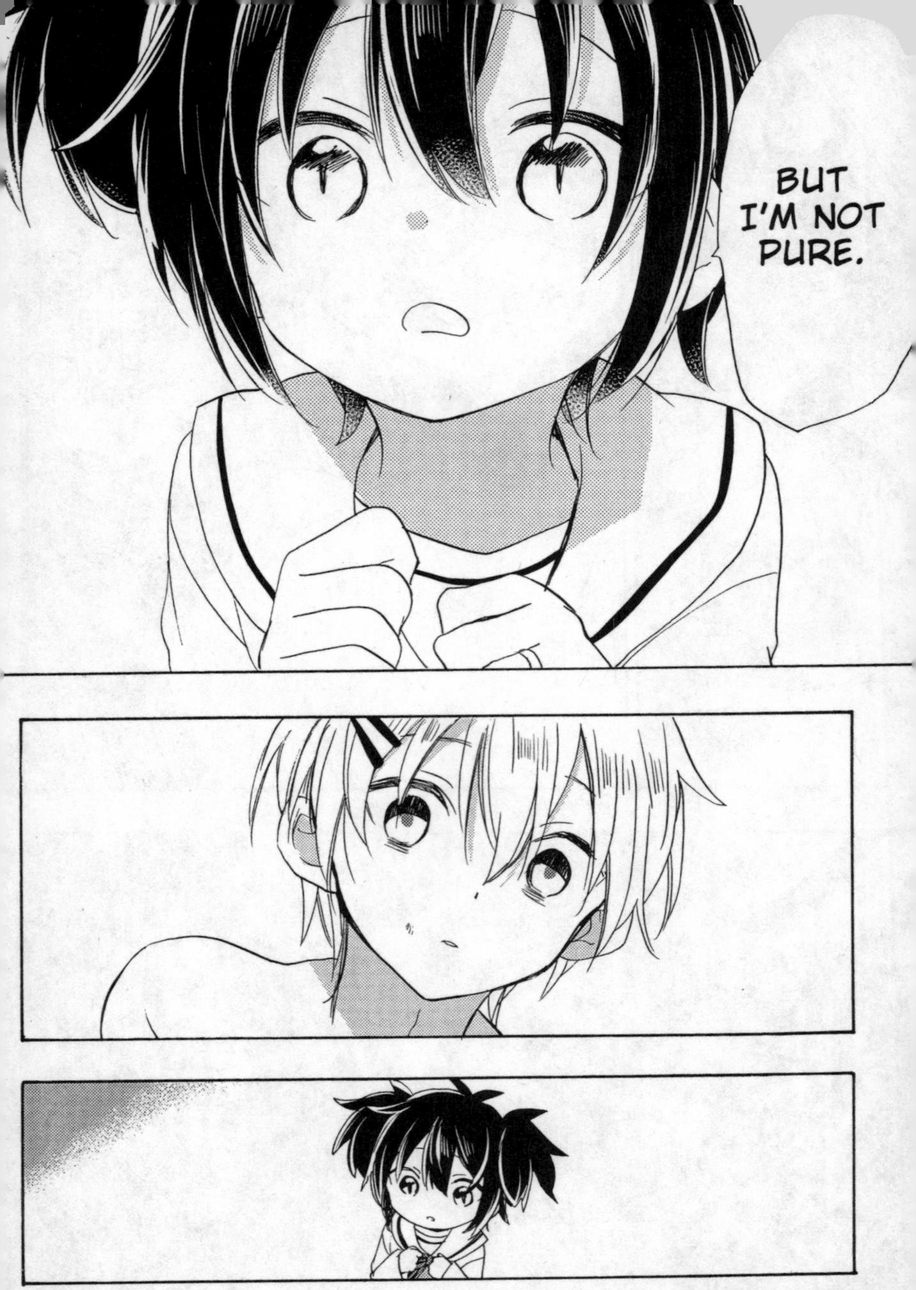
BUT I'M NOT PURE.

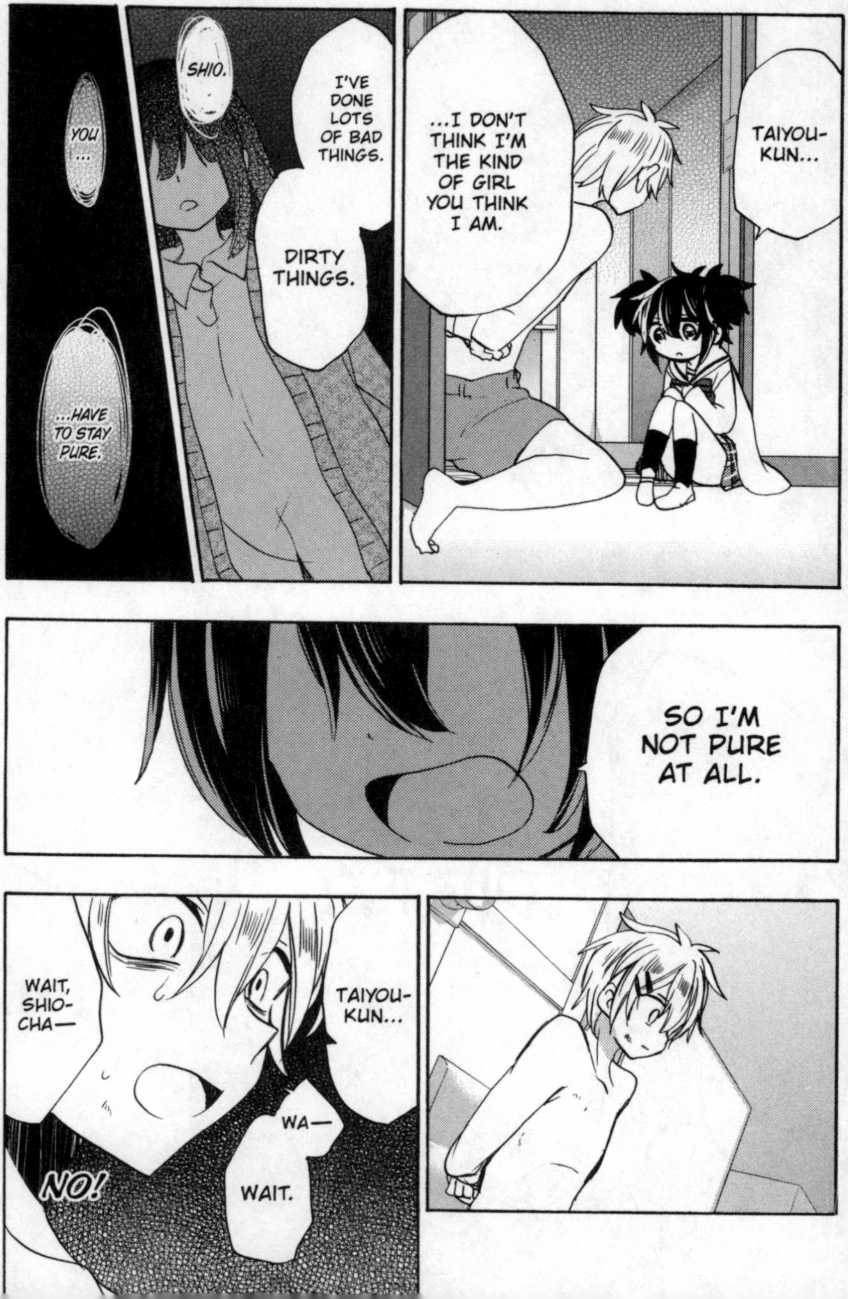
TAIYOU-KUN...
...I DON'T THINK I'M THE KIND OF GIRL YOU THINK I AM.
I'VE DONE LOTS OF BAD THINGS.
DIRTY THINGS.
SHIO.
YOU...
...HAVE TO STAY PURE.
SO I'M NOT PURE AT ALL.
TAIYOU-KUN...
WAIT, SHIO-CHA—
WA—
WAIT.
NO!

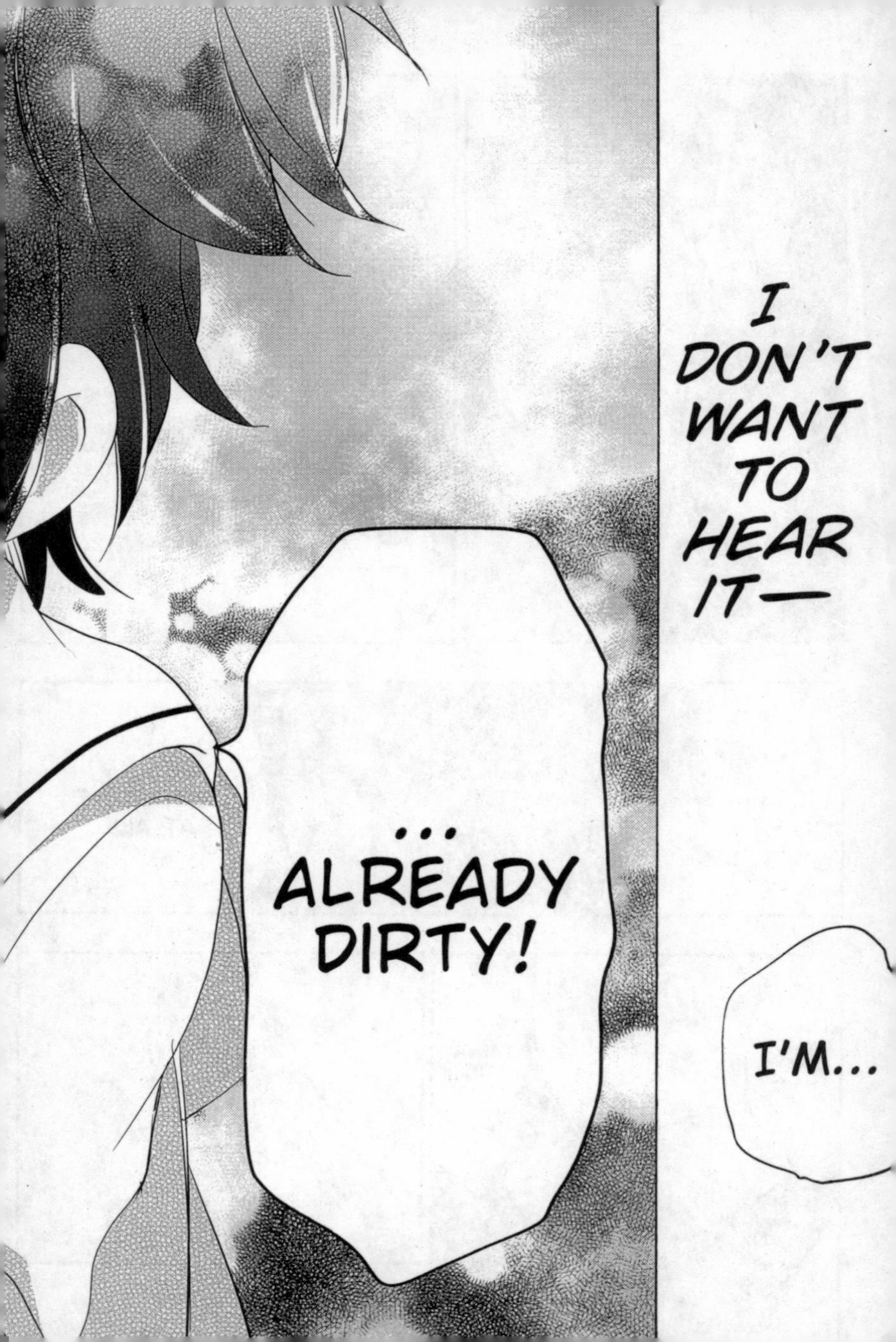
I DON'T WANT TO HEAR IT—
I'M...
...ALREADY DIRTY!

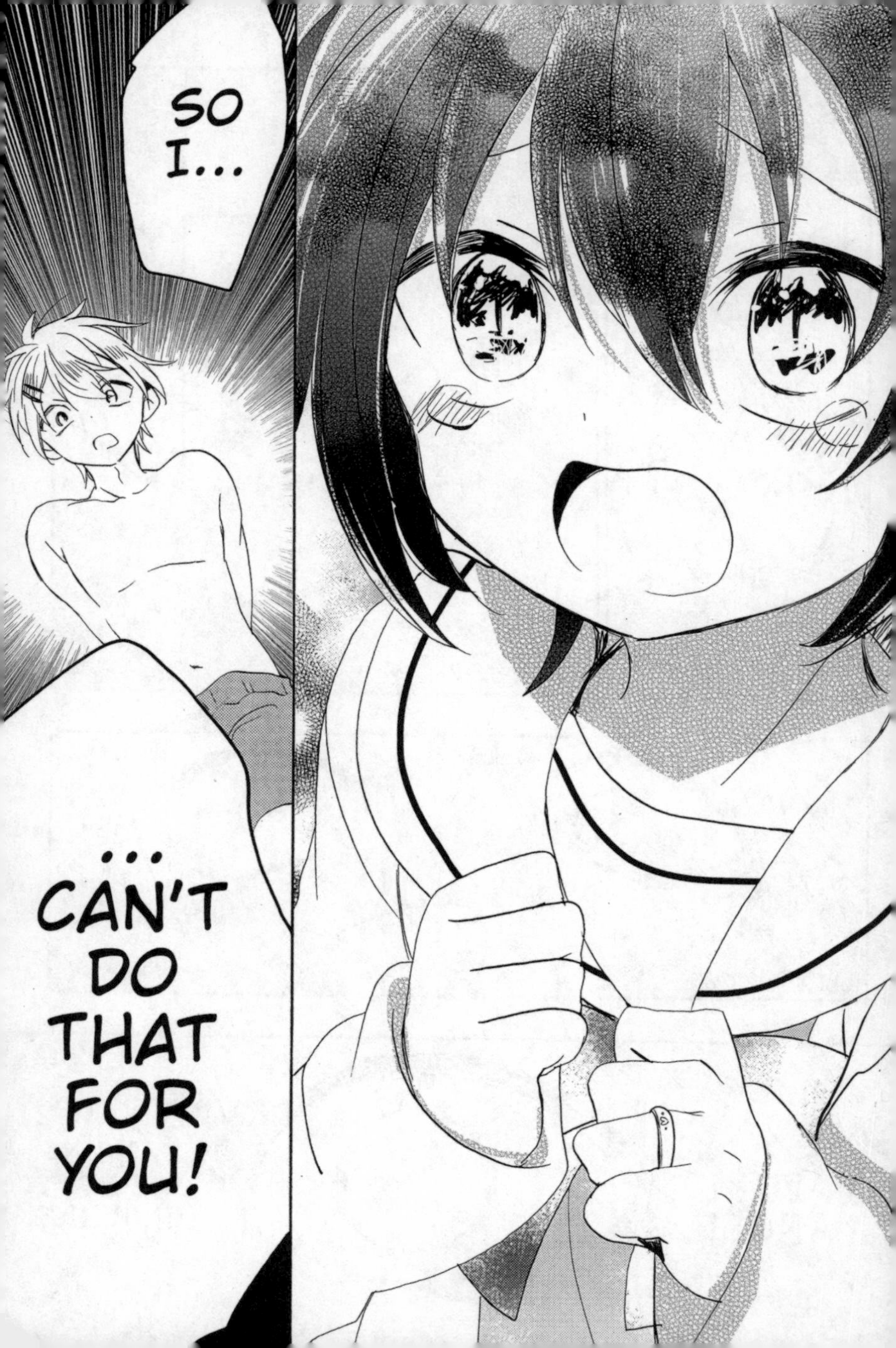
SO I...
...CAN'T DO THAT FOR YOU!

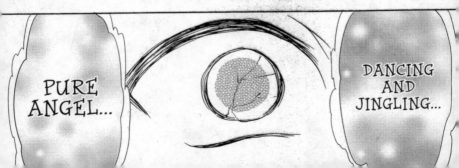

PURE ANGEL...

DANCING AND JINGLING...

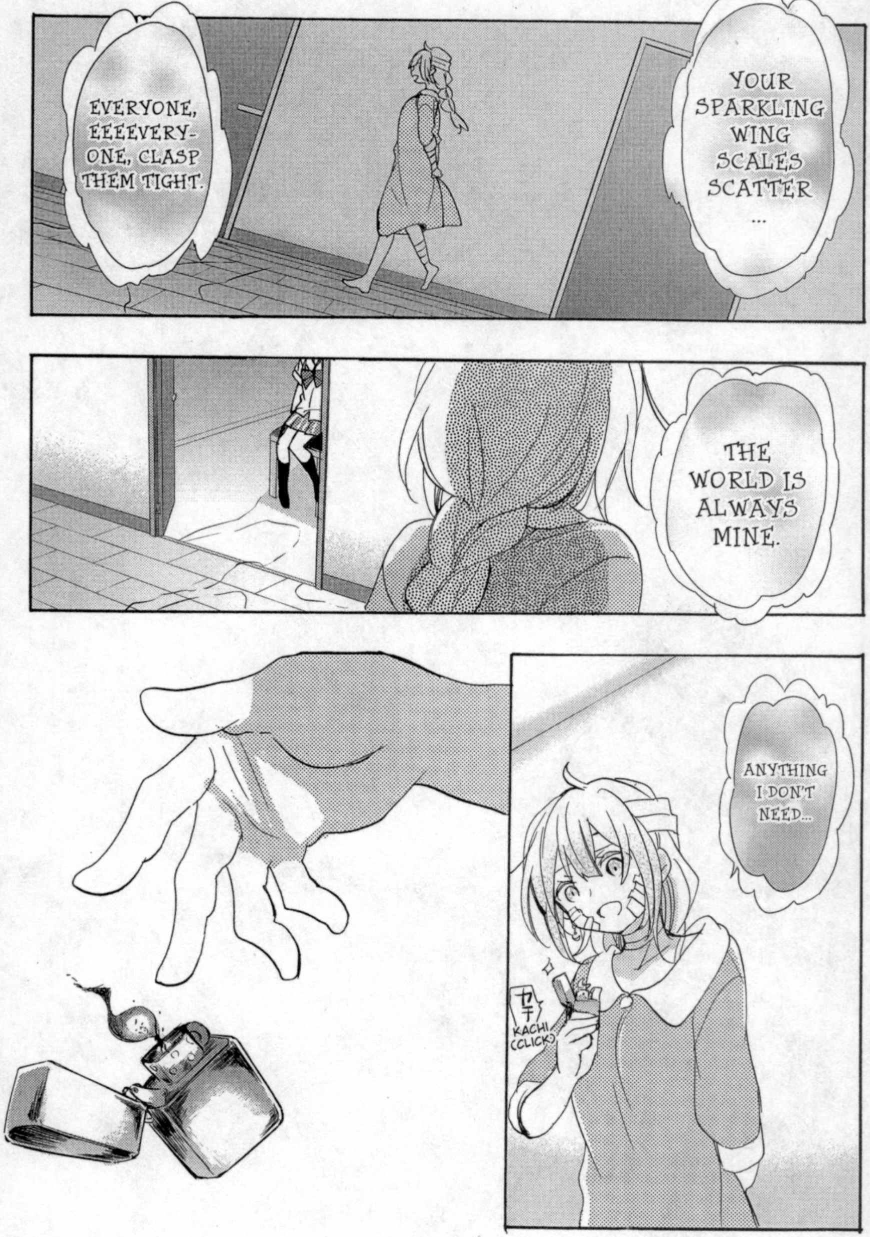
YOUR SPARKLING WING SCALES SCATTER...
EVERYONE, EEEEVERY-ONE, CLASP THEM TIGHT.
THE WORLD IS ALWAYS MINE.
ANYTHING I DON'T NEED...
カチ
KACHI (CLICK)

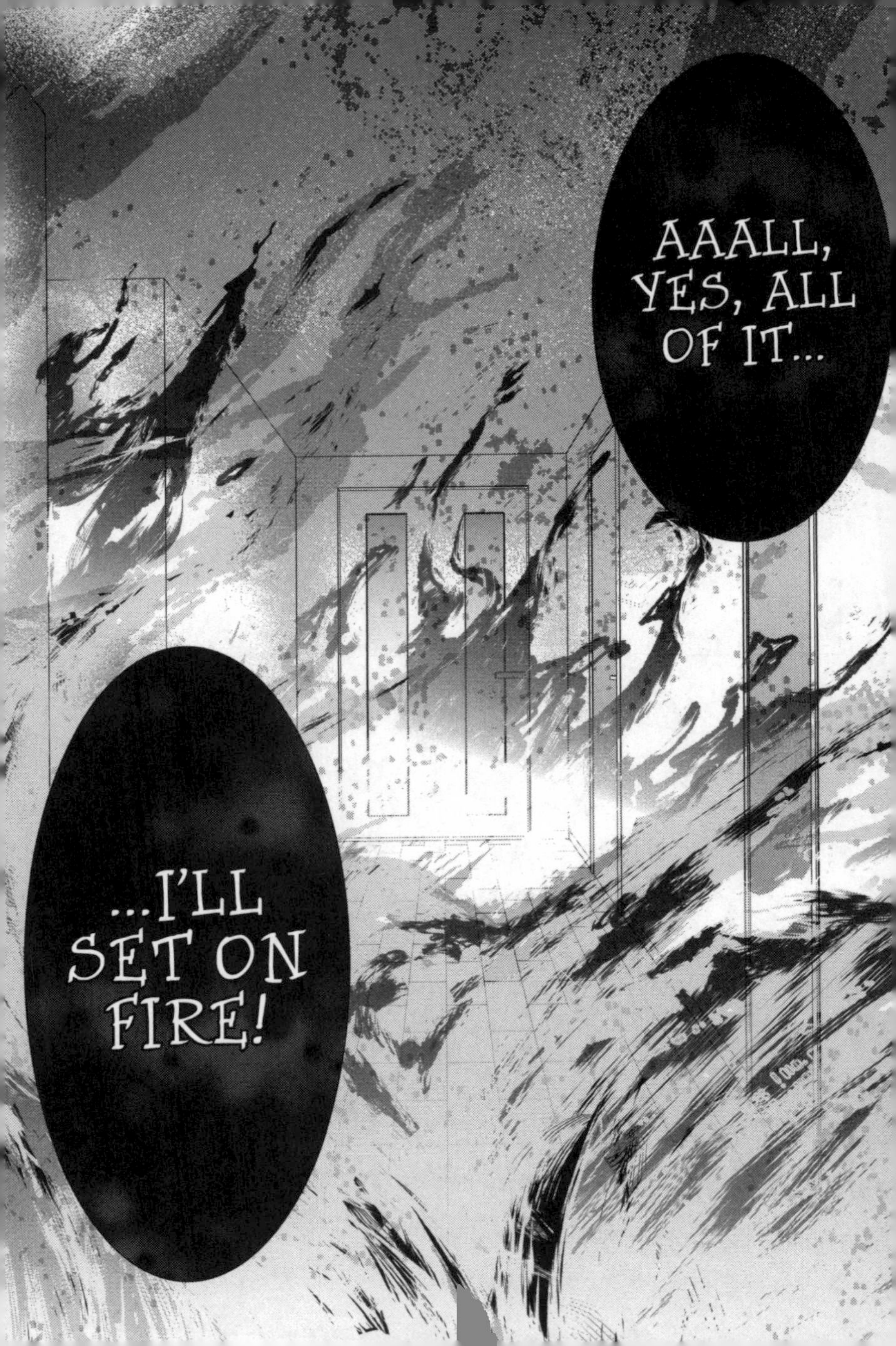
AAALL, YES, ALL OF IT...
...I'LL SET ON FIRE!

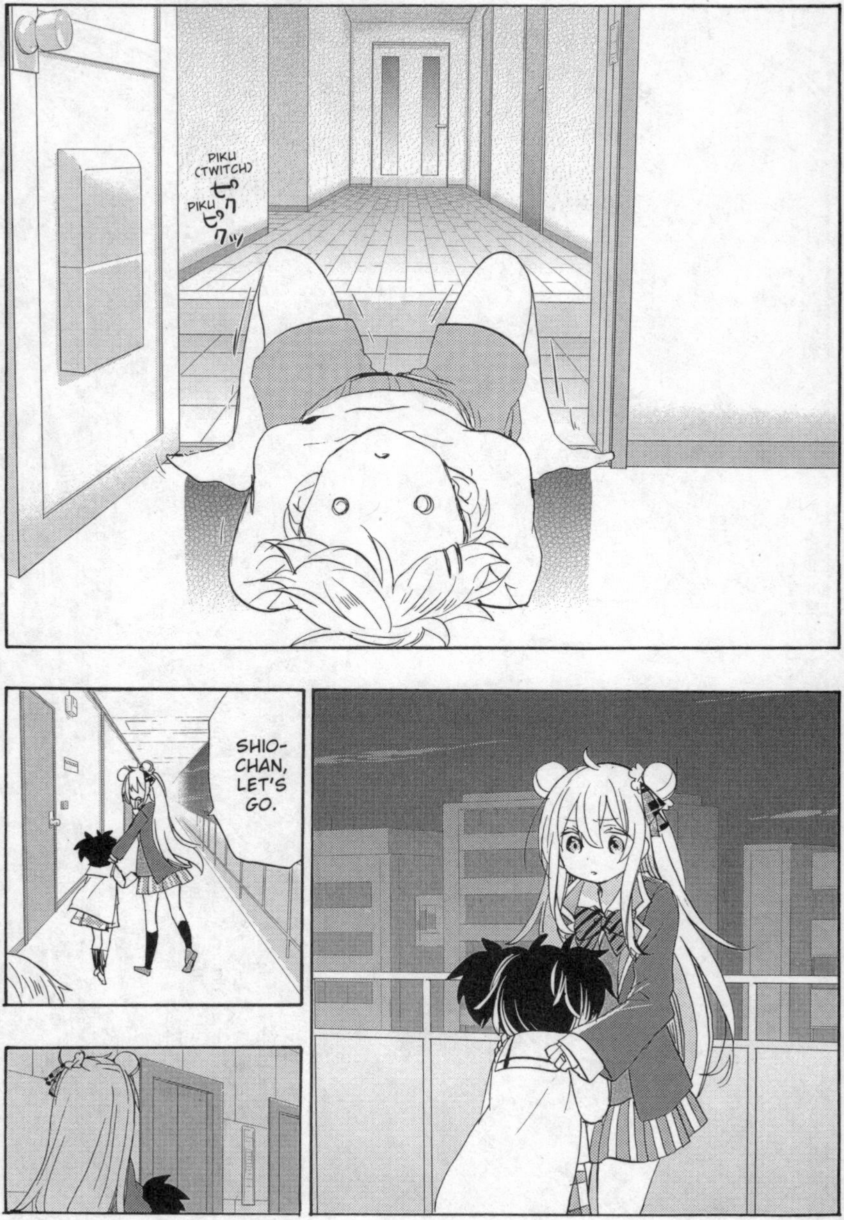
PIKU (TWITCH)
ピク
PIKU
ピクッ
SHIO-CHAN, LET'S GO.

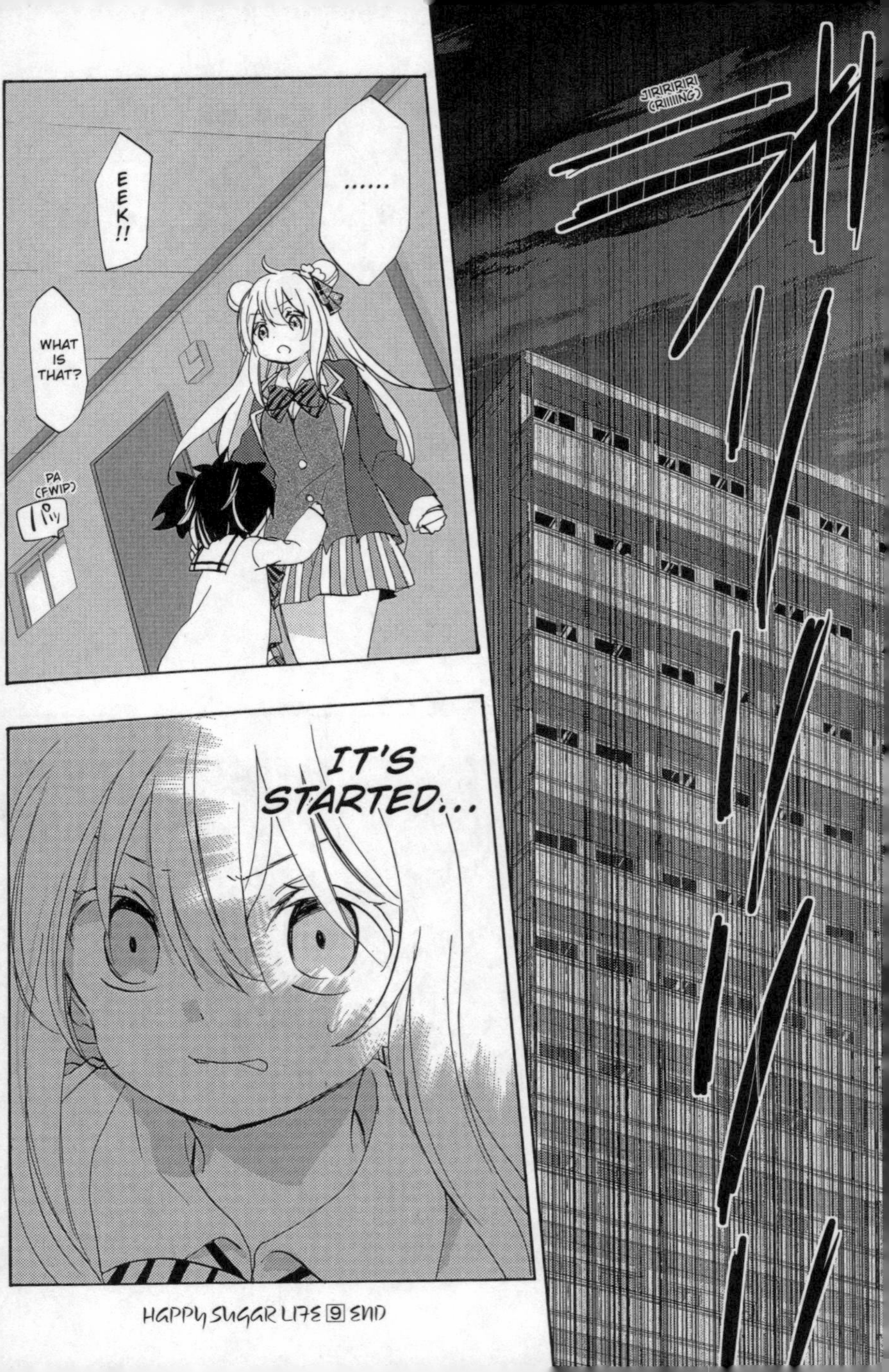
JIRIRIRIRI (RIIIIING)
......
EEK!!
WHAT IS THAT?
PA (FWIP)
パッ
IT'S STARTED...

HAPPY SUGAR LIFE 9 END

Happy
Sugar
Life

SPECIAL THANKS TO:

MY EDITOR.
MEGURU-SAMA.
TSUNAAGE-SAMA.
TADARAKU HIKARI-SAMA.
N-SAN.
THE DESIGNER.
ALL THE OTHERS INVOLVED.
THE READERS.

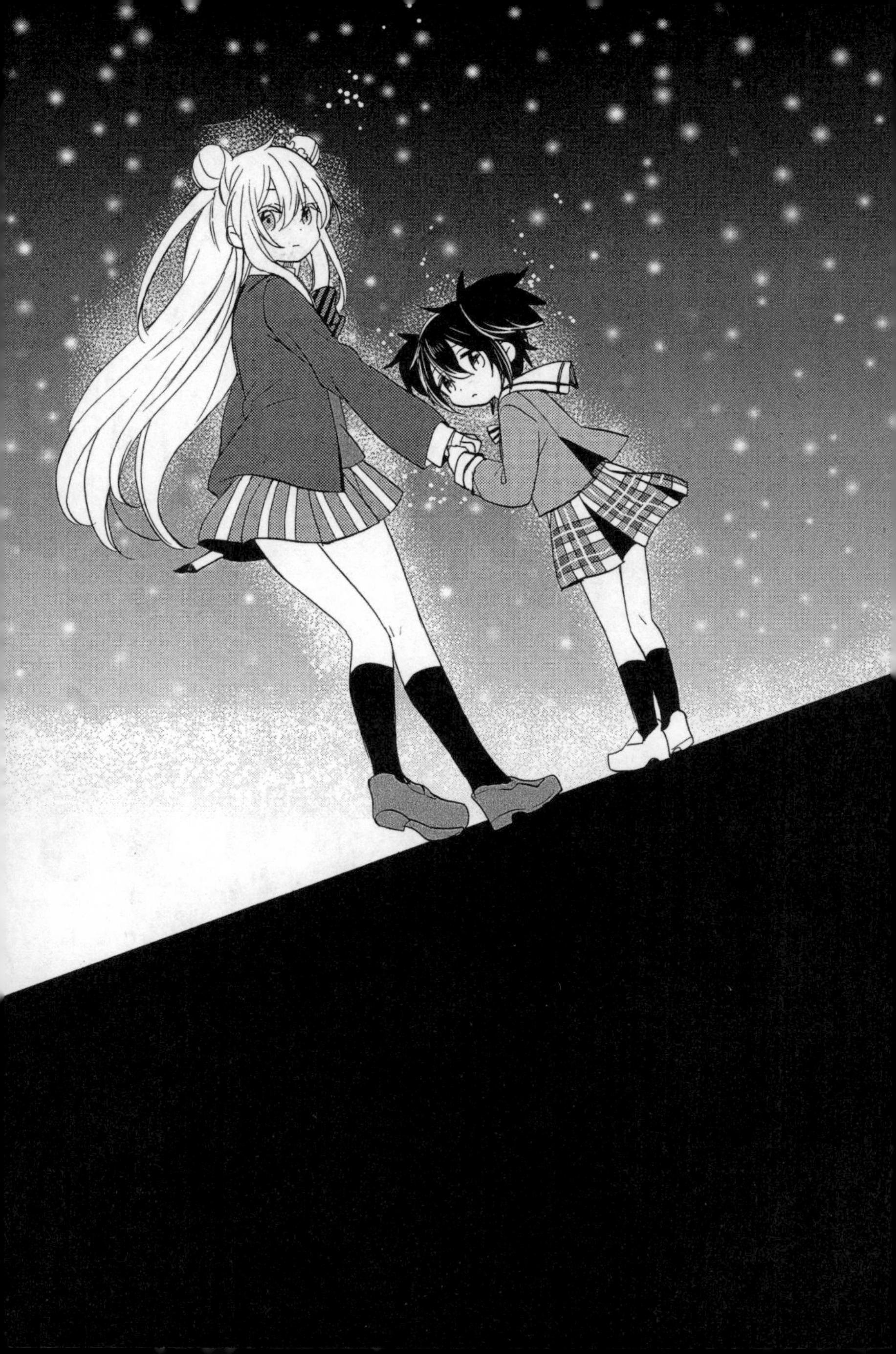

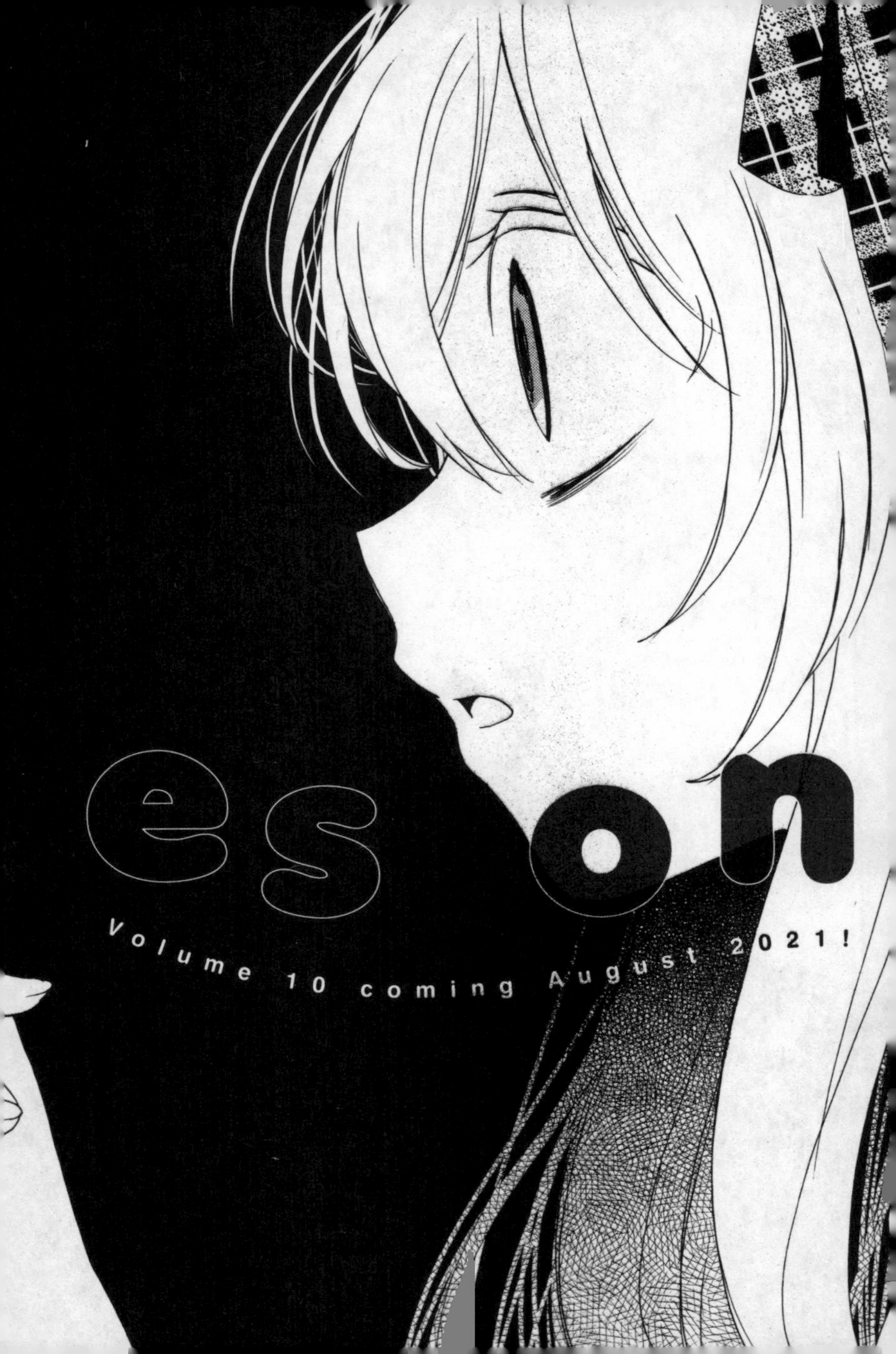
es on
Volume 10 coming August 2021!

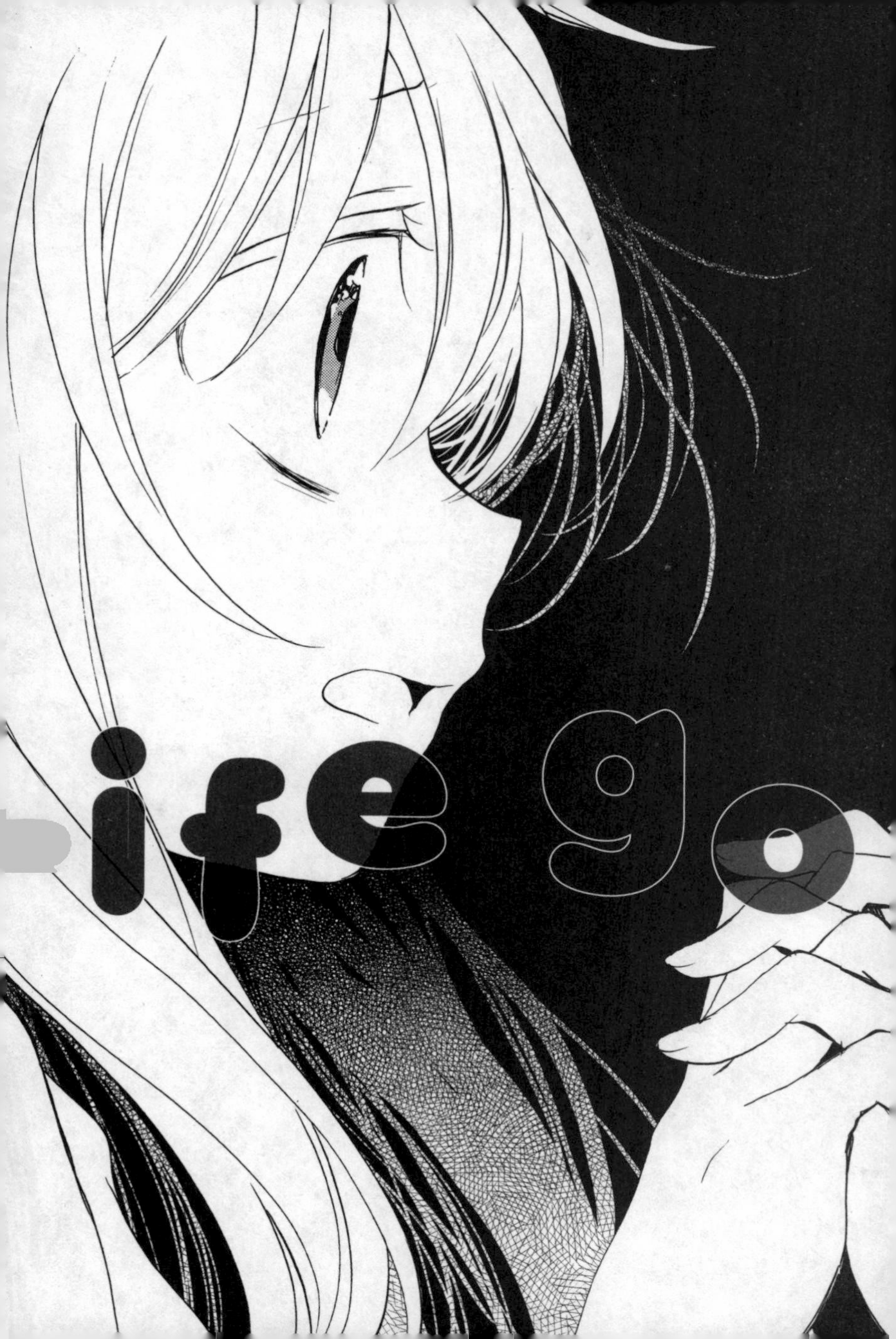
ife go

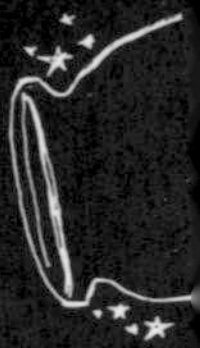

Happy Sugar Life

Tomiyaki Kagisora